IMMERSIVE JOURNALISM AS STORYTELLING

This book sets out cutting-edge new research and examines future prospects of 360-degree video, virtual reality (VR), and augmented reality (AR) in journalism, analyzing and discussing virtual world experiments from a range of perspectives.

Featuring contributions from a diverse range of scholars, *Immersive Journalism as Storytelling* highlights both the opportunities and the challenges presented by this form of storytelling. The book discusses how immersive journalism has the potential to reach new audiences, change the way stories are told, and provide more interactivity within the news industry. Aside from generating deeper emotional reactions and global perspectives, the book demonstrates how it can also diversify and upskill the news industry. Further contributions address the challenges, examining how immersive storytelling calls for reassessing issues of journalism ethics and truthfulness, transparency, privacy, manipulation, and surveillance, and questioning what it means to cover reality when a story is told in virtual reality. Chapters are grounded in empirical data such as content analyses and expert interviews, alongside insightful case studies that discuss *Euronews*, Nonny de la Peña's *Project Syria*, and *The New York Times*' VR application NYTVR.

This book is written for journalism teachers, educators, and students, as well as scholars, politicians, lawmakers, and citizens with an interest in emerging technologies for media practice.

Turo Uskali is an Associate Professor and Head of the Journalism program at the University of Jyväskylä, Finland. His research and teaching focus on the interplay of innovations and journalism, and the future of media industries.

Astrid Gynnild is a Professor and Head of the Journalism Research Group at the University of Bergen, Norway, and Principal Investigator of the ViSmedia project.

Her current research and teaching focus is on visual journalism, new technologies, and innovation foresight.

Sarah Jones is Deputy Dean at De Montfort University, UK. Sarah is listed in the top 15 global influencers in VR, is a Google Jump Creator, and has advised the UK Government on immersive technologies. Sarah has published extensively on immersive and emerging media.

Esa Sirkkunen works as a senior researcher at Research Centre COMET at Tampere University, Finland. His research focuses on assemblages of digital technologies and journalism, and on broader themes like social theory, privacy, and freedom of speech.

IMMERSIVE JOURNALISM AS STORYTELLING

Ethics, Production, and Design

Edited by Turo Uskali, Astrid Gynnild, Sarah Jones, and Esa Sirkkunen

Routledge
Taylor & Francis Group
LONDON AND NEW YORK

First published 2021
by Routledge
2 Park Square, Milton Park, Abingdon, Oxon OX14 4RN

and by Routledge
52 Vanderbilt Avenue, New York, NY 10017

Routledge is an imprint of the Taylor & Francis Group, an informa business

British Library Cataloguing-in-Publication Data
A catalogue record for this book is available from the British Library

Library of Congress Cataloging-in-Publication Data
A catalog record has been requested for this book

ISBN: 978-0-367-71329-4 (hbk)
ISBN: 978-0-367-71330-0 (pbk)
ISBN: 978-0-429-43774-8 (ebk)

Typeset in Bembo
by Newgen Publishing UK

CONTENTS

CONTRIBUTORS

Jonne Arjoranta, PhD, holds a doctoral degree in Digital Culture from the University of Jyväskylä, Finland. He specializes in philosophical hermeneutics, game studies, and internet cultures and is interested in playful politics, game hermeneutics, and geek culture. His dissertation "Real-Time Hermeneutics: Meaning-Making in Ludonarrative Digital Games" deals with the structures of meaning in digital games. He has published, for example, in *Game Studies*, *Games and Culture* and the *International Journal of Role-Playing*. He is the Editor in Chief of the *Finnish Yearbook of Game Studies*. More information about him can be found at https://jonne.arjoranta.fi.

David O. Dowling is Associate Professor in the School of Journalism and Mass Communication at the University of Iowa, and is the author of eight books and numerous articles on publishing industries and the culture of media production. His work in digital media and journalism studies has appeared in such journals as *Convergence*, *Genre*, *Digital Journalism*, *Digital Humanities Quarterly*, and *Journalism & Communication Monographs*. The impact of shifts in online culture and digital publishing industries on the multimedia narrative is the focus of *Immersive Longform Storytelling: Media, Technology, Audience* (Routledge 2019). His teaching includes courses on Digital and Gaming Culture, Critical Media Studies, and Principles of Journalism.

Siri Flatlandsmo holds a bachelor's degree in Journalism from the Department of Information Science and Media Studies at the University of Bergen, Norway. As a journalist Siri has been particularly interested in exploring the ethical implications of virtual reality on journalism. She has been a research assistant at the ViSmedia research project at the University of Bergen, and has extensive experience in digital change processes in local newsrooms.

Nina Helander is Professor of Knowledge Management and works at Tampere University, Finland as a Head of Unit of Information and Knowledge Management and as a leader of the Novi research group. Her research focuses especially on digitalization, value creation, and knowledge management. She has been leading several multidisciplinary research projects, including projects that have focused on digitalization and data-based value creation. She is also an Adjunct Professor of Information Systems at the University of Jyväskylä.

Pasi Ikonen, MA, is Project Researcher and has worked on numerous research projects on journalism at the Department of Language and Communication Studies at the University of Jyväskylä, Finland. He has studied drone journalism and virtual reality, and edited the news service of journalism research, (journalismresearchnews.org). Aside from journalism, Ikonen's research interests include organizational communication and lobbying.

Ilona Ilvonen, DSc (Tech.), is a postdoctoral researcher and lecturer at the Department of Information and Knowledge Management at Tampere University in Finland. Her research interest is focused on knowledge protection and knowledge-based value creation. She has published research articles on the knowledge management and information systems fields, and considers cross-disciplinary research to be essential for understanding complex phenomena. In addition to working at Tampere University, previously Tampere University of Technology, she has worked as a visiting scholar at the University of Texas, Austin, and as a visiting teacher at the University of Jyväskylä.

Deborah G. Johnson recently retired as the Anne Shirley Carter Olsson Professor of Applied Ethics in the Science, Technology, and Society (STS) Program in the School of Engineering and Applied Science at the University of Virginia and as researcher in the ViSmedia project at the University of Bergen. Best known for her work on computer ethics and engineering ethics, Johnson's research examines the ethical, social, and policy implications of technology, especially computers and information technology. Johnson's latest book, *Engineering Ethics: Contemporary and Enduring Debates*, will be published by Yale University Press in 2020.

Jussi Karhu, MSc, is currently a Unity engineer at Varjo, Finland. He has previously worked as a research assistant at the University of Tampere. He has designed and developed virtual reality experiences in numerous research projects. He has also created tools for user research using technologies like eye-tracking. Karhu also worked as a researcher in the VIRJOX project.

Otto Kauhanen, MSc in Human-Technology Interaction, is an experience specialist and sustainability ambassador at Cybercom Group. Kauhanen worked as research assistant at the University of Tampere in the VIRJOX project.

Chelsea Kelling is a UX-Designer and doctoral student at the University of Tampere, Finland. She is passionate about design and aims to change the world for the better through the creation of innovative interactions and unique experiences. She has worked on the VIRJOX project exploring service creation, human-centered design, and lean/agile design processes for emerging technologies. She holds a master's degree in Human-Technology Interaction from the University of Tampere and a BS in Psychology from Missouri State University.

Raine Koskimaa, PhD, is a Professor of Contemporary Culture Studies at the University of Jyvaskyla, and Vice Director of the Finnish Centre of Excellence in Game Culture Studies. He conducts research in the fields of game studies, digital literature, transmedia storytelling and digital culture. He is the co-founder of the *Cybertext Yearbook* and the author of *Digital Literature: From Text to Hypertext and Beyond*. Koskimaa has published widely, especially on digital culture and digital literature, and his writings have been translated into several languages. His current research interests are eSports, games and transmedia, and time and temporality in games.

Vesa Lindqvist is a strategic partner manager at Sanoma Corporation in Finland. In his work he has focused on business strategy, product management, mobile marketing, and product marketing. He has participated in engaging services for the virtual reality research project VIRJOX as one of the funders' representatives. He holds a BSc in Information Systems and Economics from Brunel University London.

Lars Nyre is a Professor of Media Design, Journalism and Technology at the Department of Information Science and Media Studies, University of Bergen, Norway. He is also a Professor II of Media Studies at the University of Stavanger, Norway. In the first part of his career, Lars Nyre researched sound in the media, and wrote his doctoral dissertation on radio and music recording. In 2008, he published *Sound Media: From Live Journalism to Music Recording* (Routledge). In recent years, Nyre has worked with media design and innovation pedagogy to explore the potential of new technologies in journalism. Along with students and colleagues, Nyre has explored creativity tools, drones, artificial speech, virtual reality, eye-tracking, and robots, and has published a number of articles on these topics. Read more about Lars Nyre and his publications here: www.uib.no/persons/Lars.Nyre.

Marko Siitonen is Associate Professor and specializes in digital and intercultural communication at the Department of Language and Communication Studies, University of Jyväskylä, Finland. He heads an international MA degree program on language and intercultural communication. He is currently the Chair of the Digital Games Research section of the European Communication Research and Education Association (ECREA), and is associated with the Academy of Finland-funded Centre of Excellence in Game Culture Studies. His research spans from technology-mediated communication at work, to newsgames, to communication in online communities.

Markku Turunen is a Professor of Interactive Technology. He leads a research group on Pervasive Interaction and an MSc program on Human-Technology Interaction. His background is in computer science and human-computer interaction. He has strong expertise on the design, development, and evaluation of interactive systems for different user groups and settings. He has been involved in more than 60 externally funded research projects, including several projects on different XR-technologies, such as interactive omnidirectional videos, 3DVR, and AR/MR.

Heli Väätäjä, PhD, is Principal lecturer and heads the master's degree program in Leadership of Technology Know-How at Lapland University of Applied Sciences, Finland. She started a new master's degree program, Specialist in Knowledge Management, in 2020. She also currently acts as a postdoctoral researcher at Tampere University working on virtual reality, emotions, and data in journalism. She has authored in total over 80 peer-reviewed international journal articles, book chapters, and conference articles. Her research in journalism focuses on novel media technologies and data, as well as on experiential aspects.

Joel Vanhalakka is an MSc in Business and Technology and a data consultant at Solita Oy, with a background in research at the Tampere University of Technology, where he spent more than a year researching value creation and business models in virtual and augmented reality. As a result, he published his master's thesis "Value Creation in Virtual and Augmented Reality" and was the main author of a paper called "Utilizing Knowledge Networks in VR/AR Solution Creation", which was presented at the European Conference for Knowledge Management in April 2017 in Barcelona, Spain.

Jorge Vázquez-Herrero is a PhD Research Fellow at the Faculty of Communication Sciences, Universidade de Santiago de Compostela (USC). He is a member of Novos Medios research group (USC) and the Latin-American Chair of Transmedia Narratives (ICLA–UNR, Argentina). He was visiting scholar at Universidad Nacional de Rosario, Universidade do Minho, University of Leeds and Tampere University. His research focuses on digital interactive narratives of nonfiction – mainly interactive documentary – micro-formats and transmedia, and immersive and interactive narratives in online media.

Joakim Vindenes is a PhD candidate at the Centre for the Science of Learning & Technology at the University of Bergen, Norway. His research focuses on design of Virtual Reality (VR) technology for various purposes, including memory, learning, and storytelling.

1

INTRODUCTION

What is immersive journalism?

Astrid Gynnild, Turo Uskali, Sarah Jones, and Esa Sirkkunen

Immersive technologies are opening gateways to virtual realities that might change journalism forever. In the virtual world, journalism balances on the edge between imaginary approaches to fact-based creation and extended options for fakes. The journalistic maneuverings between reality and virtual reality are particularly intriguing to work with because they put the truth-seeking values of journalism into play. How can immersive technologies be applied to improve meaningful reporting and investigate storytelling in journalism? How can skills and knowledge of virtual reality empower news professionals? And how can journalism codes of ethics help shape the new platforms, shape a future in which journalism continues to play an important role in society?

Immersive journalism got a breakthrough in 2018, when virtual reality presentations were included in the series that was awarded the Pulitzer Prize in explanatory journalism. The staff of The Arizona Republic and USA Today Network were honored for "vivid and timely reporting that masterfully combined text, video, podcasts and virtual reality to examine, from multiple perspectives, the difficulties and unintended consequences of fulfilling President Trump's pledge to construct a wall along the U.S. border with Mexico". The symbolic effect of highlighting the value of virtual reality as a complementary tool in journalism was significant.

With this book we wanted to provide a comprehensive overview of immersive technologies in journalism at the turn of the 2020s. Immersive journalism is still in its infancy and it is so far uncertain in what ways and to what extent the immersive approach will expand in the years to come. As journalism scholars we believe that an important aspect of journalism research is to critically, constructively, and creatively investigate the potential implications of emergent technologies in journalism, even before they are widely adopted in societies. Thus, the volume builds on international research projects that started in 2016 and also integrates the latest research results by other scholars in the field.

Immersive journalism relates closely to the mobile expansion in global society. It is based on the premise of ubiquitous smartphones and is marketed as the new game-changer in the communication and media industry. Major news organizations around the world are experimenting with new opportunities for virtual presence and engagement among users – from daily 360-degree news videos to award-winning short VR documentaries. Immersive journalism is often called an "empathy machine" as well. Its audiovisual narratives have proved to be extremely effective in causing strong emotions among its users.

Originally, the term "immersive journalism" was coined by Nonny de la Peña et al. (2010, 291), and defined as "the production of news in a form in which people can gain first-person experiences of the events or situation described in news stories". In this book, immersive journalism is defined more broadly as the use of immersive technologies, like 360-degree video, virtual reality, augmented reality, cinematic reality, and mixed reality in journalistic storytelling. Immersive journalism is an experiential approach that allows users to experience, and subsequently become immersed in, stories created not in the real world but in a virtual, augmented, or mixed reality.

When discussing immersive technology we thus refer to a broad spectrum of visual approaches in journalism. At the one end we have experiences created by 360-degree cameras. Whilst often called VR, 360-degree experiences are, more accurately, spherical films that allow interactivity through looking around and choosing where to look in an environment. At the other end of the immersive spectrum we have virtual reality (VR), which is more often than not computer-generated. With the VR experiences, there is more agency in the environment. Users may choose to take different paths, move more freely and interact with characters. To add to the terminology complexity, the umbrella term "cross reality" (XR) is gaining popularity, especially among engineering scholars and computer scientists. Cross reality refers to new forms of reality content creation in which all the above technologies may be mixed; digital objects are brought into the physical world and physical objects are brought into the digital world.

Because of its no-distance-at-all illusion, virtual reality experiences feel more real than other forms of journalistic storytelling. Evans (2019, 11) argues that VR is "a medium that offers something – immersion, interaction, even co-presence – that other media cannot due to the degree of intimacy and interaction that VR can achieve". Presence is a distinctive quality distinguishing immersive technologies from traditional film, computer games, television, and documentary. In journalism, the competitive advantage of immersive storytelling lies in its ability to create a sense of emotional connections to people, events and places. Bailenson (2018) argues that in the case of climate change deniers, for instance, the only way to change someone's mind is to put people in a position to directly experience something in order to "see the light". The perception of presence is derived from the notion of suspending all disbelief in the world (Pimental &

Texaria 1993), and one of a mediated world that is not mediated (Lombard & Ditton 1997).

Immersive journalism is thus a powerful new way to capture the attention of a multitude of users. The interactive traits of immersive technologies include hot spots that easily "teleport" users to new locations. The rapidly increasing options for virtually influencing audiences provide the journalism institution with genuinely new and extremely powerful storytelling tools. The need for ethical storytellers on multiple platforms will most likely grow in the years to come: journalism proves itself relevant to society by demonstrating that news professionals are at the forefront of immersive innovations, rather than passively observing what is going on. For journalism to provide knowledgeable storytelling and prove relevance, experiential approaches with new technologies would profit by starting from within; journalism innovation leads to innovation journalism (Gynnild 2014).

Immersive technologies are empowering in that they make journalism more relevant. In the era of touchscreens, individuals are used to navigate with their fingertips, and with immersive technologies new kinds of navigation, for example gazing, are easily added. At this point in history, audiences still expect journalism stories to be accurate, credible, and ethical. Even though immersive technologies are still in their infancy, we already know that users are easily persuaded by visual messages. Our brain believes so strongly in what it sees in VR that we might not be able to distinguish fake news from real news. Falsified videos of authorities such as former president Obama are hardly able to be differentiated from authentic clips (Diakopoulos & Johnson 2019), and boundaries between storytelling and storyliving are potentially getting blurred not only in gaming and social media but in journalism in general.

Immersive journalism experiences have evolved rapidly since 2012 when Nonny de la Peña provided the first, animated immersive journalism experience at the Sundance Film Festival. The video was a story on a diabetic man collapsing while standing in line at a food bank in Los Angeles. In 2015, immersive journalism´s most innovative beat was probably *The New York Times*' mini-documentary *The Departed*, which could be downloaded to viewers' smartphones via the NYTVR app. When used via Google Cardboard it offered a glimpse of the possibilities with mobile immersive journalism. In 2016, the Oculus Rift or HTC Vive offered the first high-end head-mounted display of immersive journalism experiences. By that time expensive HMDs also needed powerful computers and cables attached to the user. Only two years later, however, the first affordable stand-alone VR devices started to pour into the markets like Oculus Go, XiaomiMi VR, and Lenovo Mirage Solo. Three years later, in 2018, virtual storytelling was already on the list of Pulitzer winners in the United States, as the staffs of the Arizona Republic and USA Today Network were awarded the Explanatory Reporting prize.

Futurists and tech optimists have since then envisioned that immersive technologies will disrupt education, travel, health, and the media on a global scale. Leading tech companies have invested heavily in virtual reality since 2014, and CEOs have been hoping that users would quickly adapt to the new devices, applications, and platforms. But, as media history has taught us many times, consumers' behavior is hard to change. Sometimes it takes decades to happen. This was true with the adoption of radio, television, internet, smartphones, and obviously also with immersive-technology-related devices such as wearables. Smartwatches, smart glasses, and smart rings are heavily marketed, but are still used mainly by innovators and early adopters. The marketing hype of virtual reality and other immersive technologies has not yet, at the turn of the 2020s, materialized into reality – at homes or in our daily lives. The number of people who have not ever tried HDMs is still far beyond those who have. By 2018, the total number of active virtual reality users was estimated to be about 170 million. About 28 million VR devices (head-mounted displays) were sold that year, and 34 million were projected for the year 2019 (Statista.com 2019a). Compared to the numbers of smartphones, of which more than three billion copies were sold in the same year (Statista.com 2019b), the use of virtual reality content is still, rightly, quite marginal in a global perspective.

Naturally, the experienced delays in public response have created uncertainties about future investment, not least in the media business. So far, a widespread hypothesis is that the equipment is too big and complicated, and that it creates a form of loneliness that has to be resolved for it to take off. Even the first step, of putting the head-mounted display on the face for the first time, has been a threshold for many people. And, if their first immersive experience was like a rollercoaster ride, they might have undergone virtual simulation sickness, also known as motion sickness, a phenomenon which hopefully will be resolved at later stages of technological development.

Indeed, as human beings we have interacted with media content in different ways. Already during the Stone Age, the cave paintings offered immersive experiences. In 1838, stereoscopic photos were used after Charles Wheatstone's research demonstrated that the brain processes two different two-dimensional images from each eye into a single object of three dimensions. When two images are viewed side by side through a stereoscope, it gives a sense of depth and immersion. Later, individuals have experienced immersion in many other forms, from books, radio, films, television, computers, game consoles, and even smartphones. Immersion has been at the heart of a body of scholarly work; by bringing together immersion and interactivity, it is argued that total art can be achieved in virtual reality, with the emphasis lying in narrative (Evans 2019). Evans (ibid.) has narrated a short cultural history of virtual reality, starting from Victorian panoramas and ending with Second Life's computer-generated worlds and avatars designed by Linden Labs in 2003. Second Life was not yet an immersive VR experience, though; rather, a kind of social gaming through the screen of a PC.

In the last few years, immersive journalism has started attracting vanguard journalism scholars inquiring into emergent technologies and their influence in journalism. (See, for example, Sirkkunen et al. 2016; Jones 2017; Sundar et al. 2017; Sánchez Laws 2017; Bosworth & Sarah 2019; Aitamurto el al. 2018; Kukkakorpi 2018; Aitamurto 2019; Hassan 2019; Mabrook & Singer 2019; Pavlik 2019; Sánchez Laws 2019.) In the first wave of immersive journalism research, the production consisted mainly of conference papers, master's theses, and journal articles. Our investigations suggest that this opening phase of the new research field lasted from 2010 to 2019, when there was a notable shift in research investment. In the second wave the research field expanded into building more coherent overviews of immersive journalism via larger works. Melissa Bosworth and Lakshmi Sarah (2019) conducted an impressive number of interviews, analyzed and classified respectable numbers of immersive narratives and news. Their book offers an excellent review of virtual reality, augmented reality, and mixed reality storytelling cases from recent years. John V. Pavlik (2019) argues that a new form of mediated communication has emerged along with virtual reality, haptic technologies, interactive documentaries and drone media, and introduced the new terms "experiential news" and "experiential media". Ana Luisa Sánchez Laws (2019) emphasizes the importance of theorization in immersive journalism on the implications of full bodily experiences.

This edited volume continues and enlarges the scope of immersive journalism research from 21 authors representing scholars from five countries (Finland, Norway, the United Kingdom, the United States, and Spain). The publication is the first international and interdisciplinary joint-venture project aiming at understanding the many layers of immersive journalism storytelling. The approaches vary from comprehensive case studies via philosophical discussions on the premises and perils of emergent technologies to a broad spectrum of perspectives on immersive journalism from professional practitioner, researcher, and educator perspectives.

Much of the research developed for this volume derived from two internationally ongoing research projects, and the volume also gathers the latest analyses from other scholars studying the implications of immersive technologies in journalism. News streams related to immersive journalism have been systematically monitored for several years, with the internet as the most valuable data source.

In the project "Engaging Services in Virtual Reality (VIRJOX)" at the University of Tampere and University of Jyväskylä in Finland we developed, designed, and evaluated journalistic storytelling concepts for VR with an agile design process (Väätäjä et al. 2018). The same group has continued to explore the various ethical aspects of immersive journalism in a follow-up project (EMORES).

The four-year project "Visual Surveillance Technologies in the News Media (ViSmedia)" at the University of Bergen, Norway, is grounded in the framework of Responsible Research and Innovation (RRI). RRI is a methodological framework that helps facilitate the co-creational, collaborative resources of universities, industry, education, and civic society (Owen et al. 2012, Stilgoe et al. 2013). The RRI is applied to different stages of technological research and innovation. The framework guides processes in which the involved actors engage in mutual actions to find sustainable solutions to the grand challenges of our time. Collecting empirical data on emergent technologies, prompting public debate, adjusting the course, and providing responsible foresight is thus a main aim of RRI.

The volume further conceptualizes immersive filmmaking practices, using original productions as examples, including *The Town that Blew Away* (Jones, Aesthetica

Film Festival, 2017) and Google-supported Digital News Initiative projects on VR Journalism, including the *Coventry Blitz* VR.

The 16 chapters are divided into four sections that deal with essential issues of immersive journalism: trends and experiential practice, ethics, production and design, and education.

In the first section, an overview of immersive journalism is presented. Although we are seeing the presence of immersive journalism in every continent (Sánchez Laws 2019), there is a limited understanding of practices and case studies in Latin America and Asia. The United States is certainly leading the way as the main testbed for media content. These ideas are picked up in the first section. Esa Sirkkunen, Jorge Vázquez-Herrero, Heli Väätäjä, and Turo Uskali explore the use of 360-degree videos in journalism, through a content analysis drawing on the practices of *The New York Times* and *Euronews* together with interviews with journalists making immersive content. This is followed by a case study that focuses on the work of *Euronews*. Joakim Vindenes and Astrid Gynnild analyze the production and workflows in *Euronews* and how they have applied a low-cost approach to immersive journalism. In the final chapter of this section a global overview of immersive journalism is presented by Sarah Jones. In this, the need for accessibility is highlighted to bring the technology to different communities so that experiences are authentically created.

It is then that we move to arguably one of the most important sections: ethics. It begins with a chapter by Turo Uskali and Pasi Ikonen, who summarize what we know about the emotional implications of virtual reality experiences. Their discussion is followed by a case study on *Project Syria*. *Project Syria* was created by Nonny de la Peña in 2014 and uses virtual reality technologies to put the audience "on scene", enabling people to feel as if they are truly witnesses to the violent events in Syria. In this case study, Siri Flatlandsmo and Astrid Gynnild concentrate on accuracy in immersive journalism and why this is implied in VR experiences. Then follows a chapter by Deborah Johnson, who discusses emerging technologies in the light of anticipatory governance and ethics. It then focuses on the potentials for surveillance and manipulation of virtual experiences and the impact that this can have on an audience.

The claims that immersive journalism can be an empathy machine have been central to arguments for news industries to develop the technology in order to engage new audiences. In the final chapter of this section Sarah Jones explains why immersive journalism does not necessarily increase empathy and instead needs to be thought of in new ways for the technology and journalism to reach new audiences.

We move then to look at the production and design of this emerging form of journalism. With the demand on journalists to become multi-skilled and tell stories across platforms, it is important to reflect and critically analyze the production processes within immersive journalism and the implications around this.

This section begins with David Dowling looking at the concepts of place-based journalism. It considers the implications for interactivity and production aesthetics and how branding plays a role within production. A second case study by

Ilona Ilvonen, Joel Vanhalakka, and Nina Helander follows the creation of value in immersive journalism in *The New York Times* and their VR application NYTVR. The process of design is the focus of the next chapter by Chelsea Kelling and six other contributors from the project VIRJOX. The chapter culminates in building the hierarchy of needs of user experiences, something that designers should take seriously into account when developing immersive journalism and immersive products in general.

A lot of scholarly thought around immersive media has come from game studies, and there is certainly a lot that can be learned within immersive journalism from these traditions. In Chapter 12, Jonne Arjoranta, Raine Koskimaa, and Marko Siitonen take a look at pioneering examples of immersive gaming and how these impact journalism. This is developed further in the following chapter, where the focus turns to Augmented Reality. Within AR, we are looking at the application and situating of digital objects within our own environment. Pasi Ikonen and Turo Uskali focus on how this now plays a role in journalism.

The final section concerns teaching and learning. For educators reading this book, there is a need to continue to ensure that students are familiar with new trends and skills. It is important that students are thinking critically about emerging technologies and how it can reach new audiences, but also that core journalistic skills are not lost within the excitement of a new technology. In the first in this section, Turo Uskali and Pasi Ikonen provide an overview of teaching approaches in five different countries and how the educators bring immersive journalism into the classroom. This is followed by a chapter by Lars Nyre and Joakim Vindenes, who discuss immersive journalism as witnessing. They conceptualize the designs and strategies behind first-person experience in VR journalism and present experiments from an innovative pedagogy approach to teaching journalism.

The book ends with a chapter on the future of immersive journalism. As the technology develops quickly, it is important to think more broadly about the implications of immersive journalism on the media industry. To this end, trends and future trajectories for immersive journalism are analyzed, looking at where and how this industry, which is full of questions, debates, concerns, and opportunities, can develop and establish itself in responsible ways.

References

Aitamurto, T. 2019. "Normative Paradoxes in 360-degree Journalism: Contested Accuracy and Objectivity." *New Media & Society 21*(1): 3–19.

Aitamurto, T., Z. Shou, S. Sakshuwong, J. Saldivar, Y. Sadeghi, & A. Tran. 2018. "Sense of Presence, Attitude Change, Perspective-Taking and Usability in First-Person Split-Sphere 360-degree Video." In: *Proceedings of the 2018 CHI Conference on Human Factors in Computing Systems*. New York: ACM.

Bailenson, J. 2018. *Experience on Demand: What Virtual Reality Is, How It Works, and What It Can Do*. 1st ed. New York: WW Norton & Company.

Bosworth, M. & L. Sarah. 2019. *Crafting Stories for Virtual Reality*. London: Routledge.

Diakopoulos, N. & D. Johnson. 2019. "Anticipating and Addressing the Ethical Implications of Deepfakes in the Context of Elections." October 23. Available at SSRN: https://papers.ssrn.com/sol3/papers.cfm?abstract_id=3474183 [Accessed 15 March 2020].

Evans, L. 2019. *The Re-Emergence of Virtual Reality*. 1st ed. London: Routledge.

Gynnild, A. 2014. "Journalism Innovation Leads to Innovation Journalism: The Impact of Computational Exploration on Changing Mindsets." *Journalism 15*(6), August: 713–30. doi:10.1177/1464884913486393

Hassan, R. 2019. "Digitality, Virtual Reality and the 'Empathy Machine'." *Digital Journalism*, published online 2 January. doi:10.1080/21670811.2018.1517604

Jones, S. 2017. "Disrupting the narrative: Immersive journalism in virtual reality." *Journal of Media Practice 18*(2–3): 171–185. doi:10.1080/14682753.2017.1374677

Kukkakorpi, M. 2018, n.p. "Immersive Journalism: Presence and Engagement in Conflict News Stories: Close Reading of The New York Times' Virtual Reality Stories." Master's thesis. Finland: Media and Communication Studies, University of Helsinki.

Lombard, M. & T. Ditton. 1997. "At the Heart of It All: The Concept of Presence." *Journal of Computer-Mediated Communication 3*(2). September.

Mabrook, R. & J.B. Singer. 2019. "Virtual Reality, 360-degree Video, and Journalism Studies: Conceptual Approaches to Immersive Technologies." *Journalism Studies 20*(14), January. https://doi.org/10.1080/1461670X.2019.1568203

Owen, R., P. Macnaghten, & J. Stilgoe. 2012. "Responsible Research and Innovation: From Science in Society to Science for Society, with Society." *Science and Public Policy 39*(6): 751–760. https://doi.org/10.1093/scipol/scs093

Pavlik, J. V. 2019. *Journalism in the Age of Virtual Reality: How Experimental Media Are Transforming News*. New York: Columbia University Press.

Pimentel, K. & K. Teixeira. 1993. *Virtual Reality: Through the New Looking Glass*. Windcrest/McGraw-Hill/TAB-Books.

Pulitzer.org. 2018. "Staffs of The Arizona Republic and USA Today Network." www.pulitzer.org/winners/staffs-arizona-republic-and-usa-today-network [Accessed 15 March 2020].

Sánchez Laws, A.L. 2017. "Can Immersive Journalism Enhance Empathy?" Published online 20 October. *Digital Journalism* 1–16. doi:10.1080/21670811.2017.1389286

Sánchez Laws, A.L. 2019. *Conceptualizing Immersive Journalism*. London: Routledge.

Shin, D. & F. Biocca. 2017. "Exploring Immersive Experience in Journalism." *New Media & Society* 1–24. doi:10.1177/1461444817733133

Sirkkunen, E. & T. Uskali. 2019. "Virtual Reality Journalism." In: T.P Vos & F. Hanusch (eds), *The International Encyclopedia of Journalism Studies*. Hoboken, NJ: Wiley Blackwell.

Sirkkunen, E., H. Väätäjä, T. Uskali, & P.P. Rezaei. 2016. "Journalism in Virtual Reality: Opportunities and Future Research Challenges. Academic Mindtrek '16." In: *Proceedings of the 20th International Academic Mindtrek Conference*. New York: ACM, pp. 297–303.

Statista.com. 2019a. "Unit Shipments of Virtual Reality Head-mounted Displays Worldwide from 2017 to 2018 and in 2022 (in million units)." www.statista.com/statistics/509154/head-mounted-displays-worldwide-shipments/ [Accessed 22 September 2019].

Statista.com. 2019b. "Number of Smartphone Users Worldwide from 2016 to 2021 (in billions)." www.statista.com/statistics/330695/number-of-smartphone-users-worldwide/ [Accessed 22 September 2019].

Stilgoe, J., R. Owen, & P. Macnaghten. 2013. "Developing a Framework for Responsible Innovation." *Research Policy*. *42*(9): 1568–1580. https://doi.org/10.1016/j.respol.2013.05.008

Sundar, Shyam S., Jin Kang, & Danielle Oprean. 2017. "Being There in the Midst of the Story: How Immersive Journalism Affects Our Perceptions and Cognitions." *Cyberpsychology, Behavior, and Social Networking 20*(11): 672–682.

Väätäjä, H., M. Turunen, I. Ilvonen, E. Sirkkunen, T. Uskali, C. Kelling, T. Keskinen, A. Burova, V. Mäkelä, & J. Karhu (eds). 2018. *VIRJOX. Engaging Services in Virtual Reality*. Finland: Tampere University of Technology. https://tutcris.tut.fi/portal/en/publications/virjox(9bf3cfba-f2be-4ecf-a800-b7ca8c04faad).html [Accessed 14 October 2019].

PART I

Storytelling

2

EXPLORING THE IMMERSIVE JOURNALISM LANDSCAPE

Esa Sirkkunen, Jorge Vázquez-Herrero, Turo Uskali, and Heli Väätäjä

Current drivers of 360-degree journalism have been mostly curious about the new medium, its possibilities, and are exploring business opportunities. The early adoption of such technology is often a matter of brand-building – that is, news organizations experimenting with virtual reality (VR) want to demonstrate that their digital strategies are forward-thinking (Watson 2017). After interviewing representatives from leading US newspapers, Bosworth and Sarah (2019, 226) also conclude, "among major media companies that failing to experiment in immersive and experimental stories will mean losing a race".

Thus far, 360-degree journalism has been generally a testbed for the most prominent media companies. For example, the BBC produced the very first entirely 360-degree TV episode of the technology program *Click* in March 2016. One crucial factor driving these experiments has been the activity of tech companies like Samsung and Google, who sponsored major journalistic institutions such as *The New York Times* and *Euronews* in 2017. Major platforms like Facebook and YouTube have already built platforms for 360-degree content with the possibility for users to publish content themselves. The process of platformization (Helmond 2015; Nieborg and Poell 2018) of 360-degree content and consumption is well underway.

This chapter starts with an overview of 360-degree journalism genres. We especially explore the relationship between conventional journalism and 360-degree productions. Our hypothesis is that the general narrative conventions and ethical principles of journalism are reflected in the evolving 360-degree journalism. We continue with questions regarding production and narration based on interviews with journalists making immersive journalism. We discuss suitable topics, production processes and narrative options concerning immersive journalism, especially 360-degree journalism. The data for this chapter contains findings of projects in which we have analyzed more than 100 360-degree stories (Sirkkunen, Uskali, & Väätäjä 2017 a,b; Vázquez-Herrero & López-García 2017; Sirkkunen & Vázquez-Herrero

2018). We have analyzed the 360-degree journalism of CNN, *USA Today*, *The New York Times*, *Euronews*, the BBC, *The Wall Street Journal*, *The Guardian*, *El País*, and *Dagens Nyheter*. Additionally, we have interviewed 13 experts in immersive journalism from 2016 to 2019. Those interviewed come from the US (4), UK (1), Sweden (1), and Finland (7). Interviewees were chosen from various kinds of journalistic organizations (YLE, *Helsingin Sanomat*, *Dagens Nyheter*, the AP, Frontline), with a few people from VR production and gaming companies, tech companies, and academic teachers of VR. The interviews were done face-to-face, recorded, and conducted along a semi-structured questionnaire, each interview lasting 20 to 60 minutes.

Evolving genres

We have analyzed 360-degree content by topic, length, narration strategies, and immersive features in each 360-degree story. Analyzing various characteristics like sound, camera movement, and immersion, we wanted to grasp the multimodal (Kress 2010) affordances of 360-degree as a medium. From these findings, we built tentative genres of 360-degree journalism. We want to underscore that we are not trying to build a permanent taxonomy of 360-degree journalism. Our understanding of the genre concept highlights its unstable, dynamic nature (Kress 2010, 133). We have identified three tentative genres: *360-degree live*, *360-degree news*, and *360-degree documentaries*. We will also touch briefly on the fourth genre, *360-degree fiction*, when it is produced by media companies and disseminated on the same platforms as the journalistic pieces. We will give short descriptions of each genre in the following.

First, *360-degree live* can be compared to live television or radio in that 360-degree equipment transmits live footage, and the sound flows from an interesting environment. It gives users options to look around and obtain a full panorama of the event. For example, 360-degree live has been used to transmit NBA games and other sports events, concerts, town meetings, and political spectacles such as President Donald Trump's inauguration in 2016. However, live streaming in 360-degree is not a genre solely for media houses. Moreover, user-generated 360-degree live on YouTube, Periscope and Facebook is becoming increasingly popular (Schaerlaeckens 2017; Steinberg 2018; Cohen 2018).

Perhaps the most-produced genre of 360-degree journalism thus far is *360-degree news*. With a duration from one to three minutes, users can visit distant places, explore the wonders of nature and art exhibitions, or visit war zones and refugee camps. The most active newsroom has been *The New York Times*, which in 2016–18 produced 351 360-degree news pieces, following *Euronews* with 144 pieces (Sirkkunen & Vázquez-Herrero 2018). Samsung sponsored both companies. *The New York Times*' project The Daily 360 was shot across 57 countries by 200 different journalists. According to *The New York Times*, the videos gathered 94 million views on Facebook and two million views on YouTube (Willens 2017).

In our analysis, we found an interesting difference in storytelling between *The New York Times* and *Euronews*. *Euronews* has adopted 360-degree as part of their reporters' work process. This means *Euronews* reporters use narration more familiar from TV reporting, for example journalists' voiceover narration or reporting visibly on the spot. *The New York Times* chose a different path. *The New York Times'* reporting lets sources tell their stories and keeps the journalist mostly invisible and silent, as Figure 2.1 shows.

When analyzing 100 360-degree news videos by *The New York Times* and *Euronews*, we identified three different narration strategies (Sirkkunen & Vázquez-Herrero 2018). Following Jones (2017), we call the first two *reporter-led* and *source-led narration* (Figure 2.1). The first means the reporter is present either as a voiceover or visible in the footage. Source-led narration means the journalist/reporter is visually or vocally absent and a person tells his or her story as the only narrator. The third – also quite common – is to let the user see and hear the 360-degree content without significant interruptions from journalists or sources. We called this *invisible/neutral narration* (Sirkkunen & Vázquez-Herrero 2018). Notably, journalists partially control this third strategy by placing the camera, directing events, cutting footage and adding possible textual information or sounds.

The next subgenre is *360-degree documentaries* (for example, *Underworld: A Virtual Experience of the London Sewers* or *6x9* by *The Guardian*) come close to extensive 2D documentaries regarding the amount of work and money spent on production. The duration of video documentaries varies and is mostly between four to 20 minutes. Compared to 360-degree news, more varied narrative strategies and styles are used.

Another offshoot worth mentioning is *360-degree fiction*. Based on our observations, it is mainly *The New York Times* who has produced them. Of course, many other 360-degree production houses have focused on animated fiction, drama, or short fiction stories. As such, publishing fiction may be a wise move for

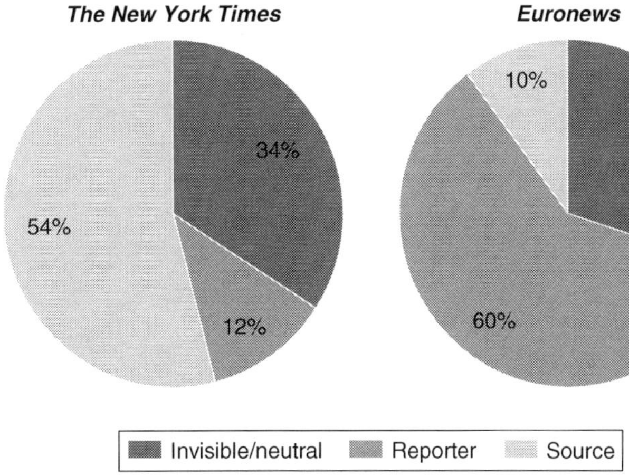

FIGURE 2.1 Narration strategies of *The New York Times* and *Euronews*.

a journalistic platform, because fiction broadens the scope of the content available and attracts new users to a company's VR content. Good examples of 360-degree fiction are *Lincoln in the Bardo*, a version of the novel by George Saunders, or *LA Noire* short stories, in which a user is no casual observer but a character in a bar of 1940s' Los Angeles. Other examples of fiction content on 360-degree are *Alento* (RTVE) and *Cervantes VR* (RTVE). Interestingly, factual journalism and fiction have appeared on the same platform before, for example in the pre-history of modern journalism in the late 19th century, when novels and poems were published first as serial stories in newspapers and magazines.

As mentioned, the field is emerging, and borderlines between tentative genres are in flux. To illustrate this dynamically evolving field, we formed a fourfold table based on the importance of photorealistic effects (the visual representation of time and space of the news) in Figure 2.2. We placed genres evolving from photorealism (upper left) to emotional realism (in the center) and finally to fiction (lower right) to illustrate the differences and continuities between genres. The fourfold figure illustrates also the interaction between documentary and fiction genres – a process that has happened previously in the history of journalism, for instance in the early development of the television documentary (see, for example, Cutrin 1993).

In conclusion, in 360-degree live and 360-degree news the photorealistic tradition is more prevalent, while in 360-degree documentaries a wider array of narrative means is allowed. For example, in the beginning of spherical VR journalism, some prominent documentarists have been using animated characters and environments with real, on-the-spot audio recordings. One pioneer, Nonny de la Peña, has coined the concept of behavioral realism (de la Peña 2017, 2) to mean the sense of presence in the story is more important in creating authenticity for the photorealistic environment, for instance.

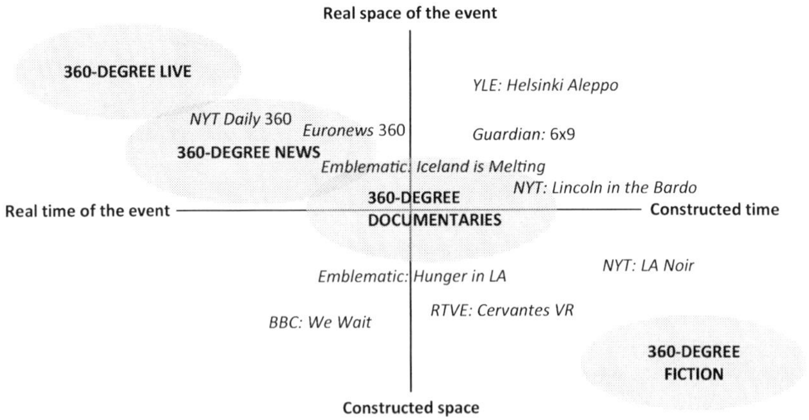

FIGURE 2.2 Some 360-degree productions illustrated fourfold. The figure depicts how different codes, canons of rhetoric and narration strategies are applied in different 360 journalism subgenres.

Our genre analysis does not say much about the intentions and experiences of the actual creators of 360-degree journalism. To get more insight into such creations, we conducted a small number of expert interviews.

Start with witness test

In interviews, we focused on the process of making VR journalism concerning the following four themes: what kind of topics are suitable for VR journalism, what kind of staff is required for making VR, the principles of VR storytelling, and the main problems concerning the publication of VR stories. In the following, we introduce key findings from interviews and connect those to our content analysis results presented earlier and interviews published elsewhere.

In our analysis of *Euronews*, the topics in 360-degree news vary from Europe's politics and social problems such as climate change to human interest stories about exciting experiences in exotic environments. Topics in *The NYT Daily* included politics, but also more broadly social problems, minorities, culture and art in experientially interesting surroundings (Sirkkunen & Vázquez-Herrero 2018).

How do VR professionals themselves define topics suitable for more immersive storytelling? There are various ways to make these decisions. For example, in CNN's newsroom, before starting to make a 360-degree story, journalists evaluate news topics using a pattern they call *the witness test*. Only topics in which the environment is interesting and creates strong experiences for users should be chosen. Jason Farkas from CNN emphasizes the importance of visceral experiences – for example, jumping out of planes or running with bulls in Pamplona (Watson 2017).

Ville Juutilainen, a journalist from the Finnish national broadcasting company YLE's Plus Desk, believes giving the user a presence in a new environment is the key to successful VR/360-degree journalism. According to him, the same principle can be used in nearly all themes and topics, from sports to politics, the economy, or future urban visions. VR can be particularly useful in visualizations in which one must give users a sense of size or scale.

> It is not only what you see but also from whose angle you see it. If we think about my making a VR story on how pedestrian crossings are insecure for children, I can make the adults look the same from a familiar place down here *(from a child's perspective)*. We can literally play with different perspectives, which will definitely raise some questions.
>
> *Juutilainen 2017*

Matilda Hanson from the Swedish newspaper *Dagens Nyheter* emphasizes the same feature of providing ways for users to perceive the news from different angles than they have normally used, which can be the very asset of VR journalism.

> Therefore, it's very much the physical experience of almost a presence in these different areas of the world where people don't get to go normally.

> I think it is also a matter of transparency. We do not frame the way we do as photographers. [...] There's so much that we frame and so much that we cut out (*in normal two-dimensional journalism*) because we think this is the important story but, in a way, the readers miss out a lot of things that would make them empathise and understand the world better.
>
> *Hanson 2017*

As with an interview (Willens 2017), *The New York Times'* Marcelle Hopkins, Executive Director of Virtual Reality, highlights the importance of interesting and extraordinary places that lure users to make a visit with 360-degree technology. She thinks that the environments work better than, for example, 360-degree interviews. When using the 360-degree headsets, users also appeared to stay longer exploring the 360-degree environment than watching the same material on flat video (Willens 2017).

Additionally, environments should have something extra for users to experience. Even by 2016, Paul Cheung, then from the AP, had learned that most of the happenings like fashion shows or exhibitions do not bring extra value when documented with 360-degree equipment. However, 2D footage is often sufficient for documenting these kinds of occasions in which the focus is fixed onstage. "The rule of thumb is 'would you look around you in a certain situation?' If the answer is yes, then maybe there is an opportunity to create a VR experience" (Brackebush 2016).

Duration is also an important factor. According to Paul Cheung, AP journalists have shifted to shorter news videos, as they seem to work better on social media platforms. However, this does not mean that long form is banned in AP, but longer stories are used, for example, in feature topics (Brackebush 2016).

As a summary of what makes good 360-degree journalism, we state that it is the ability to offer a strong feeling of presence and something to be perceived by the senses. Picking the right, interesting locations worth exploring is also crucial. The third important feature is the possibility of showing the world from an alternative or complementary point of experience. Good-quality sound and footage are also important factors to produce a sense of presence and immersion. A producer from the Finnish production house Zoan, Laura Ala states: "Sound creates easily a half of the virtual reality experience. It is a useful tool in guiding the users as it is in real life also" (Ala 2019; see also Bosworth & Sarah 2019, 180–193).

From simple to complicated work processes

The consensus in the field is that VR operations are complicated and expensive. This is true with longer productions, but one can also start experiments with a lower budget. A good way to start inexpensively is to make shorter pieces first and then gradually expand into more complicated and longer productions. For example, *Euronews* has started to train its journalists to shoot 360-degree routinely, with only a short introduction. (See more in Chapter 7.)

The process of making VR stories can sometimes be very slow. However, it need not necessarily be so. The 360-degree live cast is the fastest way to get content published on platforms like YouTube or Facebook. The 360-degree content can be quite a fast way to disseminate important news if there is a limited amount of post-production. For example, the BBC already was able to use 360-degree footage in reporting the Bataclan terror attack in Paris 2015. Zillah Watson and her colleague filmed, edited, and published the footage on YouTube and Facebook within hours (Watson 2015).

Ole Krogsgaard from *Euronews* goes against the current wisdom, stating that interviews, when properly done, also can be interesting content in 360-degrees. Some prominent VR journalists have been avoiding 360-degree interviews, but Krogsgaard thinks that it can be a good and cost-effective way to expand the spectrum of 360-degree content. *Euronews* has also experimented with easy-to-use editing tools like web-based VR editor Fader to lower the threshold for journalists to start editing more complicated stories themselves (Krogsgaard 2017 a,b,c).

There are also other VR strategies than *Euronews*' "keep it simple and cheap". Many of our interviewees have mostly been doing longer VR productions. Compared to documentaries made for TV, a VR documentary takes even more work because of the extra pre-planning and laborious post-production. Because the tools and programs used are developing rapidly and no general standards have developed yet, a wide variety of cameras, editing technologies, and programs are utilized. Many of the tools used come originally from game production like Unity, a development platform for multiplatform games and interactive contents. Hence, all kinds of new expertise and skills are needed when producing the content to VR.

Some companies make only a few VR productions per year. For example, PBS's *Frontline* program in the US has traditionally focused on investigative stories and documentaries. In 2015, it started to produce VR documentaries in collaboration with VR studio Emblematic Group, funded by the Knight Foundation (Wang 2015). In the interview, producer Benedict Moran explained that Emblematic Group has produced a couple of ten-minute-long VR documentaries per year (Moran 2016). In September 2019, the *Frontline* website contained 14 360-degree documentaries; the last (*Greenland's Glaciers Are Melting Faster Than Expected*) was published in September 2018.

Dagens Nyheter has started with a small VR staff and two full-time workers who get occasional help from other sections in the newsroom. *DN* started publishing VR stories in December 2016 and has published so far (at September 2019) 20 360-degree documentaries, each lasting from four to nine minutes.

In conclusion, concerning the use of staff, much, of course, depends on the general strategy and the resources. For example, *Euronews* can make a substantial amount of 360-degree news with relatively cheap equipment and short introductions to journalists on making 360-degree. Conversely, expensive documentaries like those by Emblematic Group have taken months to finish.

There are several open-ended questions for anyone considering starting a VR production. One substantial challenge is how to make content available to users. So far, one can apply several strategies. A news outlet can create an app to publish VR content. This is good in that the outlet can control its app, which is a more stable platform for more complex VR productions, but bad because it means users must download the app before perusing the story. The downloading process may be one hindrance to getting people to experience the content.

The news outlet can use already-existing VR platforms like Google's YouTube VR, Facebook's Oculus Rift, Samsung's Gear VR, the HTC Vive Headset, or Sony's PlayStation VR. Thus, making a version for each platform will add to production costs. Moreover, the platforms may take a share of the potential revenues derived from, for example, advertising connected to VR viewing. It is also unclear whether the tools of the big platforms are collecting user data.

Finnish journalists Ville Juutilainen and Jussi Pullinen both underscore that the whole process of making VR journalism should be based on open standards and platform independence.

> Open technology solutions that are not parts of larger ecosystems are especially in the interest of national media companies [...] such equipment and technologies that you can use inside your own system without the risk of the information being transferred to somewhere outside.
>
> *Pullinen 2019*

Thus far, one of the successful ways of making journalistic VR is to collaborate with a platform like Samsung Gear VR and gather sponsors to cover expenses, as *The New York Times* does (more about this in Chapter 11).

According to journalism educator Robert Hernandez, the biggest bottleneck for adapting VR in newsrooms is the culture of fear, especially fear of the costs of producing VR.

> The biggest problem that I see still is culture. Not necessarily accepting VR – I think there is a lot of acceptance of VR. But there is cultural fear of the cost of producing VR. And I encourage newsrooms to look at the low-end cameras. To start producing those experiences, because there are a lot of things that you can learn in terms of where to place the camera, how to hide it, placing, framing, that you can do and learn on low-end cameras before you get in the high-end cameras, before you are going to immersive experiences, so it is not a lot of money to start. But a lot of people have that roadblock: oh my God, it costs tens, hundreds, thousands of dollars.
>
> *Hernandez 2017*

"Unlike traditional storytelling"

One of our main findings from the content analysis has been that the longer and more developed 360-degree documentaries are more versatile concerning narrative structure (also Sánchez Laws & Utne 2019). This means that, while some editors of longer documentaries remain within the photorealism convention, others have taken more liberties with animated characters and surroundings (de la Peña 2017). In those cases, credibility has been maintained, often with an authentic soundtrack or by carefully modelling and animating real circumstances. When technical affordances expand from 360-degree to more interactive ones, as is the case in volumetric VR, journalists have taken more freedom to explore ideas outside of standard documentary journalism.

One of the dilemmas that 360-degree and VR narration in general raise is how to balance the narrative function of journalism and the immersive effect that the technology affords. The sensory or affective thrill is not the only goal of immersive journalism; there is also an informational context to be given for the user to understand her experiences. Some signs of this dilemma are the aforementioned differences between the narration of *Euronews* and *The New York Times*' Daily 360 that we found in our analysis.

For journalists, it may take some time to understand the distinctions between writing linear text and writing for 360 and VR generally. Ville Juutilainen thinks that, at some point, writing for VR comes closer to writing game scripts than journalism. However, when writing stories, it is crucial to maintain journalistic principles. According to Juutilainen, there are assorted views and occasional disputes in the Finnish Broadcasting Company's graphics department on how photorealistic VR productions should be. The pioneering VR journalist Nonny de la Peña has argued that the full photorealistic illusion of reality is not the only prerequisite of credibility. Carefully crafted animations can give sufficiently good impressions of reality if the story is interesting and immersive (de la Peña 2017).

Jannicke Mikkelsen, a Norwegian visual journalist living in London, has shot and directed various VR documentaries with high-end equipment. One of her works is a VR documentary *VR the Champions* about the rock band Queen's concert in Barcelona, captured with a rig with 20 GoPro cameras and 70 microphones. She highlights the distinctions between VR and cinema narration.

> It is very much unlike traditional storytelling. [...] One difference I've noticed is that I don't need establishing shots. I can just throw people into a situation. I don't have to say, like in the Queen film, this is a stadium and we are in Barcelona. Cut all that away. Just put them into their concert. It works better.
>
> *Mikkelsen 2017*

According to Mikkelsen, *VR the Champions* works with few cuts because a concert is a familiar space and situation for users to experience and get ecstatic about the music and the band.

Noora Heiskanen has been working in a Finnish VR company, Teatime Productions, which produced the much-discussed 360-degree *Helsinki Aleppo* published by the national broadcaster YLE. It depicted how the center of Helsinki would look if it was destroyed as Aleppo was during recent years. Noora Heiskanen thinks that the novelty of VR lies simply in users' freedom to explore footage as they wish.

> It is important to give enough space and time for the user to explore and accept that he/she can look elsewhere or to interpret the story differently. There has to be a good reason for using VR production instead of traditional video. Maybe it is just that you do not have to follow a certain narrative.
>
> *Heiskanen 2017*

One important feature is whether the narration – and technological affordances of the solution in question – give real agency to the user or whether he/she is a godlike figure who can only observe what is happening. So far, for example, the possibilities of interactivity in 360-degrees are very limited. Another technical restriction is the quite poor user experience that cheap cardboards may offer. There is the danger that users become disappointed with the poor quality and decide to avoid also high-end VR content in the future.

Conclusions: different epistemologies for different genres

During content analysis, we were able to detect several tentative genres: 360-degree live, 360-degree news, 360-degree documentaries, and 360-degree fiction. We found that different canons of documentary and narration strategies are utilized in different genres. For example, in short 360-degree news the journalistic code is very much based on the tradition of television news journalism, whereas in longer documentaries journalists are allowed more liberties – like using animated characters, building stylized environments, etc. We also found some justification for our hypothesis that general journalistic norms are reflected in immersive journalism. First, the topics chosen seemed to follow the journalistic canon used in news genres in general. Second, 360-degree live and short 360-degree news rely mostly on news realism and the photorealistic tradition. The tradition of photojournalism is also reflected in discussions as to whether it is allowed to edit footage and, if yes, how far the editing can go (see Aitamurto 2019). The discussion of realism shows that the defining process of immersive journalism is still very much in progress. On one hand, for example, Aitamurto (2019) emphasizes the importance of the realistic code of ethics of 360-degree news: in short, to represent *what is* rather than *what if*. Conversely, for instance, Sánchez Laws and Utne (2019) point out that journalists cannot claim authenticity regarding 360-degree content for synthetically reconstructed pieces. The credibility of stories like de la Peña's *One Dark Night* and *Hunger in L.A.* or *The Guardian's 6x9* is, rather, based on the audience's trust in journalists and on the embodied cognition produced when using immersive journalism pieces (SánchezLaws & Utne 2019).

It is still unclear if 360-degree technology will develop as a serious genre of immersive journalism. Importantly, after Samsung's sponsorship ended, the number of productions diminished dramatically, both in *The New York Times* and *Euronews* (Sirkkunen & Vázquez-Herrero 2018). The peak year of producing 360-degree news by *The New York Times* (281) and *Euronews* (73) was 2017. In 2019, *The New York Times* made only a couple of 360-degree news articles, and *Euronews* about 20.

As the declining figures show, it seems unlikely that short 360-degree news will soon become a major genre of immersive journalism. In addition, the viewer statistics on YouTube reveal that 360-degree has remained quite marginal compared to 2D news videos consumed simultaneously. However, the 360-degree technology has served as an important testbed for journalism and its core ideas and ideals.

Overall, it seems that VR indeed offers several new opportunities for journalistic storytelling, and 360-degree is the first linear step on that path. There may be an evolution in progress from eyewitnessing and experiencing visceral effects towards more complicated narrative elements found in games and fiction, including spherical sound and eventually more interactive VR features. With what kind of devices we will consume these new contents remains to be seen.

References

Aitamurto, T. 2019. "Normative Paradoxes in 360 Journalism: Contested Accuracy and Objectivity." *New Media & Society 21*(1): 3–19.

Ala, L. 2019. Focus group discussion with VR experts, 25 February 2019, in Helsinki.

Bosworth, M. & L. Sarah, 2019. *Crafting Stories for Virtual Reality*. New York: Oxford, UK: Routledge.

Brackebush, J. 2016. "What the Associated Press Has Learned from a Year of VR." *Digiday*. https://digiday.com/media/aps-learned-vr-360-videos/ [Accessed 14 October 2019].

Cohen, A. 2018. "NBA's New Chinese Broadcast Deal with Migu Will Include Virtual Reality." *Sporttechie.com*. www.sporttechie.com/nba-chinese-broadcast-deal-migu-includes-virtual-reality/ [Accessed 1 September 2019].

Cutrin, M. 1993. "Packaging Reality: The Influence of Fictional Forms on the Early Development of Television Documentary." *Journalism Monographs* (137), February: 1–37.

de la Peña, N. 2017. "Towards Behavioral Realism: Experiments in Immersive Journalism." In: J. Aston, S. Gaudenzi, & M. Rose (Eds.), *I-Docs: The Evolving Practices of Interactive Documentary*. New York; Chichester, UK: Columbia University Press pp. 206–221.

Hanson, M. 2017. Interview with Esa Sirkkunen, 10 May 2017, in Helsinki.

Heiskanen, N. 2017. Interview with Esa Sirkkunen, 15 March 2017, in Helsinki.

Helmond, A. 2015. "The Platformization of the Web: Making Web Data Platform Ready." *Social Media + Society 1*(2): 1–11.

Hernandez, R. 2017. Interview with Turo Uskali, 21 June 2017, in Vienna.

Jones, S. 2017. "Disrupting the Narrative: Immersive Journalism in Virtual Reality." *Journal of Media Practice 18*(2–3): 171–185. doi:10.1080/14682753.2017.1374677

Juutilainen, V. 2017. Interview with Esa Sirkkunen, 10 April 2017, in Helsinki.

Kress, G. 2010. *Multimodality*. New York: Routledge.

Kroksgaard, O. 2017a. "This Is How *Euronews* Trains Journalists in the 360." *Medium*. https://medium.com/journalism360/this-is-how-euronews-trains-journalists-in-360-36cf663e4ea1 [Accessed 1 September 2019].

Kroksgaard, O. 2017b. "Experimenting with WebVR Fader and Interactive 360-degrees in a Newsroom." *Medium*. https://haptic.al/experimenting-with-webvr-fader-and-interactive-360-videos-in-a-newsroom-3f08ebcd710b [Accessed 1 September 2019].

Kroksgaard, O. 2107c. "Doing Interviews in 360 Degrees." *Medium*. https://medium.com/journalism360/doing-interviews-in-360-videos-d3902f5c031 [Accessed 1 September 2019].

Mikkelsen, J. 2017. Interview with Esa Sirkkunen, 26 April 2017, in Tampere, Finland.

Moran, B. 2016. Interview with Turo Uskali, 26 September 2016, in Stanford, CA, USA.

Nieborg, D. & T. Poell. 2018. "The Platformization of Cultural Production: Theorizing the Contingent Cultural Commodity." *New Media & Society 20*(11): 4275–4292.

Pullinen, J. 2019. Focus group discussion with VR experts, 2 May 2019, in Helsinki.

Sánchez Laws, A.L. & T. Utne. 2019. "Ethics Guidelines for Immersive Journalism." *Frontiers in Robotics and AI*. https://doi.org/10.3389/frobt.2019.00028

Schaerlaeckens, L. 2017. "Virtual Reality Is the Future of Soccer Broadcasting, and It's Already Here." *Yahoo.com*. https://sports.yahoo.com/news/virtual-reality-is-the-future-of-soccer-broadcasting-and-its-already-here-014744043.html [Accessed 1 September 2019].

Sirkkunen, E., T. Uskali, & H. Väätäjä. 2017a. "From Witnessing to Experiencing? Exploring the First Wave of 360-degree Journalism." Presented at the IAMCR World Conference, Cartagena, Colombia, 16–20 July 2017.

Sirkkunen, E., T. Uskali, & H. Väätäjä. 2017b. "The Making of Journalistic VR: 'It Is Very Much Unlike Traditional Storytelling.'" Presented at the Nordmedia Conference, Tampere, Finland, 17–19 August 2017.

Sirkkunen, E. & J. Vázquez-Herrero. 2018. "Exploring the First Waves of VR-journalism." ECREA 2018, Lugano, 2 November 2018.

Steinberg, L. 2018. "Virtual Reality Is Leading the Sports-Tech Wave." *Forbes.com*. www.forbes.com/sites/leighsteinberg/2018/07/31/virtual-reality-the-forefront-of-the-tech-wave-sweeping-over-sports [Accessed 1 September 2019].

Vanian, J. 2017. "Google Is Experimenting with Virtual Reality Advertising." *Fortune 500*, 28 June 2017. http://fortune.com/2017/06/28/google-virtual-reality-advertising [Accessed 1 September 2019].

Vázquez-Herrero, J. & X. López-García. 2017. "Immersive Journalism Through Mobile Devices: How Virtual Reality Apps Are Changing News Consumption." In: Á. Rocha., A. Correia, & H. Adeli et al. (eds.), *Advances in Intelligent Systems and Computing 571*. Cham, Switzerland: Springer, pp. 3–12.

Wang, S. 2015. "Frontline Is Diving Deeper into VR with $580,000 from the Knight Foundation." *Niemanlab.org*. www.niemanlab.org/2015/12/frontline-is-diving-deeper-into-vr-with-580000-from-the-knight-foundation [Accessed 1 September 2019].

Watson, Z. 2015. "Filming 360-degrees in Paris." *BBC News Labs* Report.

Watson, Z. 2017. *VR for News: The New Reality?* Digital News Project. Oxford, UK: Reuters Institute for the Study of Journalism, University of Oxford. https://reutersinstitute.politics.ox.ac.uk/our-research/vr-news-new-reality [Accessed 15 March 2020].

Willens, M. 2017. "One Year in: What The New York Times Learned from Its 360-Degree Video Project,"The Daily 360. *Digiday*. https://digiday.com/media/one-year-new-york-times-learned-360-degree-video-project-daily-360/ [Accessed 1 September 2019].

3

CASE *EURONEWS*

A low-cost approach to immersive storytelling

Joakim Vindenes and Astrid Gynnild

This chapter investigates the approaches of a particularly innovative immersive journalism actor, the pan-European news organization *Euronews*. Since early 2016, *Euronews* has systematically experimented with immersive storytelling using consumer-grade 360-degree cameras. The study identifies the tools, emerging work practices and content of experimental immersive journalism over a one-and-a-half-year period. Furthermore, the study analyzes the ways in which 360-degree videos are less editor-directed than their regular video equivalents, which is in itself an indication of a new form of selective consumer freedom on what to watch in the immersive video environment. The analysis is based on qualitative interview data with leaders and practitioners at *Euronews* and subsequent content analysis of 95 published 360-degree video productions. Based on the two empirical datasets, we critically discuss the advantages and disadvantages of low-cost approaches to 360-degree news production.

With the increasing availability and popularity of virtual reality (VR) technology, there has been a rapid rise in the use of 360-degree videos for journalistic purposes. Referred to as VR journalism, immersive storytelling and disputably immersive storyliving (Maschio 2017), the VR technology demonstrates journalistic potential in that it "promises to bring audiences closer to a story than any previous platform" (Aronson-Rath, Milward, Owen, & Pitt 2015). However, even if the increasingly available and lightweight 360-degree technology has caused a surge in video journalism in the last few years, creating immersive productions is a very challenging task for most newsrooms.

In the early literature on the potentials of immersive technologies in journalism, researchers frequently turn to the lack-of-time-and-tools argument to explain why immersive journalism so far is less widespread in the newsrooms than predicted by early adopters. The Knight Foundation's 2016 report on VR journalism suggests that the use of 360-degree video is less prevalent in small and medium-sized news organizations owing to the time and effort required to create VR stories (Doyle, Gelman, & Gill 2016). The report suggests that for VR to become more prevalent, tools that reduce the burden of production and post-production are required. In their state-of-the-art paper, Sirkkunen, Väätäjä, Uskali, and Rezaei (2016) concur that for smaller news organizations to be able to embrace this medium, "rapid work processes should be ideated, developed, and trialed" (6).

In another report on the use of VR technology in journalism, the Tow Center suggests that using simpler equipment would bring down costs and "[widen] the swath for the number of people who can produce VR" (Aronson-Rath et al. 2015, 7). In addition to making hardware available, however, the research so far has indicated the necessity of gaining more knowledge about production processes to fully understand the potential of VR technology. Aronson-Rath et al. (2015) further point out that "the industry desperately needs evidence of the platform's benefits and information about the necessary skills, practices and equipment" (26).

In the few years since the first VR reports were published by the Knight Foundation and the Tow Center, however, technologies for capturing as well as distributing 360-degree content have become more readily available. Although the medium was previously explored almost exclusively through well-produced documentaries provided by professionals outside of the news organizations, larger newsrooms increasingly experiment with producing their own content using consumer products.

A report by Reuters Institute mentions *The New York Times*, CNN, *USA Today*, BBC, and *Euronews* as organizations adopting a model different from well-produced documentaries, instead using low-cost cameras with auto-stitching of the images (Watson 2017). This new approach to immersive storytelling with 360-degree video is attainable for a wider range of organizations and will therefore be important in exploring the new medium's potential for conveying journalism. Moreover, rapid and affordable processes seem to be a prerequisite for the adoption and usage of VR technologies across the journalism field as a whole.

The aim of the case study in this chapter is to first investigate the ways in which easily accessible immersive journalism tools are actually applied in a large newsroom such as *Euronews*. Based on these empirical data, we reflect on and discuss the lessons learned from *Euronews*' emerging immersive journalism content production that might be applicable to small-to-medium-sized news organizations. Only by critically discussing and possibly intervening in current practitioner experiments can ongoing research support the creative, constructive, and continued exploration of immersive journalism. Thus, detailed studies of ongoing productions are, in our opinion, a basic research challenge because the medium has distinctly unique features that must be explored in practice to reveal its potential.

In this chapter, we first present *Euronews* and its experimental approaches to immersive storytelling, detailing their organizational structure, workflows, and technologies used. Next, we present an analysis of 95 videos resulting from this practice, identifying issues such as coverage, production choices, video context, and the role of the journalist. Finally, based on the documented approach and analysis, we discuss the advantages and disadvantages of the evolving 360-degree video production approach in *Euronews* and comment on potential future work.

Euronews

Euronews is a European multilingual news bureau with an operating base in Lyon, France. The agency is the most watched news channel in Europe ("About *Euronews*" n.d.). In addition to traditional broadcasting, the bureau hosts an online news site with a distinct focus on video reports. The main purpose of *Euronews* is to cover news events in Europe from a "pan-European" perspective, meaning that they attempt to disseminate news from Europe as a whole, rather than from the perspectives of the individual countries in Europe. *Euronews*' first television broadcast was distributed in 1993 in English from Lyon. By the turn of the millennium, *Euronews* had extended its distribution to English, French, German, Italian, Spanish, and Portuguese. Since 2013, *Euronews* has provided news in 13 European languages. The majority (60%) of *Euronews* is owned by the Media Globe Networks (Dziadul 2015; "About *Euronews*" n.d.), while 25% is owned by Universal Studios Limited (NBC News) (Atkinson 2017; "About *Euronews*" n.d.). In total, *Euronews* employs more than 500 journalists of 30 different nationalities, and their television news reaches 430 million homes across 133 countries.

In early 2016, *Euronews* began publishing 360-degree videos. According to Editor-in-Chief of Digital Platforms, Duncan Hooper, the news organization envisioned that VR would empower the audience, which was stated as an explicit editorial goal: "we want to let them make their own decisions, not tell them what they should be watching, not tell them what they should be thinking" (Flueckiger 2016). The same argument lies latent in some of *Euronews*' regular, flat video formats as well in the "No Comment" series ("flat" videos are defined as video in traditional formats such as 4:3 or 16:9 as opposed to spherical videos). The series, which is one of *Euronews*' signature programs, disseminates video clips of events without presenting a certain view or comment on the footage. Ideally, it is up to the users to interpret the cases that are covered. On its website, the news bureau states that its "strong belief is to empower audiences to forge their own opinion" ("About *Euronews*" n.d.).

The immersive trend

Euronews is one of the many large organizations that experiment with producing journalism in 360 degrees, and a growing number of online newsrooms are fueling this process. They are also engaged in international experiments with immersive journalism. In 2016, *Euronews* partnered with Samsung to promote their cameras through use. This collaboration made it financially easier for *Euronews* to start experimenting with 360-degree video as part of their workflow. Moreover, Google News Lab–through its Digital News Initiative–has immersive storytelling as one of its focus areas; together with the Knight Foundation and Online News Association,

Google News Lab launched Journalism 360, "an initiative of thought leaders, practitioners, and journalists dedicated to accelerating immersive storytelling in news" ("Journalism 360" n.d.).

In 2017, Google News Lab delivered over US $250,000 to projects investigating ideas within this domain. The aim was "to discover ideas that grow immersive storytelling to advance the field of journalism–that inform and encourage news organizations to innovate, experiment and learn" ("Journalism 360 Challenge" 2017). In their call for grant applications, the Knight Foundation wrote that they were "primarily looking for projects that will yield lessons and 'how-tos' for the field of journalism" ("Journalism 360 Challenge" 2017). Information about the required equipment, technology, and workflow is important for organizations to experiment.

In addition to grants, Journalism 360 encourages the sharing of experiences and practices of immersive storytelling. On its Medium collection ("Journalism 360" n.d.), dozens of articles and case studies on immersive storytelling are present that serve as a resource bank for emerging VR journalists. Some of the articles were written by *Euronews'* journalists and editors who partake in this initiative. To further develop their editorial workflow, *Euronews* also received support from the Google Digital News Initiative Grant.

To experiment or not to experiment

Watson (2017) reports that the key issues of the news organizations heavily investing in VR, such as through the launching of apps, have been brand innovation and future market positioning. By contrast, organizations that hold back on VR investments might benefit from less risk-taking because technologies are quickly evolving and immersive journalism still is a highly experimental news approach. Watson (2017) reports, however, that most of the organizations from which she collected data endorsed the view that smaller news organizations ought to themselves experiment to understand the benefits of VR. With simple consumer cameras, this experimentation can be done without great risks, creating a middle ground between the full leap into the unknown and holding back on any experimentation. *Euronews* approached their experimentation with 360-degree video something akin to this middle ground. According to the Editor-in-Chief of Digital Platforms, Duncan Hooper, they were not going to build their app because it is a big gamble (Flueckiger 2016) and, if they were going to fail, they wanted to fail cheaply (Scott 2016). Moreover, they would not hire an external team of experts but were dependent on innovative, visual work practices that were possible to implement within the existing organizational resource frames.

Euronews' immersive journalism practices

The identification of the emerging immersive journalism practices of *Euronews* is based on the direct and indirect qualitative interview data with diverse professionals involved in the organization's 360-degree video productions. In addition to analyzing the comprehensive material of online interviews and articles in which *Euronews*' journalists have shared their experiences with 360-degree video production, we conducted three in-depth, virtual interviews with the VR editor of *Euronews* and two VR journalists. To obtain an overview of the work processes of a lightweight 360-degree camera production, we first identify the typical editorial steps, followed by a content analysis of the disseminated videos in the collected data material.

The 360-degree videos at *Euronews* are produced in various ways, depending on the journalist's experience and affiliation with the organization. In general, the decision to make a 360-degree production is prompted either by a news event that requires immediate visual action or by a journalist who approaches the VR editor with a pitch. When the idea is actualized, the VR editor will initiate a quick discussion with the reporter before a decision on producing a 360-degree video is made or hire a freelance reporter to make the video. During the subsequent idea exchange with the journalist, the following questions are raised: 1) How can the story be done in 360 degrees? 2) To what extent is the potential 360-degree video production realistic in terms of cost? 3) Have any similar stories been done before? 4) To what degree is the potential story newsworthy? As soon as the topic, angle, and journalist's time expenditure are decided, the journalist will undergo introductory technical training, unless he or she is already an experienced VR reporter. After one hour of technical instructions on how to use the equipment, the journalist is sent off with a checklist that contains practical tips for executing the production (Krogsgaard 2017). In short, the checklist explains several important aspects of the production, such as the following: 1) cleaning of lenses, 2) appropriate camera settings, 3) aligning of the camera, 4) optimal camera placement relative to motive (height and depth), 5) correct lighting for each camera lens, 6) microphone use under varying conditions, and 7) practices for backup and charging. The checklist can be viewed in its entirety online, where it is shared with other 360-degree enthusiasts (Hooper 2017). In addition to bringing the Samsung GEAR 360-degree cameras to the shoot, the journalist brings a light tripod, a zoom h2n recorder, an iRig mic lav and a Samsung S6 phone for controlling the camera from afar and previewing the shots. It goes without saying that the journalists selected for such a job do have some visual experience before heading off to a job with the checklist and the camera equipment, although they might not be specifically proficient in 360-degree video productions. According to the VR editor, using existing resources and workflows within the organization is a key factor when producing 360-degree videos.

When the shoot is done, the VR journalist is expected to hand over the footage to the online news desk. At *Euronews*' section for footage processing, the raw material is stitched in the Gear 360 Action Director (license included with camera purchase) and edited in Edius and After Effects, the software that *Euronews* uses for their traditional videos. The VR journalists are not supposed to directly engage in the editing process albeit serve as supervisors on the edit of the provided footage.

The journalists prepare the piece and meet with the editor to guide the process while writing the final script to the text article and/or the voiceover of the video. When the edit is done, the video is sent to the graphics department, where the names of the relevant people, places, etc., are added to the video report. If the video has a voiceover, this is recorded in up to 13 languages, in parallel with the video editing.

When *Euronews* stresses the necessity of integrating 360-degree videos with the existing production workflows, the production costs, even with lightweight cameras, appear to be a main challenge. The data collected in this study indicate that the quickest turnaround time for the shooting and editing process is three full days. The shooting and stitching are done on the first day; the second day involves the editing and writing of script; on the third day, the voiceover is recorded and the videos are exported and uploaded. Often, however, the process stretches over a week because time-sensitive material is not often covered in 360-degree and other productions have priority. A freelance video reporter doing jobs for *Euronews* explains, "360-degree video is one of the storytelling tools I use, I would like to do much more of it, but there is not yet as much demand for it". He points to the fact that most newsrooms do not have budgets for full-time 360-degree video journalists. Moreover, he emphasizes that 360-degree videos should be "one solely for stories that are visual and/or places that are hard to access". "For me, 360-degree video production is just one of my freelance gigs", he says.

The editorial strategy for the 360-degree stories produced by *Euronews*' web of freelance journalists is illustrated by the following example: A freelance web journalist in a European country was asked by *Euronews* to produce a 3–4 min 360-degree video on a natural phenomenon. The story was part of a European-wide project. When agreeing on the assignment, the journalist was instructed that *Euronews* wanted as little journalistic presence as possible, with no stand-ups and only one interview. The video was supposed to be as country-specific as possible and present no general statements on the news beat. Reflecting back on this particular job assignment, the journalist commented, "editorially, they let me free to build my own story".

However, according to the journalist, the fee was quite low for the amount of work that went into the project, so he agreed that *Euronews* would take care of the post-production while he delivered the raw materials and a detailed script. In addition to putting the video together, the digital department at *Euronews* took care of translating the piece into 12 languages before dissemination.

When *Euronews*' 360-degree videos are complete, they are generally uploaded to Facebook, YouTube, *Euronews*' own websites and a platform called Veer.tv–one of the largest content communities for VR wherein *Euronews* has over 83,000 followers. *Euronews* uses the OmniVirt player, a subscription service, to distribute the videos on their websites and app.

In summary, the editorial quality of 360-degree videos at *Euronews* is thus taken care of mainly at the online news desk. That is, regardless of whether the raw material is produced by staffers or freelancers, the content production is centrally managed and appears to have specific characteristics. Having presented the tools and workflow of 360-degree video productions at *Euronews*, we move on to the content analysis of the 360-degree videos produced by the news organization.

Video content

In this section, we will further discuss the immersive videos at *Euronews* through an analysis of some storytelling content grips of the bureau's 360-degree videos. The data material consists of 95 pieces of 360-degree videos in which we identified the topics of coverage, production choices, verbal contextualizations, and techno-narrative structures. To compare 360-degree videos and "flat" videos, the analysis is followed by a comparison to 20 selected flat videos on similar topics from the website www.euronews.com. Note that the 360-degree videos analyzed here represent the early stages of *Euronews*' experimentation with 360-degree videos and actually include the first 95 pieces of production. We chose the period from 16 February 2016 to 11 July 2017 because it best represents what we wanted to capture in this chapter: the transition and adoption of *Euronews* into 360-degree video production. *Euronews* has continued its production of 360-degree and as of August 2019 has published over 170 videos.

Topics

Based on content, *Euronews*' 360-degree videos span wide on topics comprising arts, politics, humanitarian issues, culture, and sports. "Culture", which includes cultural events, festivals, and concerts, was actually the most prominent topic in 25% of the videos. Political issues were highlighted in 19% of the videos–mainly owing to a 360-degree series that focused on the 2017 French presidential election. Humanitarian issues, such as refugee camps, natural disasters, and war zones, were featured in 12% of the videos. Apart from these more classical categories, there was a substantial group of videos comprising "curiosities": for instance, a tour of Hitler's car or a beer brewery in the Arctic. Such clips are very popular and constitute 21% of the videos. Moreover, 11% of the productions might be classified as "travel", which simply aimed to present a certain location to the user. Sports and arts constituted the least popular categories, holding 3% and 5% of the productions, respectively. Another striking feature that surfaced in the identified categories was the lack of time-sensitive content: the 360-degree cameras were simply not used as a news-gathering tool in the initial phase of the immersive productions at *Euronews*. It can be discussed whether this somewhat surprising tendency was attributable to turnaround constraints or editorial choices; nevertheless, none of the 95 videos featured any particularly time-sensitive content.

Verbal contextualizations

Doing a 360-degree production implies more than disseminating visuals, meaning imagery. Each video, just like any other journalistic clip, is contextualized within reality by means of verbal text elements such as headlines and introductory information of time, place, and event. Such verbal contextualizing elements largely affect how the overall journalistic message is perceived (Gynnild 2014; Gynnild 2018). In terms of the accompanying texts, the 360-degree videos in this study contained only approximately half the number of words compared with flat videos. In other words, the 360-degree productions provided notably less textual information (164 words per video) than the flat videos (289 words per video). This tendency may indicate that 360-degree videos are considered by the online news desk to be a more stand-alone format than flat videos. It might also indicate that the aim of covering issues by 360-degree videos is to experiment with visual storytelling that requires less verbal contextualization.

The verbal decontextualizing aspect of the 360-degree approach is illustrated, for instance, by *Euronews*' coverage of Bocuse d'Or, the unofficial French world championship of culinary arts. Whereas *Euronews*' 360-degree report from the event contained 55 words, their flat video from the same event contained 148 words. Moreover, while the flat video comprised several interviews, clips of the chefs in action and a voiceover, the 360-degree video featured only shots from the celebration, providing glimpses of the atmosphere and audience surrounding the competition. In this way, the 360-degree video narrative appeared more simplistic than the in-detail interviews provided in the flat videos. This particular video serves as a clear example of a 360-degree production conducted "on top of" a normal TV production, as *Euronews* often tends to do. The approach may indicate that the 360-degree video as a medium did not have competitive advantages in terms of conducting interviews and presenting a consistent story from the championship event; it served more as a spectator approach to the Bocuse d'Or, a complementary story. The findings also indicate that employing the 360-degree video camera is a more inexpensive way to provide an online story that harvests views simply because of the novelty of the medium itself and not its actual production value. As the journalists were already on the scene, placing a 360-degree camera at the scene could be a simple way to get an additional story at a low cost.

Another interesting feature that surfaced during the textual analysis was the extent to which the articles mentioned the medium of capture as part of the news story. In total, 71% of the videos contained either explicit ("A 360-degree visit to...") or implicit mentions ("Take a look around...") to 360-degree video in the headlines or preamble. This is a way of referring to the story as interplay between the user and available content and leaning towards a greater user-oriented focus of video content. However, in terms of contextualization, it also means that the medium is itself a substantial part of the message or newsworthiness of the story, or at least that it is something that may fill sensation criteria in the early stages of immersive journalism. Although this can be relevant information for the user, one may also be critical towards such a presentation if the medium is not necessarily well fit for the content it should cover. One may argue that such types of sensational journalism do not add any value if the medium itself is the sensational element.

Narrative structures

The final aspect of the analysis focuses on the narrative structures of the videos: in what ways the online news desk chooses to portray the content. We isolated four different ways of narrative conveyance present in the 360-degree videos: 1) text in the article, 2) journalist or interview object addressing the camera/user, 3) graphical overlays on the video, and 4) voiceovers. These different narrative conveyances were often combined. Voiceover was used in a third of the videos, and the content of the voiceover was often the same as the accompanying text. Overlaying graphics were used in 45% of the videos to present the names of places and persons in the video.

In terms of the use of voiceovers and graphics for narration, such as name tags, locations, and other facts, the 360-degree reports were quite similar to the flat videos. However, the 360-degree videos do not appear to have clearly developed formats in terms of graphical representation such as intros and vignettes with logos. This feature may be attributable to the fact that the medium does not have any strong traditions within the organization and that the recurrent formats have not yet been developed. Very few of the 360-degree videos in the data material provide any specific format introduction to present the topic of the video. An exception was identified in *Euronews*' 360-degree reports on the French presidential election, which were created in cooperation with Google News Lab. In these nine episodes, *Euronews* and Google News Lab experimented with the same format throughout all the episodes. *Euronews*' VR editor explained, "we kept the format of the episodes the same throughout. You have an intro with journalists talking to the camera, then switch to the entrance of the place, introduce the subject, then dig in. The template gives us a sense of cohesiveness" (Redhohl 2017). Most of the 360-degree videos did not experiment with such a way of presenting the subject, which represents a definitive shift away from the ways that *Euronews* produces their flat videos.

Further, it should be noted that in our sample, the journalist was visible in 45% of the 360-degree videos and only in 33% of the flat videos. (These results are in alignment with those of Sirkkunen et al., see Chapter 6.) The surprisingly high degree of journalist presence in 360-degree videos compared with flat videos may be attributable to the differences of format between 360-degree and flat videos. In flat videos, it is easier to remove the clips of the journalist when editing, for example, by displaying only the answers to questions in interviews. In 360-degree videos, by contrast, journalist visibility cannot simply be removed from the scene. Therefore, the edits are more a question of either/or from beginning to end. The narrative style has to be decided before the shoot: should the story be told by focusing on an atmospheric scene without a journalist, perhaps with a voiceover? Or should the journalist be talking to the camera or an interview object? In 360-degree videos, it is not ideal to show a journalist in the background of the scene looking at the smartphone while controlling the shot. Such shots usually give the user a feeling of an item placed in the production set rather than that of getting immersed in an experience. There is thus less room for in-between levels of journalistic appearance in 360-degree videos as the explicit mediator of the experience, although implicitly the journalist has already made a selective choice of shots and edits.

Editorial choices

The greatest difference between the 360-degree videos and their flat video equivalents at *Euronews* is found in the number of shots/clips per video. The 360-degree videos had an average of 7 shots, whereas the flat videos had an average of 19, even when the 360-degree videos were, on average, 1 minute longer. The 360-degree videos had an average clip duration of 23 seconds, whereas the flat videos' average was 6 seconds. The relatively longer duration of each shot in the 360-degree video appears to ensure the user the time to orient within the video-sphere and explore the environment it depicts. While the journalist can still select what the user will perceive by placing the camera accordingly, the 360-degree sphere cannot be perceived all at once. The agency of what this selection will be is distributed to the user; thus, the nature of the medium restricts the ability of the journalist to secure a given linear narrative. Using multiple shots of smaller duration, panning, zooming, and/or even having a moving camera, may feel disorienting to the users viewing the video through a head-mounted display. Such given technical restrictions on building up a narrative in 360-degree videos have been discussed widely in the field (Aronson-Rath et al. 2015; Doyle et al. 2016).

Concluding remarks

In this chapter, we have presented a qualitative analysis of *Euronews*' intent and practice in immersive journalism through producing 360-degree videos. The data material demonstrates how *Euronews* uses readily available consumer technology in their experimental approaches towards immersive journalism with 360-degree lightweight cameras. Moreover, the bureau has systematically integrated 360-degree video production into their already existing workflows and trained their journalists and video editors in the new necessary skills. Through an analysis of 95 360-degree videos, we have identified how the 360-degree videos are far less editorially directed than their flat video equivalents, which offers a room of opportunity for the consumer to choose what to watch in the virtual environment. The analysis took into consideration the role of the journalist, topics of coverage, and context in which the 360-degree video is presented. We critically discussed how the medium may be used to fulfill sensation criteria and how the 360-degree videos are less contextualized than their flat video equivalents. Based on the datasets investigated in this study, we conclude that the biggest obstacle to ubiquitous immersive journalism news dissemination is still the time-consuming aspects of the 360-degree productions. By integrating such productions with already existing workflows, time expenditure is minimized as far as possible. Issues of time and cost are, however, still a challenge in journalism as a whole and become more evident when adopting and experimenting with new media for news dissemination. Further, the added value of such simplified, centrally edited 360-degree videos could still be questioned. Editors and journalists need time to develop formats and get a feel for the topics that are more suited for the medium than others. Such issues might partly explain why small and medium-sized news organizations tend to hesitate when it comes to investing heavily in the further development of immersive journalism.

References

About *Euronews*. 2019. *Euronews.com*. http://euronews.com/about [Accessed 11 April 2019].

Aronson-Rath, R., J. Milward, T. Owen, & F. Pitt. 2015. "Virtual Reality Journalism" [Technical report]. Columbia Journalism School, Tow Center. www.cjr.org/tow_center_reports/virtual_reality_journalism.php"https://www.cjr.org/tow_center_reports/virtual_reality_journalism.php#executive-summary [Accessed 15 March 2020].

Atkinson, C. 2017. "NBC News Names New President, Buys $30M Stake in *Euronews*." *New York Post*. https://nypost.com/2017/02/14/nbc-news-names-new-president-buys-30m-stake-in-euronews/ [Accessed 11 April 11 2019].

Doyle, P., M. Gelman, & S. Gill. 2016. "Viewing the Future? Virtual Reality in Journalism" [Technical report]. Knight Foundation. https://knightfoundation.org/reports/vrjournalism [Accessed 30 January 2019].

Dziadul, C. 2015. "Sawaris Family Gains Control of *Euronews*." *Broadbandtvnews.com*. www.broadbandtvnews.com/2015/07/09/sawaris-family-gains-control-of-euronews/ [Accessed 13 August 2019].

Flueckiger, S. 2016. "What *Euronews* Learned from Experimenting with 360 Video." *Wan-ifra.org*. https://blog.wan-ifra.org/2016/10/19/what-euronews-learned-from-experimenting-with-360-degree-video [Accessed 13 August 2019].

Gynnild, A. 2014. "Surveillance Videos and Visual Transparency in Journalism." *Digital Journalism 15*(4): 449–463.

Gynnild, A. 2018. "The Visual Power of News Agencies." *Nordicom Review* 38: 25–39.

Hooper, D. 2017. "*Euronews*' Tips for Filming with Samsung Gear 360." LinkedIn.com. www.linkedin.com/pulse/euronews-tips-filming-samsung-gear-360-duncan-hooper [Accessed 30 January 2019].

Journalism 360-degree Challenge. 2017. Knight Foundation. https://knightfoundation.org/challenges/journalism-360-challenge [Accessed 11 April 2019].

Journalism360. n.d. *Medium.com*. https://medium.com/journalism360 [Accessed 11 April 2019].

Krogsgaard, O. 2017. "This is How *Euronews* Trains Journalists in 360." *Medium.com*. https://medium.com/journalism360/this-is-how-euronews-trains-journalists-in-360-36cf663e4ea1 [Accessed 30 January 2019].

Maschio, T. 2017. "Storyliving: An Ethnographic Study of How Audiences Experience VR and What That Means for Journalists." Google News Lab. https://newslab.withgoogle.com/assets/docs/storyliving-a-study-of-vr-in-journalism.pdf [Accessed 11 April 2019].

Redhohl, S. 2017. "Q&A with Thomas Seymat about *Euronews*' 360 French Election Coverage." *Immersiveshooter.com*. www.immersiveshooter.com/2017/05/10/qa-with-thomas-seymat-about-euronews-360-french-election-coverage/ [Accessed 30 January 2019].

Scott, C. 2016. "Lessons from 360-degree video experiments at *Euronews*." *Journalism.co.uk*. www.journalism.co.uk/news/lessons-from-360-degree-video-experiments-at-euronews/s2/a682590/ [Accessed 11 April 2019].

Sirkkunen, E., H. Väätäjä, T. Uskali, & P.P. Rezaei. 2016. "Journalism in Virtual Reality: Opportunities and Future Research Challenges." In: *Proceedings of the 20th International Academic Mindtrek Conference*. New York: ACM, pp. 297–303. doi:10.1145/2994310.2994353

Watson, Z. 2017. *VR for News: The New Reality?* Digital News Project. Oxford, UK: Reuters Institute for the Study of Journalism, University of Oxford. https://reutersinstitute.politics.ox.ac.uk/our-research/vr-news-new-reality [Accessed 15 March 2020].

4

GLOBAL PERSPECTIVES OF IMMERSIVE JOURNALISM

Sarah Jones

> VR is such a fascinating medium for journalism because two huge factors of VR are the feeling of transporting you to some place, and secondarily, but just as importantly, connecting you to the people inside of that place.
>
> *Chris Milk 2015*

Technology companies like Oculus and Samsung have been instrumental in driving immersive journalism forward. With support in the form of development funding, news organizations have been encouraged to look at how immersive journalism can develop in the virtual reality space. This has been evident in the form of initiatives like Oculus' VR for Good and HTC Vive's VR for Impact. Technology companies have seen journalism and factual storytelling as a way to reach a new audience, away from the gaming and computer science industries where it has previously dominated. There has been indicative support for this. With *The New York Times* sending 1.2 million headsets to subscribers in November 2016 and virtual reality (VR) units or studios developing in companies like Al Jazeera, BBC and *The Guardian*, new ways of using the technology to drive journalism have been identified.

At the heart of this is the widespread belief that VR has the potential to change perspectives in understanding stories. It is the idea that stories told through VR can "transport viewers to places and events – to understand the world in new ways" (Watson 2017, 7). In the seminal paper on immersive journalism, Nonny de la Peña defined it as the production of news where "people can gain first-person experiences of the events or situation described in news stories" (2010, 291). The ability and impact that transporting an audience to a different place to engage in a news story in a direct way is contextualized in conversations around empathy and ethics, as discussed in Chapter 5 and 8 respectively in this book. What needs to be understood here is the positioning of immersive journalism in a global context.

With this in mind, this chapter analyzes the importance of immersive journalism to understand global issues and perspectives and the challenges that this raises when faced with a global digital divide. Through a series of case studies, immersive journalism practices from across the world will be identified and the impact that this has on the journalist, the journalism, and the experience.

The global context for immersive journalism

Journalism is about stories. It is about taking people to different places, providing information, and allowing for an objective account of a story to be told. The first wave of VR in the 1960s focused on the possibilities with the advancement of the technology. It was in the second wave, when the technology was more advanced and organizations like NASA could start to utilize it for education and training, that we saw the first ideas emerge around how VR could be applied to media practices. The early work on the ideas ofVR (Hamit 1993; Rheingold 1991) began introducing VR as the next logical step for communications, with Biocca and Levy (1995) theorizing that VR would enable journalists to "conquer time and space" by creating "a sense on the part of audiences of being present at distant, newsworthy locations and events". When narratives are developed to transport an audience to different places and cultures, the necessity to understand the global context of immersive journalism is clear.

What is evident, though, is the digital divide: the idea that there is an inequality in access and information to communication technologies. In 2019, there are still groups in America with limited access to the internet, with 30% of rural America still lacking what the Federal Communications Commission consider as adequate broadband (Politico 2018). This includes communities within certain income brackets, ethnicities, and geographical locations, which then has implications for employment, education, and the economy. It is even more prevalent when we look at the digital divide globally, where the "Internet has developed unevenly throughout the world" (Guilen & Suárez 2005, 681).

The 2018 Digital Use Suite (We Are Global and Hoot Suite, Kemp 2018) showed slight improvements in the distribution of internet access across the world. Internet penetration rates are found to be still low across Central Africa (12%) and Southern Asia (36%), but they are also the fastest-growing regions for adoptions. The number of users in Africa has increased by more than 20% year on year. Users in Benin, Sierra Leone, Niger, and Mozambique have also more than doubled in one year.

When considering the global digital usage in the context of journalism, the number of mobile phones is also important to consider, a valuable addition to the journalist's toolbox and something that will be discussed later in this chapter. The same report found more than two-thirds of the global population has a mobile phone, but still below 50% in Central Africa. The connection speeds vary considerably, which is important to note when this is looked on as a tool for digital storytelling and connectivity. Norway, Singapore, and the United Arab Emirates all boast speeds in excess of 50 Mbps, compared with Bangladesh at 5.2 Mbps andVenezuela at 7.9 Mbps.

The rise of digital journalism, responding to changes in platforms and technologies, has been as a direct result of the use of mobiles, as well as by innovations in digital narratives (Vázquez-Herrero & López-García 2017), so the existence of a digital divide raises concerns around representation of voices when considering the global context of immersive journalism. There is an increase in the adoption of digital journalism, but the divide will continue to exist when countries cannot freely access the technology.

The 2018 ICFJ report, The State of Technology in Global Newsrooms, addressed some of these challenges, providing a clear indication of the ways in which the digital divide is impacting news production and consumption. The findings of the report detail the digital media skills used regularly in the newsroom. What is classed as first-tier skills are those used by at least half of the newsrooms across the world and include stories and comments on social media (72%) and using digital photography (61%). Video production skills and audio production skills are classed as second-tier skills, used by at least one-third of newsrooms. Video skills are used in 49% and audio 42%. Mobile reporting is used in 34% newsrooms. The third-tier skills are where we find journalists working with VR and 360-degree video, however it is represented in only 21% newsrooms.

New revenue models for news businesses have adapted and changed over the past decade (REF) and this is especially difficult for newsrooms in developing countries. More than 70% of organizations in sub-Saharan Africa and Latin America/Caribbean found this to be a major challenge in adapting to new revenue models (ICFJ 2018). The rise of immersive journalism and virtual reality platforms was found to be particularly problematic and the biggest challenge for newsrooms in South Asia (53%), East/Southeast Asia (47%) and sub-Saharan Africa (46%). It was the least of a challenge for newsrooms in Europe, with only 15% finding it problematic.

With 21% of global newsrooms reporting to be using VR, this may be more down to teams experimenting with 360-degree filming or still photography on a tilt-and-rotate platform on social media. Certainly previous studies (Jones 2017) demonstrate the number of newsrooms producing VR regularly is significantly lower. The concern is around representation, with the question needing to be asked as to how do we ensure stories are being represented by journalists on the ground? The majority of stories produced within an immersive journalism format are usually around issues in the developing world (Jones 2017) to allow the idea of working in someone else's shoes, or essentially meeting the purpose of journalism "to provide people with information they need to understand the world" (Kovach & Rosenstiel 2014). It is essential to show that work is being done on the ground by journalists to establish immersive journalism practices in a global context.

Immersive journalism for a global perspective

With support from organizations like Journalism 360, Oculus and Vive, organizations have been able to develop immersive journalism practices. Through analysis of these organizations the potentiality of immersive journalism to offer authenticity of the story is understood. The organizations that have been developing since 2015 onwards are all committed to storytelling from a diverse range of voices to prevent the portrayal of communities and cultures through a foreign lens, something that will now be discussed.

Electric South was developed to build an ecosystem of immersive journalists in Africa. Based in Cape Town, South Africa, the organization operates under the belief that "new technologies must open up spaces for original voices and underrepresented narratives" (Electric South). The argument for this came out of a need for diversity and inclusivity within emerging media. As Kopp argued in 2017, "the problem is there is no balance in the African narrative being told – the pieces were all made by people from North America and Europe and they were not telling the whole story" (Kopp 2017).

The challenges facing the developing world in diversifying storytelling through new technologies is clear. As Kopp argues, it is harder and more expensive to buy equipment, it is harder to get the equipment in and out of countries, visas are expensive and difficult to get, the community is small so it is harder to share resources, there are barriers and complications for distribution, and phones have limited data or WiFi connectivity.

Despite the challenges, the global need for creating networks of diverse immersive journalists is evident as a way to avoid blind spots that emerge if only one group of society dominates a particular field, and it is through an ecosystem of inclusion that avoids this (Sinclair 2017). Through a residency approach, immersive storytellers in Africa have come together annually since 2015 with Electric South to collaborate, develop skills and look at emerging media forms to tell stories. The programs have been supported by the Ford Foundation. As one participant said following the 2018 camp, "they plant the seed for the new generation to come" (Afande 2018).

Although not specific to immersive forms, the workshops cover augmented reality, virtual reality, machine learning, and depth kit perceptions. It means that the participants are contributing to the development of immersive media, how it is used, produced, and consumed, before the rules have been set. As mainstream journalism has developed, it has relied on learning from previous traditions of narrative, imagery and style, whether online formats (Steensen 2010), radio and podcasting (Berry 2016; Cwynar 2015) or television (Wood 1986; Tuchman 1978). The rules in immersive media still have not been set and as RYOT co-founder Bryan Mooser (in Hernandez 2017) argues "journalism is changing". Due to the complexities of the combination of technical, artistry, and journalistic understandings, there is a collaborative approach with no one skillset dominating. This is allowing for inclusivity and levelling the playing field for diversity. As Kombo Chapfika, an Electric South 2018 participant, said, "there are no rules, the hierarchies haven't been fully set yet".

Similarly, it echoes the driving force behind Contrast VR, perhaps one of the most established immersive studios, with the explicit mandate to promote diversity and inclusivity in immersive journalism.

Contrast VR was founded in 2017 as the immersive studio of Al Jazeera. It originally began as the testing lab within Al Jazeera Digital with the aim to explore emerging technology and how that could be used for more immersive storytelling and, specifically, for journalism. Zahara Rasoul is the Editorial Lead, noting in 2018 that the main challenge is an understanding of what can be done; we have the tech but you don't have the storytelling that is actually going to have the impact that we think the technology combined with the storytelling can have" (Rasoul 2018).

The aim for Contrast is authenticity and to use immersive journalism as a way to break down the view of stories being told through the lens of a foreign reporter. Through a project where cameras and training were provided, they sought to enable journalists who did not have access to the kit to take charge of their own narratives.

> One of the goals of Contrast is to be able to enable local journalists and storytellers to take charge of their own narratives and to tell their own stories rather than only foreign journalists going into a place and telling those stories.
>
> *Rasoul 2018*

The initiative, *My People, Our Stories*, has trained filmmakers across the Za'atari refugee camp, South Sudan, and Rio de Janeiro, Brazil. It is seeking to add authentic voices to the concerns around representation in the media, something that has been the subject of a large body of academic research in recent years (Krimsky 2002; Heinrich 2012; Joye 2009), where there has been a disparity in the voices and tone of stories when presented through a foreign reporter's lens. This was clearly reflected in the comments from one of the Contrast VR workshops,

> When residents of the favela see a local journalist that is covering a story, they trust that the narrative won't be stereotyped or told in a distorted way. But when there is a journalist from outside there is a relationship of fear and even revolt, as favelas and their residents are almost always depicted as marginalized by the corporate media.
>
> *Thamyra Thâmara, in Contrast, Medium 2018*

More than 100 journalists and filmmakers have been trained by Contrast in two years (Contrast 2018) using the technology to give agency to different communities. Joi Lee, a Contrast producer, argues, "when those impacted by the issue are at the forefront of shaping the narrative, the stories become more informed and nuanced to reflect the realities on the ground" (Lee, Contrast 2018).

The above two case studies demonstrate the interest and desire to develop skills and expertise in immersive media to promote diversity and inclusivity. This is applicable in terms of content but also within the development of an emerging field. However, despite a range of workshops and interest in showing work, without securing funding for developing immersive content, the market becomes fragmented. There is a need for creators to continually develop and build on work, testing new methods and technologies as they develop, otherwise there are no resources for people to get better (Kopp, in conversation 2019). The impact that this is having in the Global South is clear. There is government resource in countries including Canada (CMF), France (CNC), and the UK (Creative XR), so the industry is developing. With funding limited in the Global South for development and production, "people aren't building a body of work" (Kopp in conversation 2019).

Distribution is also a key concern with finding and engaging audiences to show and make immersive media more accessible. Electric South has taken this with a top-down and bottom-up approach by targeting museums and art galleries at the top end and libraries and community spaces at the bottom. The driver has been to take it out of "self-selecting" spaces (Kopp, in conversation 2019) and to ensure that access to technology finds a wide group of people. It is a similar approach to that of NowHere Media in India and the VR experience, Love Matters India (www.lovematters.in). With technological challenges in the infrastructure, the experience needed to have an offline distribution channel for maximum impact. The experience was launched in restaurants in Delhi and Mumbai. In a partnership with the Delhi Metro, viewing booths were set up with mobile-based headsets, but there were challenges with electricity and limitations to streaming experiences.

Research in the case studies has shown the challenge for immersive journalism across the world is aligned to technological capabilities and the digital divide. With a significant need to promote diversity and inclusivity within the news medium, it can be argued that lessons from the rise of mobile journalism can help embed the industry to offer diverse voices and native narratives.

The influence of mobile journalism

There is tradition in using emerging technology to diversify journalistic practices. Since 2008, the rise of mobile journalism has empowered journalists across the world to tell stories. Early research (Bivens 2008) examined how traditional journalistic practices were beginning to be influenced by mobile technologies and, through an ethnographic study of 40 newsrooms, found the role that the citizen journalist played through documenting events on mobile devices to aid "reporting of contested topics or regions fraught with accessibility issues" (113). Studies on early adopters (Koponen & Väätäjä 2009) found the benefits for journalists, particularly for efficiency. Mobile allowed great access to documentary stories, particularly in places where traditional media crews were banned (Quinn 2013), so this has proved valuable in countries with poor media freedom and also by allowing reporters to get closer to the story (Karhunen 2017). The same study described mobile-led stories as being "more genuine", "authentic", "more intimate", "faster", and "more informal" (Karhunen 2017, 118).

There has been an increase in the number of media organizations wanting to recruit journalists with mobile-making skills (Wenger et al. 2014), though concerns around the professionalization has been questioned with particular reference to expert knowledge, professional autonomy, routines, and the influence of external organizations (Blakenship 2016).

It is necessary to put to one side the questions concerning quality, workflows, and techniques as this is not the focus of this chapter. However, it is important to consider how the rise of mobile journalism has enabled diverse voices to reach new audiences and capture a new form of journalistic storytelling. Mudliar et al. (2013) studied how the use of mobile technologies enabled rural communities in India to become active participants in issues that they were facing. Previously excluded, with the discourse largely taking place on television and in newspaper editorials, an interactive voice forum called CGNet Swara allowed communities to record messages of local interest, as well as to listen to messages that others had recorded. Although seen as a tool for citizen journalism and public engagement, the research found that communities felt that it was a "tool that carries complaints forward and helps in their resolution" (ibid., 72).

The impact of equipping people with skills to report on what is going in their location is nowhere more prominent than in Egypt, where there has been a long history of bloggers and activists chronicling events and demonstrations against the then President Hosni Mubarak, which were not covered on mainstream media. The impact was clear with blogs becoming powerful sources of information and also lobbying with the ability to reach international audiences (Levinson 2005). However, concerns around government intimidation and fragmentation with competition is often addressed (Hamdy 2009; Isherwood 2008; Radsch 2008).

Hashtag Our Stories was formed in September 2017, with the company mission set out as follows: "A global network of mobile storytellers creating videos about people changing their worlds". With the same ethos as Contrast VR, Hashtag Our Stories has been working to equip people with the skills necessary to broadcast their stories on platforms that have a global audience. The company, led by Yusuf Omar, has trained more than 2,000 mobile journalists in 140 countries to tell mobile stories which are then curated on the company's social platforms. The plan for the organization is to cover stories and voices that are "specifically looked at, often been talked about, but seldom been talked to" (2019).

In a similar vein to the work at Contrast VR and Electric South, on-the-ground training in communities has meant that there are more journalists to do "good factual reliable and authentic journalism" (2019), reaching 6 million people across their social platforms. They believe this is a more authentic way than through the lens of foreign journalists, as replicated in the mission behind Contrast VR. As with Contrast VR and the research that emerged from citizen journalism in the Arab Spring, it is built on the idea that diversity in voices enables a more authentic journalistic voice. Despite operating with the digital divide, Omar believes projects like this are breaking the barriers of entry into the ecosystem.

Concluding thoughts

The genre of immersive journalism is very much still emerging. Studios and news organizations have been identifying ways of working and discussing how stories are best told and the editorial guidelines that should be followed (all discussed throughout this book). It is clear that there are no set rules yet and so immersive journalism is very much in a period of experimentation. *The New York Times* supported Daily 360 stories for a one-year period (2017–2018), and *The Guardian* developed a VR lab, before resting it whilst the industry finds its place. The implication of this is that journalists from all over the world can be experimenting to find the voice of immersive journalism, without being dominated by the narrative of Silicon Valley (Kopp 2019).

As has been evidenced through movements in video and mobile journalism, opening access to technology is diversifying narratives and including more perspectives into the journalistic voice. Through specific organizations operating in the Global South, training is being offered to diverse communities to enable an authenticity to storytelling that is not being delivered through a foreign lens. This is allowing journalism to expand on the mixed narratives that have emerged from digital journalism practices. Immersive journalism now sits alongside these with calls for access to technology to enable a narrative and experimentation with story forms that breaks the digital divide. It is clear in the case studies presented that this work is being done by Contrast VR and Electric South offering examples of where there is talent emerging within this technology. It is important for this work to be continued as digital technology breaks down barriers in making and consuming news, as indicated in Elite Truong's Nieman Lab Report (2016): "to ensure that news reports have impact, we'll need to connect with readers because we reflect the readers".

Immersive journalism is not just about taking audiences to places that they haven't been or to afford them the opportunity to "walk in someone else's shoes". It is about opening up technological barriers so there is diversity and inclusivity in the voices telling sto for a true immersive experience.

References

Afande 2018, in Electric South, www.electricsouth.com [Accessed 15 January 2020].

Berry, R. 2016. "Podcasting: Considering the evolution of the medium and its association with the word 'radio'." *Radio Journal: International Studies in Broadcast & Audio Media, 14*(1): 7–22.

Biocca, Frank & Mark R. Levy. 1995. "Communication applications of virtual reality." In: F. Biocca & M.R. Levy (eds.), *LEA's Communication Series: Communication in the Age of Virtual Reality.* Hillsdale, NJ: Lawrence Erlbaum, pp. 127–157.

Bivens, R.K. 2008. "The Internet, mobile phones and blogging: How new media are transforming traditional journalism." *Journalism Practice, 2*(1): 113-129.

Blankenship, J.C. 2016. "Losing their 'mojo'? Mobile journalism and the deprofessionalization of television news work." *Journalism Practice 10*(8): 1055–1071.

Contrast VR, in https://ajcontrast.com [Accessed 15 January 2020].

Cwynar, C. 2015. "More than a 'VCR for radio': The CBC, the Radio 3 podcast, and the uses of an emerging medium." *Journal of Radio & Audio Media 22*(2): 190–199.

de la Peña, N., P. Weil, J. Llobera, E. Giannopoulos, A. Pomés, B. Spanlang, D. Friedman, M.V. Sanchez-Vives & M. Slater. 2010. "Immersive journalism: Immersive virtual reality for the first-person experience of news." *Presence: Teleoperators and Virtual Environments 19*(4): 291–301.

Guillen, M.F. & S.L. Suárez. 2005. "Explaining the global digital divide: Economic, political and sociological drivers of cross-national internet use." *Social Forces 84*(2): 681–708. CiteSeerX 10.1.1.649.2813. doi:10.1353/sof.2006.0015

Hamdy, N. 2009. "Arab citizen journalism in action: Challenging mainstream media, authorities and media laws." *Westminster Papers in Communication & Culture 6*(1).

Hamit, F. 1994. *Virtual reality and the exploration of cyberspace*. Carmel, Ind. Sams Publishing.

Heinrich, A. 2012. "Foreign reporting in the sphere of network journalism." *Journalism Practice 6*(5–6): 766–775.

Hernandez, R. 2017. "Virtual reality – the shift from storytelling to storyliving is real." https://medium.com/journalism360/virtual-reality-the-shift-from-storytelling-to-storyliving-is-real-ff465c220cc3 [Accessed 15 January 2020].

ICFJ. 2017. www.icfj.org/sites/default/files/2018-04/ICFJTechSurveyFINAL.pdf [Accessed 5 January 2019].

Isherwood, T. 2008. "A new direction or more of the same?" *Arab Media & Society*. September. Available at www.arabmediasociety.com/topics/index.php?t_article=230&p=1 [Accessed 5 January 2020].

Jones, S. 2017. "Disrupting the narrative: Immersive journalism in virtual reality." *Journal of Media Practice 18*(2–3): 171–185. doi:10.1080/14682753.2017.1374677

Joye, S. 2009. "The hierarchy of global suffering: A critical discourse analysis of television news reporting on foreign natural disasters." *Journal of International Communication 15*(2): 45–61.

Karhunen, P. 2017. *Closer to the Story? Accessibility and Mobile Journalism*. Oxford, UK: Reuters Institute for the Study of Journalism, University of Oxford.

Kemp, S. 2018. "Digital Use Suite." https://wearesocial.com/blog/2019/01/digital-2019-global-internet-use-accelerates [Accessed 15 January 2020].

Koponen, T. & H. Väätäjä. 2009. September. "Early adopters' experiences of using mobile multimedia phones in news journalism." In; *European Conference on Cognitive Ergonomics: Designing beyond the Product---Understanding Activity and User Experience in Ubiquitous Environments* .VTT Technical Research Centre of Finland, p. 2.

Kopp, Ingrid. 2017. "Who is VR for? " https://immerse.news/who-is-vr-for-20b3f077a912

Kovach, B. and T. Rosenstiel. 2014. *The Elements of Journalism: What Newspeople Should Know and the Public Should Expect*. California, CA: Three Rivers Press.

Krimsky, G.A. 2002. "The view from abroad: The foreign media are covering the war on terror through lenses that differ dramatically from those used by their American counterparts." *American Journalism Review 24*(1): 54–58.

Levinson, C. 2005. "Egypt's online voices of dissent." *Christian Science Monitor* 13 (10 Oct.). www.alternet.org/story/24525 [Accessed 8 March 2019].

Mudliar, P., J. Donner, & W. Thies. 2013. "Emergent practices around CGNet Swara: A voice forum for citizen journalism in rural India." *Information Technologies & International Development 9*(2): 65.

Politico. 2018. "Digital Divide in America." *Politico.com*. www.politico.com/agenda/story/2018/02/07/digital-divide-in-america-graphic-000639 [Accessed 8 March 2019].

Quinn, S. 2013. *Knowledge Management in the Digital Newsroom*. Oxford, UK: Focal Press.

Radsch, C. 2008. "Core to commonplace: The evolution of Egypt's blogosphere." *Arab Media & Society 6*: 1–14.

Rasoul, Z. 2018. "Contrast VR." https://medium.com/ajcontrast/welcome-to-contrast-vrs-weekly-blog-52842a10d8a2

Rheingold, H. 1991. "Virtual reality: exploring the brave new technologies." Simon & Schuster Adult Publishing Group.

Sinclair, K. 2017. *Weforum.org*. www.weforum.org/agenda/2017/06/artificial-intelligence-code-better-world/ [Accessed 8 March 2019].

Steensen, S. 2010. "Online journalism and the promises of new technology: A critical review and look ahead." *Journalism Studies 12*(3): 311–327.

Tuchman, G. 1978. "Television news and the metaphor of myth." *Studies in Visual Communication 5*(1): 56–62.

Vázquez-Herrero J. & X. López-García. 2017. "Immersive journalism through mobile devices: How virtual reality apps are changing news consumption." In: Á. Rocha, A. Correia, H. Adeli, L. Reis, & S. Costanzo (eds), *Recent Advances in Information Systems and Technologies. WorldCIST 2017. Advances in Intelligent Systems and Computing 571.* Cham, Switzerland: Springer.

Watson, Z. 2017. *VR for News: The New Reality?* Digital News Project. Oxford, UK: Reuters Institute for the Study of Journalism, University of Oxford.

Wenger, D., L. Owens, & P. Thompson. 2014. "Help wanted: Mobile journalism skills required by top US news companies." *Electronic News 8*(2): 138–149.

Wood, W. 1986. "Consumer spending on the mass media: The Principle of Relative Constancy reconsidered." *Journal of Communication 36*(2): 39–51.

PART II
Ethics

5

THE IMPACT OF EMOTIONS IN IMMERSIVE JOURNALISM

Turo Uskali and Pasi Ikonen

One of the starting motivations for developing the very concept and practice of immersive journalism was concern about the audiences' general apathy toward news reporting. As Nonny de la Peña et al. (2010, 298) stated in their seminal paper, "An important role of immersive journalism could be to reinstitute the audience's emotional involvement in current events". As a documentarist, de la Peña was more familiar with "emotional literacy" than an average news reporter, for example (see Pantti 2010, 176).

Virtual reality (VR) experiences indeed trigger emotions more effectively than many traditional forms of media content, according to many scholars (Doyle et al. 2016; Sundar et al. 2017; Bailenson 2018; Schilowitz 2017; Evans 2019, 4.) Therefore, one of the core challenges of immersive journalism, even still in its infancy, is the potential to cause strong emotions, positive and negative, in its audience. Every novel communication form creates new concerns. Like any transformative technology, VR comes with significant risks.

This chapter draws from journalism studies, health sciences, and ethics. We first outline the contemporary emotional turn in journalism studies. Second, we summarize the results of studies of the effects of VR treatments and other health-related issues. Third, we focus on ethical questions in relation to immersive journalism, especially pondering the need for possible updates and fine-tuning for traditional journalism ethics. Finally, based on the aforementioned perspectives we draft some instructions and ethical guidelines for immersive journalism.

The study of emotions is nothing new. Scholars in psychology and sociology were among the pioneers, starting with William James in 1884 (Wahl-Jorgensen 2019, 4). According to the Oxford English Dictionary (2019), emotion is a strong mental or instinctive feeling "deriving from one's circumstances, mood, or relationships with others". In communication and business studies, marketing has led the way in studying emotions. According to Andrew McStay (2016, 4) "advertising and emotions have always professionally gone hand-in-hand".

Mervi Pantti (2010, 169), who was among the first scholars to examine the role of emotions in journalism, has argued that emotionality in journalism and academic research has typically been seen as lowering the basic standards of the craft. It has been perceived as linked more to entertainment, tabloid journalism, or sensationalism, than serious, fact-based narratives.

There have been several roadblocks to studying emotions in journalism, according to Karin Wahl-Jorgenson (2019, 29–30), especially the professional ideal of objectivity, which has been traditionally defined as "the polar opposite of emotion". She divides scholarship on journalism and emotion into three categories: 1) understanding how journalistic practices are shaped by emotion and emotional labor, 2) studying emotion in journalistic texts, and 3) studying audience emotional engagement with news (ibid., 30). She concludes that "despite the persistence of the ideal of objectivity, emotional storytelling is, in fact, central to the world-making powers of journalism" (ibid., 35).

Good stories, images, and videos have always captured emotions, and thus emotions have always been explicitly or implicitly present in many journalistic works, especially in longer forms of storytelling, nonfiction human interest stories, and TV documentaries. Crisis reporting has also traditionally offered many emotional experiences via photographs, films, and videos (Pantti 2010, 172–173.)

In a similar vein, Chris Peters (2011) has argued that news has always been emotional, but journalists have not been able to show their own emotions, even in times of distress. Furthermore, Peters has emphasized that one of the most significant changes with reference to emotions in journalism practice has been that the "diversity of emotional styles, the acceptability of involvement on behalf of the journalist, and attempts to involve the audience have become more explicit" (ibid., 299).

By focusing on the emotive influences of immersive journalism, this chapter relates to the growing body of research literature that is forming the newest turn in journalism studies: emotion (Pantti 2010; Peters 2011; Beckett & Deuze 2016; Lindgren 2017, 127–144; Wahl-Jorgensen 2019; Nikunen 2019.) Moreover, the term "affective turn" is already in scholarly use (Lindgren 2017, 127; Wahl-Jorgenson 2019, 30).

Charlie Beckett and Mark Deuze (2016, 1) have argued, for example, that "as journalism and society change, emotion is becoming a much more important dynamic in how news is produced and consumed". Interestingly, Beckett and Deuze have not referred directly to VR, potentially the most immersive and emotional new technology available for journalistic storytelling.

The question of emotional manipulation

This shift toward more emotive public communication and media culture could be explained by the rise of the internet and social media, which have enabled new emotional communication forms and habits (Peters 2011, 301; Lindgren 2017, 128).

In addition, mobile phones' real-time messaging in the 1990s, and especially the use of emoticons, i.e., emotion icons, has paved the way for the use of emotions in digital communication. Of course, for centuries love letters and other forms of emotional correspondence were a common private practice. In that sense there is nothing new but the magnitude, intensity, and real-time feedback of the messages.

José van Dijck et al. (2018) have used the term "platform society" to illustrate how online platforms and societal structures are already intertwined. They have also emphasized that the platform companies often bypass old organizations and regulations (ibid, 1). Interestingly, they have not mentioned how the platform companies have already heavily invested in immersive technologies, potentially the next phase of human communication systems (see also Chapter 8). According to Frank Biocca and Mark Levy (1995, 127), already in the early 1990s introductory VR books often described VR as "the next logical step in the history of communication".

Platform companies' powerful position has already led to some serious ethical discussions. For example, Facebook has been blamed particularly for massive-scale emotional tests (Kramer et al. 2014; Jouhki et al. 2016) and for being the main publishing platform of a form of digital advertising that has been called "fake news" (Silverman 2016; van Dijck et al. 2018, 49). Increasing awareness and critical public debates have created pressures, especially in the European Union, to combat misinformation and disinformation and to regulate the platform companies (Bakir & McStay 2018, 155).

As David Hesmondhalgh (2019, xxi–xxii) has analyzed, there is a constant battle between the "doomed dinosaurs", traditional cultural industries including media organizations, and their "crucial frenemies", the IT industries. He writes that "it is increasingly obvious that the new world of digital networks has some extremely worrying aspects", such as in terms of surveillance.

In addition, according to McStay (2016, 1–3), "emotiveillance" has already been tested in reality, for example emotional surveillance by advertisers. In London in 2015, marketing company M&C Saatchi produced an advert for a fictional coffee brand that changed according to people's facial reactions. It was presumably the first time that data about emotions was collected automatically for improving an advert's performance. This improvement was done by replacing elements that did not bring enough positive responses.

McStay (2016, 1) has also coined the "empathic media" concept, which refers to "technologies that track bodies and react to emotions and intentions". These "empathic media" technologies include, for example, facial coding, voice analytics, VR, augmented reality, and wearables. Based on these technologies, the users' emotions could be machine-readable, and this data could be used for influence and surveillance (Bakir & McStay 2018, 155). McStay (ibid., 10) emphasizes that collecting and using intimate data raises legal and ethical questions, but he does not yet offer any answers for this "emotion-sensitive advertising".

According to Pantti (2010, 178), in television journalism the most important question regarding emotion has been "How much emotion is too much?" This is also a valid concern for immersive journalism. As the development of immersive journalism is still only in its early stages and no mass audiences exist yet, it is important to start critical scholarly examination about the potential health issues and ethical implications of immersive technologies for journalism early enough.

Virtual reality and health effects: positive and negative

Physicians and psychotherapists have been in the forefront of adopting VR technologies in their work. According to VR treatments research literature, positive results have been published already for two decades. These range from VR exposure therapy for phobias (Emmelkamp et al., 2001; Bowman & McMahan 2007; Parsons & Rizzo 2008; Diemer et al. 2015) to VR treatment for reducing pain (Hoffman et al. 2000; Hoffman et al. 2004; Malloy & Milling 2010), and, more recently, VR treatments for anxiety disorders (Opris et al. 2012).

According to the latest research, psychotherapists have used VR exposure therapy successfully to treat fear of heights (Temming 2018), fear of flying, and fear of going to the dentist (Metz 2018). In medicine, VR has had an impact on reducing pain (Hooker 2019; Savran Kelly 2018; Bailenson 2018), detecting early risks of Altzheimer's (McKie 2018), neurological conditions (BBC.com 2018), and schizophrenia (Fidelman 2018). In addition, VR experiences have proved to be helpful in meditation practices (Garone 2018).

On the more negative side, VR experiences have also been proven to cause, for example, the loss of spatial awareness, dizziness and disorientation, seizures, nausea, eye soreness, trouble focusing, and motion or simulator sickness (Bailenson 2018; Fagan 2018). The term "cybersickness" has also been used in relation to immersive journalism (LaViola 2000; Hardee & McMahan 2017).

According to Gary Hardee and Ryan McMahan (2017), there are three main theories for what causes motion sickness in VR experiences. First, the poison theory argues that during an immersive experience the body misinterprets the stimuli as a form of toxic substance. Second, the postural instability theory claims that prolonged postural instability results in motion sickness symptoms because humans are expected to maintain postural stability. Third, and perhaps the most believable of all, is the sensory conflict theory, which is based on an assumption that the body does not know how to handle mixed signals or inconsistencies in relation to motion and the body's orientation.

Psychologist and communication scholar Jeremy Bailenson, from the Virtual Human Interaction (VHI) Lab, which was founded in 2003 at Stanford University, has been one of the study pioneers of how VR experiences could lead to changes in perceptions of self and others. He has been focusing on experiments on VR since the turn of the millennium.

According to Jeremy Bailenson (2018), people's VR experiences indeed have an impact on them and have psychological effects. Of course, these effects could be both positive and negative. VR experiences could encourage empathic understanding, often understood as "perspective-taking" or "walking in another's shoes". When head-mounted display users immerse themselves in closed VR experiences, their attention drifts away from their own bodies. Bailenson also mentions that this has been useful especially for pain reduction. On the negative side, he reminds that watching and listening to VR experiences could also cause "compassion fatigue" that can trigger anxiety, nightmares, and even burnout.

In Finland, we conducted our own empirical user tests on emotional reactions to immersive journalism experiences. The first pilot was with journalism students (n = 20). Additional focus group interviews with journalism students (n = 27) and VR journalism professionals (n = 4) followed. The tests, even at this small scale, provided a clear picture of ethical challenges as well as VR journalism's potential benefits and pitfalls. Based on our own tests, including nine different mini-documentaries or immersive experiences with journalism students, the main result was that the same experiences could generate many different reactions, depending on the person and their background. Therefore, we can claim that immersive journalism stories are far more complicated, nuanced, and provide a more subjective experience than previously thought (Uskali et al. 2019).

Based on our findings, we can argue that negative motion sickness effects do exist, but they vary from person to person. Regarding immersive journalism, one important aim should always be to avoid any motion sickness effects. The easiest way to do this is just to remember not to move the cameras (see also Hardee & McMahan 2017). According to our research, surprisingly many mini-documentaries in 2018 still included segments that used 360-degree cameras in motion.

In conclusion, we argue that immersive journalism, when using the VR storytelling methods, operates in a sensitive emotional area that also needs serious consideration of ethics.

Ethical implications: a need for updates and fine-tuning

Crisis reporting has traditionally regularly offered journalism ethics cases that are also related to health questions, especially in terms of journalists' safety. Unpredictable and hazardous work environments have caused the deaths of hundreds of journalists, not only in war zones, conflict areas, or catastrophe situations, but also when investigating sensitive issues such as corruption and other crimes (Carlsson & Pöyhtäri 2017). Of course, every death of a journalist is one too many, and signals either too much risk taking or too little protection from the newsrooms and governments.

Stephen Ward (2018) has defined journalism ethics as the "responsible use of the freedom to publish; it is the study and application of the norms that should guide responsible, public journalism". Ethical considerations, especially by photojournalists, have often concentrated on the use of violent, cruel, and pornographic materials. However, other kinds of ethical issues also exist, such as questions of authenticity, truthfulness, verification, and privacy. These are also all valid concerns for immersive journalism.

Recently, more brutal and graphic images have been shared on social media platforms than have ever been broadcast on news media. But journalism ethics still matter, and all decisions should be based on ethical considerations and professional codes. Journalism ethical standards offer a valuable basis for immersive journalism practices, but, we, to some degree, agree with Ward (2018) that there is indeed a need for some updates and fine-tuning. Ward has emphasized the need to even disrupt traditional journalism ethics due to "the digital media revolution". He argues that "journalism ethics should become a new, more complex, and conceptually deeper, global ethics for responsible communication" (Ibid.).

In a similar vein, Kathleen Bartzen Culver (2015) has summarized this need for ethical updates in immersive journalism:

> In some cases, traditional ethics contested over decades help inform our judgments. But in others, the very immersion itself prompts questions we have not yet tackled in journalism.
>
> *Culver 2015*

Philosophers Michael Madary and Thomas Metzinger (2016, 5) have already warned about the manipulative power of VR technologies (see also Chapter 7.):

> The comprehensive character of VR plus the potential for the global control of experiential content introduces opportunities for new and especially powerful forms of both mental and behavioral manipulation, especially when commercial, political, religious, or governmental interests are behind the creation and maintenance of the virtual worlds.
>
> *Metzinger 2016, 5, 3*

As a senior editor at Associated Press, Tom Kent (2015) has predicted: "It's only a matter of time until VR simulation looks more and more like the actual event". Therefore, Kent has emphasized the need for transparency and also special VR ethics statements. Furthermore, he has argued that:

> Clearly, journalism's job is to bring human drama alive for distant audiences. But creating empathy is a goal beyond just telling a story. If the ultimate aim is to create emotion, a journalist could be tempted to omit balancing or inconvenient information that could interfere with the desired emotional effect.
>
> *Kent 2015*

Kent has also started a crowdsourcing project to create a VR journalism code of ethics via the Online Journalism Association. At the time of writing in summer 2019 it only consisted of Kent's introduction, in which Kent separates two types of VR journalism stories: 1) capturing the reality, or 2) aimed at more than capturing reality, for example, re-creating an actual news event. He writes: "when re-creating a news event that wasn't captured originally by VR cameras, the ethical issues are even greater". He also wonders whether VR stories including violence could cause post-traumatic stress in the viewer (Kent 2019).

Dan Robitzski (2017) has argued that many publications' first experiments with VR raise new ethical considerations, "not only about how these stories are produced, but also about the ways in which audiences experience and remember them". In the first VR stories, audiences were transported to "less innocuous situations", such as a war zone or a prison cell in solitary confinement.

Photojournalism ethics, which are based on the notion that the images should not be altered, are solid ground for immersive journalism. Another ethical question is privacy. As the video captures everything in 360-degrees, it can be challenging to hide anything or anybody; everything is on the scene, including tripods and the journalists. One can try to hide or edit content afterwards in post-production, but it raises the question of authenticity. According to Kathleen Bartzen Culver (2015), "privacy is clearly one of the largest ethical considerations for journalists with immersives, especially 360-degree video". She also reminds us that:

> Virtual reality that relies on video capture, for instance, poses the problem of incidental capture. Imagine an immersive experience designed to transport users to a Liberian hospital treating patients with Ebola.
>
> *Culver 2015*

There are constant ethical ponderings in newsrooms concerning what to show to the audience. However, in 360-degree videos and especially 360-degree real-time streams, it is harder to make any ethical decisions with that pace. In general, people are not yet aware of 360-degree cameras and their capabilities, compared with 2D devices. Also, 360-degree microphones may capture incidentally conversations or comments that are not meant for the public. In this way, the journalist should behave ethically and consider informing people at the scenes being recorded.

Protecting children: What is the right age?

The use of VR by children has created further concern (see also Paura 2018). According to Jaron Lanier (2018, 118), "there's a consensus in the VR research community that kids shouldn't get into VR before about age six, and some researchers recommend waiting until eight or nine". The health and safety guide for the Oculus Rift and Touch headsets (Oculus 2019) forbids the use of the device by children under 13 years old. The guide explains that the headset is not the proper size for children, and that younger children are in a critical period in their visual development. Children's susceptibility toward acquiring false memories is another point of concern (Bailenson 2018, 992).

In TV news, for example, warnings by the news anchors of upcoming disturbing material have often preceded the insert but without any age recommendations. So far, *The Guardian* has been one of the few news media organizations that has provided special instructions and age recommendations for immersive journalism users. It has also informed its immersive journalism audience that if they feel sick or uncomfortable, the head-mounted displays should be taken off. Furthermore, they have been advised to sit down and avoid placing any hot drinks nearby (Panetta 2016). At the beginning of an immersive experience, such as in *6x9: Solitary confinement*, a prison story, there is a warning:

> Before you watch further you should be aware that this virtual experience has disturbing material and could provoke an emotional reaction. You should take this and your comfort level into consideration before you choose to continue. You must be at least 18 years old to participate in this virtual experience.
>
> *6×9: Solitary confinement - VR experience 2016*

Another ethical issue, emphasized first by Ana Luisa Sánchez Laws (2019), is the use of children as informants in distressing news environments. Among the very first examples of immersive journalism were mini-documentaries, such as *The Displaced* (2015) and *Clouds Over Sidra* (2015), in which refugee children were the central characters of the stories (see also *Yemen's Skies of Terror* 2018). According to Sánchez Laws (ibid., 1), "the sensitivity required when presenting distressful events is even more important when working with minors as the subjects of these events". Of course, permission from the parents or other custodians should always be asked if underage persons are to be used as story subjects. This is in line with general journalism ethics.

Conclusions

It is easy to argue that immersive journalism is indeed a powerful new medium, which could have both positive and negative effects for its users. As feelings and emotions have entered research in journalism studies, immersive journalism represents a new and important study field that needs international collaboration and networks. Finally, we can perhaps even start talking about emotive immersive journalism, as emotions play an essential role in the closed virtual experiences and story narratives.

Even if research on the effects of immersive journalism is still scarce, and the user base is low, we can already argue, based on results from health sciences, that there is a need for health instructions and ethical fine-tuning in terms of immersive experiences.

Perhaps most important of all, there should be minimum ages set for immersive journalism. What the lowest age should be for immersive journalism experiences is still debatable. Motion picture and game content rating systems could also offer some guidance for immersive experiences. If there are any doubts that the content may cause psychological harm for its users, special warnings and age restrictions should be set. Of course, another question is how to control that these warnings are obeyed.

Immersive journalists should not only be aware of their own work ethics in the matter of emotive immersive storytelling but also be critically cautious toward possibly advanced and sophisticated manipulation and disinformation operations in the immersive journalism form. In ethics, special attention should be paid to the questions of suitable content and its authenticity.

References

Bailenson, Jeremy. 2018. *Experience on Demand: What Virtual Reality Is, How It Works, and What It Can Do*. 1st ed. New York: W.W. Norton & Company.

Bakir, Vian & Andrew McStay. 2017. "Fake News and the Economy of Emotions: Problems, Causes, Solutions." *Digital Journalism 6*(2), July: 154–175.

BBC.com. 2018. "Virtual reality therapy opens new horizons for neurological conditions." *BBC.com*. 28 July. www.bbc.com/news/av/uk-scotland-44987550/virtual-reality-therapy-opens-new-horizons-for-neurological-conditions [Accessed 23 February 2019].

Beckett, Charlie & Mark Deuze. 2016. "On the role of emotion in the future of journalism." *Social Media Society 2*(3), September: 1–6.

Biocca, Frank & Mark R. Levy. 1995. "Communication applications of virtual reality." In: F. Biocca & M.R. Levy (eds.), *LEA's Communication Series: Communication in the Age of Virtual Reality*. Hillsdale, NNJ: Lawrence Erlbaum, pp. 127–157.

Bowman, Doug A. & Ryan P. McMahan. 2007. "Virtual reality: How much immersion is enough?" *IEEE Computer 40*(7), July: 36–43. doi:10.1109/MC.2007.257

Carlsson, Ulla & Reeta Pöyhtäri (eds). 2017. *The Assault on Journalism: Building Knowledge to Protect Freedom of Expression*. Gothenburg, Sweden: Nordicom.

Culver, Kathleen B. 2015. "Immersive approaches pose new questions." 11 February. Wisconsin: Center for Journalism Ethics, University of Wisconsin-Madison. https://ethics.journalism.wisc.edu/category/virtual-reality/ [Accessed 9 March 2019].

de la Peña, Nonny, Peggy Weil, Joan Llobera, Elias Giannopoulos, Ausias Pomés, Bernhard Spanlang, Doron Friedman, Maria V. Sanchez-Vives, & Mel Slater. 2010. "Immersive journalism: Immersive virtual reality for the first-person experience of news." *Presence 9*(4), August: 291–301.

Diemer, Julia, Georg W. Alpers, Henrik M. Peperkorn, Youssef Shiban, & Andreas Mühlberger. 2015. "The impact of perception and presence on emotional reactions: A review of research in virtual reality." *Frontiers in Psychology 6*(26), January.

Doyle, Patrick, Mitch Gelman, & Sam Gill. 2016. *Viewing the Future? Virtual Reality in Journalism*. Knight Foundation. https://knightfoundation.org/reports/vrjournalism [Accessed 22 February 2019].

Emmelkamp, Paul M., Mary Bruynzeel, Leonie Drost, & C.A.G. van der Mast. 2001. "Virtual reality treatment in acrophobia: A comparison with exposure in vivo." *CyberPsychology & Behavior 4*(3), June: 335–339.

Evans, Leighton. 2019. *The Re-Emergence of Virtual Reality*. 1st ed. London: Routledge.

Fagan, Kaylee. 2018. "Here's what happens to your body when you've been in virtual reality too long." *Business Insider*. www.businessinsider.com/virtual-reality-vr-side-effects-2018-3?r=US&IR=T [Accessed 4 March 2019].

Fidelman, Charlie. 2018. "People with schizophrenia learn to fight their demons with virtual reality." *MontrealGazette.com*. https://montrealgazette.com/health/montreal-researcher-has-patients-fighting-their-demons-with-virtual-reality [Accessed 7 August 2019].

Garone, Sarah. 2018. "Why virtual reality is a game-changer for my meditation practice." *Brit+Co*, 15 August. www.brit.co/virtual-reality-meditation/ [Accessed 23 February 2019].

Hardee, Gary M. & Ryan P. McMahan. 2017. "FIJI: A framework for the immersion-journalism intersection." *Frontiers in ICT 4*(21), July.

Hesmondhalgh, David. 2019. *The Cultural Industries*. 4th ed. London: SAGE.

Hoffman, Hunter G., David R. Patterson, & Gretchen J. Carrougher. 2000. "Use of virtual reality for adjunctive treatment of adult burn pain during physical therapy: A controlled study." *The Clinical Journal of Pain 16*(3), September: 244–250.

Hoffman, Hunter G., Todd L. Richards, Barbara Coda, Aric R. Bills, David Blough, Anne L. Richards, & Sam R. Sharar. 2004. "Modulation of thermal pain-related brain activity with virtual reality: Evidence from fMRI." *Neuroreport 15*(8), June: 1245–1248.

Hooker, Lucy. 2019. "How virtual reality can help you manage pain." *BBC News*, 23 January. www.bbc.com/news/av/business-46964729/how-virtual-reality-can-help-you-manage-pain [Accessed 6 September 2019].

Jouhki, Jukka, Epp Lauk, Maija Penttinen, Niina Sormanen, & Turo Uskali. 2016. "Facebook's emotional contagion experiment as a challenge to research ethics." *Media and Communication 4*(4), October: 75–85.

Kent, Tom. 2015. "An ethical reality check for virtual reality journalism." *Medium.com*, 31 August. https://medium.com/@tjrkent/an-ethical-reality-check-for-virtual-reality-journalism-8e5230673507 [Accessed 15 March 2020].

Kent, Tom. 2019. "Virtual reality journalism." *Online News Association*. https://ethics.journalists.org/topics/virtual-reality-journalism-2/ [Accessed 27 September 2019].

Kramer, Adam D.I., Jamie E. Guillory, & Jeffrey.T. Hancock. 2014. "Experimental evidence of massive-scale emotional contagion through social networks." In: *Proceedings of the National Academy of Sciences of the United States of America 111*(24), June: 8788–8790.

Lanier, Jaron. 2018. *Dawn of the New Everything: A Journey Through Virtual Reality*. London: Bodley Head.

LaViola, Joseph J. 2000. "A discussion of cybersickness in virtual environments." *SIGCHI Bulletin 32*(1), January: 47–56. doi:10.1145/333329.333344

Lindgren, Simon. 2017. *Digital Media & Society*. London: SAGE.

Madary, Michael & Thomas K.Metzinger. 2016. "Real virtuality: A code of ethical conduct: recommendations for good scientific practice and the consumers of VR-technology." *Frontiers in Robotics and AI 3*(3), February: 1–23.

Malloy, Kevin M. & Leonard S. Milling. 2010. "The effectiveness of virtual reality distraction for pain reduction: A systematic review." *Clinical Psychology Review 30*(8), December: 1011–1018.

McKie, Robin. 2018. "Virtual reality to help detect early risk of Alzheimer's: Navigation skills tested through headsets may identify patients far earlier." *The Guardian*, 16 December. www.theguardian.com/society/2018/dec/16/alzheimers-dementia-cure-virtual-reality-navigation-skills [Accessed 9 March 2019].

McStay, Andrew. 2016. "Empathic media and advertising: Industry, policy, legal and citizen perspectives (the case for intimacy)." *Big Data & Society 3*(2), November: 1–11.

Metz, Rachel. 2018. "How VR is helping flyers and dental patients calm down." *CNN.com*, 10 December. https://edition.cnn.com/2018/12/10/tech/vr-dentist/index.html [Accessed 23 February 2019].

Nikunen, Kaarina. 2019. *Media Solidarities: Emotions, Power and Justice in the Digital Age*. London: SAGE.

Opriş, David, Sebastian Pintea, Azucena García-Palacios, Cristina Botella, Ştefan Szamosközi, & Daniel David. 2012. "Virtual reality exposure therapy in anxiety disorders: A quantitative meta-analysis." *Depression and Anxiety 29*(2), February: 85–93.

Oxford English Dictionary. 2019. www.oed.com/view/Entry/61249?rskey=ed1fLA&result=1&isAdvanced=false#eid [Accessed 6 September 2019].

Panetta, Francesca. 2016. "6x9: A virtual reality experience of solitary confinement – FAQs." *The Guardian*, 27 April. www.theguardian.com/world/2016/apr/27/6x9-vr-virtual-reality-experience-solitary-confinement-faqs-explainer [Accessed 10 March 2019].

Pantti, Mervi. 2010. "The value of emotion: An examination of television journalists' notions on emotionality." *European Journal of Communication 25*(2), June: 168–181.

Parsons, Thomas D. & Albert A. Rizzo. 2008. "Affective outcomes of virtual reality exposure therapy for anxiety and specific phobias: A meta-analysis." *Journal of Behavior Therapy and Experimental Psychiatry 39*(3), October: 250–261.

Paura, Angelo. 2018. "The ethical challenges of immersive journalism." *Mediashift.org*, February. http://mediashift.org/2018/02/the-ethical-challenges-of-immersive-journalism/ [Accessed 9 March 2019].

Peters, Chris. 2011. "Emotion aside or emotional side? Crafting an 'experience of involvement' in the news." *Journalism 12*(3), April: 297–316.

Robitzski, Dan. 2017. "Virtual reality and journalistic ethics: Where are the lines?" *Undark.org*, 27 September. https://undark.org/article/virtual-reality-and-journalistic-ethics-where-are-the-lines/ [Accessed 9 March 2019].

Sánchez Laws, Ana Luisa. 2019. *Conceptualizing Immersive Journalism*. New York: Routledge.

Savran Kelly, J. 2018. "Relieving real pain in a virtual world." *Cornell Chronicle*. https://news.cornell.edu/stories/2018/04/relieving-real-pain-virtual-world [Accessed 30 April 2019].

Schilowitz, Ted. 2017. "Foreword." In: John Bucher (ed.), *Storytelling for Virtual Reality: Methods and Principles for Crafting Immersive Narratives*. New York: Routledge, pp. ix–xi.

Silverman, Craig. 2016. "This analysis shows how fake election news stories outperformed real news on Facebook." *BuzzFeed News*. www.buzzfeednews.com/article/craigsilverman/viral-fake-election-news-outperformed-real-news-on-facebook [Accessed 16 November 2019].

Sundar, S. Shyam, Jin Kang, & Danielle Oprean. 2017. "Being there in the midst of the story: How immersive journalism affects our perceptions and cognitions." *Cyberpsychology, Behavior, and Social Networking 20*(11), November: 672–682.

Temming, Maria. 2018. "Are you scared of heights? Virtual reality could help. In a therapy app, an avatar coaches people through sky-high situations." *Sciencenewsforstudents.org*. www.sciencenewsforstudents.org/article/are-you-scared-heights-virtual-reality-could-help [Accessed 14 August 2019].

Uskali, Turo, Esa Sirkkunen, Chelsea Kelling, Pasi Ikonen, & Heli Väätäjä. 2019. "Testing immersive journalism experiences: Emotions and ethics." Paper presented at The Future of Journalism conference, Cardiff University, United Kingdom, 12 September.

van Dijck, José, Thomas Poell, & Martijn De Waal. 2018. *The Platform Society: Public Values in a Connective World*. Oxford: Oxford University Press.

Wahl-Jorgensen, Karin. 2019. *Emotions, Media and Politics*. Hoboken, NJ: John Wiley & Sons.

Ward, Stephen J.A. 2018. *Disrupting Journalism Ethics*. London: Routledge.

6

PROJECT SYRIA

Accuracy in immersive journalism

Siri Flatlandsmo and Astrid Gynnild

This chapter investigates opportunities and dilemmas in VR journalism through a case study of Nonny de la Peña's pioneering production, *Project Syria*, from 2014. *Project Syria* exemplifies a computer-generated imagery (CGI) experience that prompts crucial journalism concerns that still await further discussion. While de la Peña and the Emblematic Group envisioned initiating an empathetic wake-up call through innovative technological means, this case study investigates in what ways and to what extent the VR story potentially deviates from established norms of accurate journalism.

This chapter zeroes in on the particular journalism challenges of using CGI in VR by applying the main principles of a well-established code-of-ethics program in journalism. Our point of departure is thus the application of the 35 bullet points provided by the American Society of Professional Journalists (SPJ), last updated in 2014.

A crucial question in this chapter is how journalists "seek truth and report it", "minimize harm", "act independently", and, at the same time, strive to "be accountable and transparent" when doing journalism based on CGI.

Moreover, it is pertinent to question to what extent a journalism code of ethics, albeit one that has been renewed regularly since 1909, can actually serve as a relevant guideline for new technologies such as VR. Does it really make sense, at present, to maintain the normative divides between journalism as a truth-seeking approach to reality and other forms of CGI? The aim of this case study is to highlight in what ways VR specifically challenges established principles of ethics in journalism. Perhaps most importantly, the goal is to reflect on how journalists maintain their journalistic integrity while experimenting with new technologies in a time of ethical flux.

Issues of what constitutes journalism are increasingly up for renegotiation and professional boundary work (Carlson & Lewis 2020). In these cyclical rhetorical battles, discussants often push forward the ethical guidelines of journalism, understood as the existing global body of journalism ethics. A growing number of researchers and practitioners have voiced the need for updating and further developing journalism ethics in tandem with, in particular, the experimenting with emerging technological innovations (Bartzen Culver 2015; Johnson 2020; Kent 2015; Robitzski 2017; Ward 2019). However, few attempts have so far been made thus to implement new ethical norms in practice.

According to Raney Aronson-Rath of the PBS investigative series Frontline, which received a Knight Foundation grant to explore VR production and ethics with the Emblematic Group, "no established set of standards and ethics around applying journalism in VR environments currently exists" (Seijo 2017). As further pointed out by Deborah G. Johnson (see Chapter 7), during such a state of interpretive flexibility, many actors are engaged in pushing and pulling a new technology in different directions, and they negotiate "about the meaning of what is being developed as well as about designs and uses" (Chapter 7, p.165). Throughout history, various ethical codes sets have served as professional guidelines for what constitutes good journalism. The detailed guidelines are typically developed and taken care of by journalism organizations themselves; these guidelines vary from country to country, albeit with truth and accuracy seeming to be basic requirements. In the United States, the SPJ is dedicated to "encouraging the free practice of journalism and stimulating high standards of ethical behavior" (Spj.org 2019).

As *Project Syria* was created mostly in the United States by an American team, our deliberately naïve point of departure is thus the expectation that de la Peña and her crew created the piece in alignment with established ethical norms in their country. The SPJ was founded in 1909, with the mission to maintain a free press in the United States. The argument was that because "the concept of self-government outlined by the U.S. Constitution remains a reality into future centuries, the American people must be well informed in order to make decisions regarding their lives, and their local and national communities" (Spj.org 2019). The SPJ is dedicated to stimulating high standards of ethical behavior in the practice of journalism. Their Code of Ethics, which journalists are expected to follow, is revised regularly, the last update having taken place in 2014.

Project Syria is an early computer-generated VR production that, in reality, represented a breakthrough for what was coined *immersive journalism*. De la Peña applies the term "immersive journalism" on her YouTube channel when talking about *Project Syria*. De la Peña claims that "[i]t's an extraordinary opportunity to be building an immersive journalism piece about Syrian children refugees. This is one of the most pressing issues of our time" (de la Peña 2014). Only two years earlier, in 2012, de la Peña and the Emblematic Group produced the first-ever walk-around VR documentary, *Hunger in Los Angeles* (Who We Are 2016). *Project Syria*, however, was specifically developed for the World Economic Forum in Davos, an event that engages societal leaders to "shape global, regional and industry agendas" (Our Mission – The World Economic Forum 2019).

Before we dive into more details on the production, just envision going a few years back in history, before immersion became a hot topic, and imagine the following virtual jump: You are standing in your own living room, looking around at everything familiar. Then, you put on a headset packed with the latest VR technology. Suddenly, you are standing on a buzzing street in war-torn Aleppo, Syria. When you turn around, all you can see is this unfamiliar place, people you have never seen before, but you know you are there; you can hear a girl singing. Then, a bomb explodes.

There are three scenes in *Project Syria*. First, the viewers are put in the middle of a street in Aleppo. A girl is singing, and a bomb explodes somewhere close by. Chaos spreads. The second scene witnesses a food shortage at a food bank. In the third scene, the viewers are transported to a refugee camp in Jordan that slowly fills up with more and more tents and ghostlike refugees. Throughout the piece, a male voice is explaining the severity of the humanitarian crisis in Syria (Ekos VR Experiences 2016). In the following analysis, the 35 bullet points of the SPJ Code of Ethics are grouped in four categories: 1) Seek the truth and report it, 2) Minimize harm, 3) Act independently, and 4) Be accountable and transparent (SPJ Code of Ethics, 2014).

Seek the truth and report it

According to the SPJ Code of Ethics (2014), "[e]thical journalism should be accurate and fair. Journalists should be honest and courageous in gathering, reporting and interpreting information". However, what does it mean to be "accurate" when using VR? In one sense, the accuracy requirements imply that there is always a *truth* that journalism should refer to or seek to find, whereas there is less focus on perspectivizing as a chosen approach. Four years before *Project Syria* was born, de la Peña et al. (2010) had already pointed out that VR "can bring the reader or viewer 'closer to the truth'" (293). In a VICE interview after the seminal VR production, she said it all started with a video of a girl singing in Aleppo, a video that was shown to her. As her team was concerned about authenticity, they started searching for authentic footage, which in turn served as a model for creating the virtual environment in *Project Syria*. On her YouTube channel, she explains how she started working with the piece after being shown the first video:

> We then had to gather a dozen mobile phone videos taken before the explosion and during the aftermath, as well as photographic material and Google Earth images, to anchor the street where the event occurred. I then sent a team into a refugee camp on the border of Syria to collect material about children living in the camp in order to inform the second half of the piece.
>
> *De la Peña 2014*

De la Peña and her team decided to reconstruct the photographs and videos using photographic textures and 3D models made from real people's images (de la Peña 2014). Co-producer Vangelis Lympouridis explains the process in this way:

> Searching with Google Translate in Arabic, we managed to find two handicam videos of the explosion and traced the location to find out exactly where and when it happened [...]. We pulled still frames from the videos, created panoramic shots, and used those to build the Aleppo neighborhood hit by the blast. For the refugee camp, we sent a team to the camp to record the situation. The audio is all real, which really creates a sense of presence.
>
> *Malmo 2014*

The de la Peña solution to the accuracy dilemma corresponds to one of two generally accepted ways of building virtual worlds: "through video capture – recording a real-world scene – or by building the environment in Computer Generated Imagery" (Aronson-Rath et al. 2015, 12). When choosing the latter, however, inaccuracy is hardly possible to avoid: 2D images don't show everything, so the modeler has to make a decision. Just hypothesize what the backs and sides of objects look like? Or leave some things a little fuzzy to connote uncertainty? Seijo (2017) highlights the same difficulties, and poses the question of whether it is really ethical to re-enact something about which we do not have all the information (116–17). From the Code of Ethics (2014) perspective, these issues alone become problematic, as one should "[n]ever deliberately distort facts or context, including visual information", "[r]emember that neither speed nor format excuses inaccuracy", and "[c]learly label illustrations and re-enactments".

The issues of truthfulness and objectivity were a driving force in the development of *cinéma vérité* in the 1950s. The French documentarist Jean Rouchs attempted to find resolutions to these dilemmas by setting up a camera and letting it roll as long as the 16mm film roll lasted. *Cinéma vérité*'s attempts to document events objectively were nevertheless criticized because even by choosing where to set up the camera, the videos were, in reality, being edited. Thus, we suggest that VR (especially 360-degree video) in some ways builds a bridge back to the *cinéma vérité* tradition. The viewer is allowed to watch everything that is happening in front of the camera without further editing by the producers.

To avoid the ethical issues that accompany computer animation, documentarist Bryn Mooser (This Week in Startups 2015) claims that it is possible to film directly in true VR by stitching: 360-degree videos might be recorded using one 360-degree camera or by stitching together footage from several regular cameras. Mooser, who has shot several documentaries in 360, such as *Welcome to Aleppo*, explains that "if you put little GoPros all over the room, you could move around the environment". Making VR using videos instead of CGI would make the VR product look less like a game and more like the journalism we know. Mooser adds: "It's a tremendous amount of stitching" (ibid. 2015). This hints at the conflict between accuracy requirements and the fast-paced stream of news beats that journalists are expected to produce.

On the other hand, even though inaccuracy is unavoidable in VR made through CGI, is it really worse than or different from adhering to the visual documentary traditions of journalism? When a virtual environment has been artificially created, it provides the creators with large amounts of power to edit perceived reality. Just like in other kinds of journalistic storytelling, the VR journalist acts as a filter between the event and the viewer. This could be problematic if viewers perceive that they are actual eyewitnesses even when realities have already been edited. Reality is seen through the lens of a journalist, whether it is a technological one or merely a matter of perception: "The problem is that the journalist must undertake a choice of context in which to place the facts. And this choice is his own subjective choice" (Wien 2017, 5). In VR, the viewers have the freedom to choose what to focus on. However, even if the camera records everything that is visible, the viewers still cannot see what is in the street next to where the camera is set up. Deciding the location of the camera is also the journalist's choice in VR.

Minimize harm by not risking safety

According to the SPJ Code of Ethics (2014), "[e]thical journalism treats sources, subjects, colleagues and members of the public as human beings deserving of respect". As the humanitarian crises in Syria continued, it became more difficult to provide documentary video stories, and the advantages of animating virtual environments became clearer. As a VR enthusiast put it, "thanks to the rapidly growing world of virtual reality technology, there is now a way to put people outside Syria on the ground in the middle of the war without risking their safety" (Malmo 2014).

By the very nature of computer graphics, the persons depicted in *Project Syria* were anonymous. According to the Code of Ethics, anonymity should be reserved for sources who may face danger, and journalists should identify sources clearly, because "[t]he public is entitled to as much information as possible to judge the reliability and motivations of sources" (SPJ Code of Ethics 2019). However, full anonymity was not provided, as the audio was real and could still be recognized.

Anonymity which could be provided via computer graphics could be considered a good way to minimize harm because it protects the sources. With *Project Syria*, it could also be important to consider the safety of the people on the receiving end of the product, as they prepare for undertaking the role of eyewitnesses to traumatic events. Balancing the public's need for information against potential harm or discomfort is an important part of journalism. As pointed out by Aronson-Rath et al. (2015), "virtual reality can create feelings of 'social presence' – the feeling that a user is really 'there' – which can engender far greater empathy for the subject than in any other media representations". Because of the added feeling of presence, some viewers might find *Project Syria* difficult to watch. Pursuit of the news is not a license for arrogant or unduly intrusive behavior. At the same time, exactly what makes the video grueling to watch, according to de la Peña, is why it works well. She points out that the participant "is afforded unprecedented access to the sights and sounds, and possibly, the feelings and emotions that accompany the news" (de la Peña et al. 2010, 292).

Act independently through newsgames

The third category of the SPJ Code of Ethics (2014) guides reporters to act independently, and states that "[t]he highest and primary obligation of ethical journalism is to serve the public". For journalists to serve the public, the public needs to know that what they see is actually a piece of journalism. More often than not, CGI environments are associated with VR gaming, which operates far from journalism in most cases. Newsgames, by contrast, are games that "utilize the medium with the intention of participating in the public debate" (Treanor & Mateas 2009, 1). Newsgames are "not seeking to state a specific political agenda, but instead to shape the space of opinions about a current event for a group of citizens with a shared vision of public interest" (ibid., 1). *Project Syria*, however, nearly dictates what the viewers are supposed to feel through a male voice. This is a problem if *Project Syria* is considered to be journalism, but not if it is a game. Newsgames are supposed to "report and communicate about current events in a manner consistent with the theories and traditions of journalism" (Treanor & Mateas 2009, 1). The authors suggest that newsgames serve the same role as political cartoons in a video game context.

Do these clarifications imply that a journalistic VR product can be considered a newsgame as well? Once more, it becomes apparent that clarifying the genre is of great importance. While a person looking at a political cartoon will normally be aware of the biased context, a person participating in a newsgame may not recognize the bias. If the viewers know a VR production is a game, they will most likely not expect it to present facts. If they know it is journalism, they will expect to get validated information; for journalism to serve the public, the public must be familiar with the form and genre it is presented in.

A pertinent question to raise next is whether *Project Syria* has more in common with a newsgame than with other journalism genres. Computer games are, as other interactive media, "different from VR in that they are not necessarily immersive" (Aronson-Rath et al. 2015). According to the founder of Oculus VR, Palmer Lucker, games are becoming more and more realistic, and have been building up to VR for a long time (CNN Business 2015). *Darfur is Dying*, for example, is an online game situated in a refugee camp in Sudan, in which the player uses the keyboard to avoid getting caught while fetching water for the family. This story is a newsgame meant to "increase empathy for victims of genocide by positioning the player within a game environment where the hazards refer to actual tragedy" (de la Peña et al. 2010, 293). This description fits well with *Project Syria* if we take into account that empathy is one of the main goals of the production.

Project Syria was first installed at London's Victoria and Albert Museum for five days in June 2014 (Kasson 2015). Although de la Peña's work gets distributed via installations in appropriate locations, it does not have any kind of established channel where audiences can find her stories easily. With the lack of better platforms to publish *Project Syria*, the Emblematic Group uploaded the video to the gaming website Steam, where anyone could download it for free (Store.steampowered.com 2013). Here, one can observe what expectations do to the experience of a product. When *Project Syria* was uploaded to Steam, the gamers expected it to be a game.

On Steam (Store.steampowered.com 2013), users can rate and review the games. Even the users who gave the journalistic VR product a "thumbs up" rating did not like it much. A user named "kasperhviid" wrote:

> The immersion doesn't kick in. Even free, this simply isn't worth it. However, the basic idea of using VR to make a human connection to people and groups we only see described in dry news feeds is the kind of unexplored possibilities that makes me get exited [*sic*] about VR. Also, this VR experience annoyed a lot of racist nutters! For these reasons, I clicked the thumbs up – this is the kind of stuff that gives me hope for our future. But don't download – instead, imagine what this could have been.
>
> *Steam*

In a similar tone, "stuttlepress" commented:

> They say a VR headset can be an "empathy machine". This is an attempt toward that goal. It's a few very brief scenes documenting the humanitarian crisis in Syria. It feels like something that might be played on a loop in a kiosk as part of a larger exhibit. This is not a very polished experience. It is interesting for its aspirations more than for what it actually achieves.
>
> *Steam*

These gamers gave a "thumbs up" rating and pointed out options for optimizing the video as a game. However, they do not appear to be impressed. In general, *Project Syria* got poor reviews on the graphics, and was also accused of being "blatant propaganda" (Store.steampowered.com 2013). Other respondents voiced that *Project Syria* had no reason to be on a gaming platform. This may be true, because *Project Syria* was not, according to de la Peña (2014), supposed to be a game. The bad reviews on the gaming platform could be more a matter of expectations attributed to the distribution platform than a reflection on the product itself.

One of Emblematic Group's goals when creating this journalistic VR product was to emphasize discussion of the humanitarian crisis among the world's most powerful people (VICE Motherboard 2014). De la Peña claims, "if we make people understand how difficult these circumstances are, perhaps they can actually start to think about what kind of change they, too, can help bring about" (de la Peña 2014). This desire to better the Syrians' circumstances places the VR production close to propaganda or, at best, advocacy journalism; that is, journalism that advocates a cause or expresses a viewpoint. Advocacy journalism might be an issue if the ultimate aim is to create emotion, because a journalist could be tempted to omit balancing or inconvenient information that could interfere with the desired emotional effect (Kent 2015). If empathy is the goal, the journalists must have an idea of what they want the viewers to feel.

Another aspect of "acting independently" relates to perspectivizing news events. *Project Syria* does not present different perspectives on the topic. The video does not accuse anyone of causing the misery we are witnessing through the headset. *Project Syria* is a short experience, and not many words are spoken. The most frequently used words are "children", "refugee" and "Syrians". There is no information that might explain why Syrian children become refugees, nor do we get any other verbal perspectives on the war. This lack of narration supports the impression of *Project Syria* as a piece of advocacy journalism or even borderline propaganda. Even though one-sided journalism is widespread on all platforms, the tendency to highlight only one side of a story is especially problematic in immersive journalism, with its strong emphasis on empathy. The founder of Oculus VR reflects on the new ethics dilemmas in this way:

> It's going to be important for people to understand that just because something looks real in virtual reality does not necessarily mean it actually is real. You shouldn't assume it's real unless they are telling you, "This is unaltered, real, actual captured footage, and we haven't done anything." Without the assurance, you don't want to be falling into the trap of seeing something in VR, and because you feel like you're in the scene, saying, "This is how it actually happened."
>
> *CNN Business 2015*

The blurring of VR with the real world strengthens the importance of ethics for immersive journalists. Journalists are supposed to "[d]istinguish news from advertising and shun hybrids that blur the lines between the two" (SPJ Code of Ethics, 2019). As de la Peña and her crew had a clearly expressed agenda, namely to create empathy with the Syrian refugees, it raises the question of whether the journalists serve the public or the Syrian victims only. At the same time, it should be noted that the same issues hold for other journalism genres as well, particularly the coverage of war zones or other tragic circumstances.

Be accountable and transparent in the immersive world

According to the SPJ Code of Ethics (2014), "[e]thical journalism means taking responsibility for one's work and explaining one's decisions to the public". Because the imagery in *Project Syria* was computer-generated, fact-checking the sources would be complicated. Despite the producers' tedious research of factual events, how is the public supposed to trust that the events in *Project Syria* depict what really happened in Aleppo? Would it be possible, in VR, for the journalists to be fully accountable and transparent in their storytelling? These are questions that are broadly discussed, but the community is still not close to any practical solutions, as VR and reality are increasingly merging in VR productions.

De la Peña argues that true VR is "deep immersive", and that "[t]he fundamental idea of immersive journalism is to allow the participant to actually enter a virtually re-created scenario representing the news story" (de la Peña et al. 2010, 292). Aronson-Rath et al. (2015) emphasize that the promise to journalists is that VR will offer audiences greater factual understanding of a topic:

> [V]irtual reality offers the promise of further breaking the "fourth wall" of journalism, wherein those represented become individuals processing agency, rather than what Liisa Malkki has referred to as "speechless emissaries".
>
> *Aronson-Rath et al. 2015*

The authors argue that there are two aspects in particular that differentiate VR journalism from other kinds of conventional journalism: immersion and presence. Presence is defined as the feeling of being there, and is achieved "when one reacts to a virtual environment as he or she would to a physical world" (Aronson-Rath et al. 2015). According to Sirkkunen et al. (2016), presence "refers to the sense of being there, a state of consciousness, which has even been claimed to be the central goal of virtual reality". It is about the subjective feeling of how realistic a place is, and it is about observations of how people act similarly to how they would in a real environment. There is: 1) Place illusion, 2) The sensation of being and operating at a remote or virtual place, and 3) Plausibility (feeling that what is happening is really happening).

Aronson-Rath et al. (2015) define immersion as "the feeling that someone has left his or her immediate, physical world, and entered into a virtual environment". Two of the factors that promote immersion are the ease of interaction and how realistic the images are. Sirkkunen et al. (2016) describe immersion as "the extent to which the computer displays are capable of delivering an inclusive, extensive, surrounding and vivid illusion of reality". To rephrase the definitions in a simpler manner: *Immersion* is the ability to investigate the story, and *presence* is the feeling of actually being there.

When considering the journalistic content presented and consumed with VR technologies, the highest level of exactness is created visually by 360-degree videos. High-quality graphics can create seemingly realistic sensations visually in limited spaces. De la Peña et al. (2010) claim that in VR, people respond to what is happening in immersive virtual environments as if they were happening in our world, even when they know they are not real. The authors find it surprising that "this response-as-if-real occurs even though the level of fidelity with respect to everyday physical reality is severely reduced" (293–294). In deep interactive journalism, "the participant can feel that his or her actual location has been transformed to the location of the news story, and more importantly their actual body has transformed, becoming a central part of the news story itself" (de la Peña et al. 2010, 293). This kind of deep immersion makes ethics even more important, as faulty information might potentially have wide-ranging implications if the user gets confused and is convinced that certain events actually happened.

Concluding remarks

In this chapter, we have discussed reoccurring ethical challenges of using CGI in immersive journalism. Through a case study of Nonny de la Peña's pioneering VR production, *Project Syria*, it emerged that with new technologies, such as VR, issues of journalistic accuracy are in constant flux. No standards are currently set, and codes of ethics are only partially helpful in practice. While immersive journalism is becoming a powerful approach to engaging and influencing news audiences, the boundaries between journalism and other approaches to VR storytelling are increasingly blurred. Presence and immersion might leave viewers more vulnerable to the creators' potentially biased messages.

The analysis indicates that in *Project Syria*, journalistic accuracy, accountability, and transparency emerged as the most challenging dilemmas to deal with. These findings are somewhat paradoxical, as these virtues are considered particular advantages of immersive journalism.

At this point in the CGI history of immersive journalism, it is still possible for viewers to see a difference between the real world and virtual environments. Most enthusiasts agree, however, that CGI is just the beginning. When we can no longer distinguish the virtual from reality, ethical frameworks that can be adhered to will truly become imperative.

References

Aronson-Rath, Raney, James Milward, Taylor Owen, & Fergus Pitt. 2015. "Virtual Reality Journalism." Columbia Journalism School, Tow Center. http://towcenter.org/new-report-virtual-reality-journalism [Accessed 21 January 2019].

Carlson, Matt & Seth C. Lewis. 2020. "Boundary Work." In: Karin Wahl-Jorgensen & Thomas Hanitzsch (eds), *The Handbook of Journalism Studies*. New York: ICA/Routledge, pp. 123–135.

CNN Business. 2015. "Oculus Founder: Virtual Reality Will Change Journalism As…." *YouTube video*, 3:42. www.youtube.com/watch?v=znmtuVN3kFE [Accessed 9 October 2015].

Culver, Kathleen B. 2015. "Immersive Approaches Pose New Questions." 11 February. Wisconsin: Center for Journalism Ethics, University of Wisconsin-Madison. https://ethics.journalism.wisc.edu/category/virtual-reality/ [Accessed 15 March 2020].

de la Peña, Nonny. 2014. "Project Syria: An Immersive Journalism Experience." *YouTube video*, 4:13. www.youtube.com/watch?v=jN_nbHnHDi4 [Accessed 28 January 2014].

de la Peña, Nonny, Peggy Weil, Joan Llobera, Elias Giannopoulos, Ausiàs Pomés, Bernhard Spaniang, Doron Friedman, Maria V. Sanchez-Vives, & Mel Slater. 2010. "Immersive Journalism: Immersive Virtual Reality for the First-Person Experience of News." *Presence: Teleoperators and Virtual Environments* 19(4): 291–301.

Ekos VR Experiences. 2016. "Project Syria – VR Recreation – Oculus Rift CV1." *YouTube video*, 3:33. www.youtube.com/watch?v=digE62wpHOk [Accessed 7 November 2016].

Johnson, Deborah G. 2020. "Promises and perils of immersive journalism." In: Uskali et al. (eds), *Immersive Journalism as Storytelling: Ethics, Production and Design*. London: Routledge, pp. 71–81.

Kasson, Elisabeth Greenbaum. 2015. "Future Doc: Digital Storytelling, Virtual Reality and Gaming." *International Documentary Association*. www.documentary.org/feature/future-doc-digital-storytelling-virtual-reality-and-gaming [Accessed 8 March 2017].

Kent, Tom. 2015. "An Ethical Reality Check for Virtual Reality Journalism." *Medium.com*. https://medium.com/@tjrkent/an-ethical-reality-check-for-virtual-reality-journalism-8e5230673507 [Accessed 5 April 2017].

Malmo, Christopher. 2014. "A New Virtual Reality Tool Brings the Daily Trauma of the Syrian War to Life." *VI Motherboard*. https://motherboard.vice.com/en_us/article/virtual-reality-is-bringing-the-syrian-war-to-life [Accessed 4 February 2017].

Mooser, Bryn. 2015. "Bryn Mooser's RYOT.org is Using VR to Transform Journalism & Let Us Live Global Stories." This Week In Startups. *YouTube video*, 1:07:47. www.youtube.com/watch?v=WkCf6WhNQ44 [Accessed 17 September 2015].

Robitzski, Dan. 2017. "Virtual Reality and Journalistic Ethics: Where Are the Lines?" *Undark.org*. 27 September. https://undark.org/article/virtual-reality-and-journalistic-ethics-where-are-the-lines [Accessed 15 March 2020].

Seijo, Sara Pérez. 2017. "Immersive Journalism: From Audience to First-Person Experience of News." In: Francisco Campos Freire, Xosé Rúas Araújo, Valentin Alejandro Martínez Fernández, & Xosé López García (eds), *Media and Metamedia Management: Advances in Intelligent Systems and Computing 503*. Cham, Switzerland: Springer. http://link.springer.com/chapter/10.1007/978-3-319-46068-0_14 [Accessed April 25, 2017].

Sirkkunen, Esa., Heli Väätäjä, Turo Uskali, & Parisa Pour Rezaei. 2016. "Journalism in Virtual Reality: Opportunities and Future Research Challenges." In: *Academic MindTrek'16: Proceedings of the 20th International Academic MindTrek Conference*. New York: Association for Computing Machinery (ACM), pp. 297–303. doi:10.1145/2994310.2994353

SPJ Code of Ethics. www.spj.org/ethicscode.asp [Accessed 14 October 2019].

Store.steampowered.com. 2013. https://store.steampowered.com/ [Accessed May 2017].

Treanor, Mike, & Michael Mateas. 2009. "Newsgames: Procedural Rhetoric meets Political Cartoons." In: *Proceedings of DiGRA 2009*. www.digra.org/wp-content/uploads/digital-library/09300.09505.pdf [Accessed 15 March 2020].

Ward, Stephen J.A. 2019. *Disrupting Journalism Ethics: Radical Change on the Frontier of Digital Media*. London: Routledge.

Wien, Charlotte. 2017. "Defining Objectivity within Journalism An Overview." *Nordicom Review 26*(2).

7

PROMISES AND PERILS IN IMMERSIVE JOURNALISM

Deborah G. Johnson

Immersive journalism (IJ) is said to offer exciting new opportunities for storytelling by providing audiences with the experience of being present in real-world situations, experiences that are more intense and intimate than other modes of journalism such as written text or film (de la Peña et al. 2010; Aronson-Rath et al. 2015; Sirkkunen et al. 2016). A growing literature on this new form of journalism attends to an array of questions about how various kinds of equipment work, what empathy is, how participants respond, whether IJ is more effective, and more. The discourse is rife with discussion of the potential and the significance of IJ for journalists, journalism, and audiences.

The term "immersive journalism" is used broadly to refer to storytelling that uses a variety of equipment ranging from virtual reality systems with headsets and other haptic devices, to multiple flatscreen set-ups, to 360-degree video and more. In this chapter the focus is primarily on storytelling that uses virtual reality (VR) equipment, though much of the analysis is relevant to other forms of IJ.

In this chapter the discourse around IJ is critically examined with IJ viewed as an emerging technology. The chapter positions this examination as an exercise in anticipatory ethics and a form of responsible research and innovation (RRI). As is apt for an emerging technology, IJ discourse tends to emphasize the promises and perils of future development; hence, this chapter critically examines two of the major promises and their correlated perils.

Anticipatory ethics and RRI

Anticipatory *governance* refers to a movement to identify the broad social implications of emerging technologies while they are still in the early stages of development, when they can be steered away from potential negative social consequences and towards more socially beneficial designs and uses (Guston 2014). The idea is to avoid the development of technologies that are later found to be unacceptable to the public or to have negative social effects. Examples of older technologies that might have been improved by anticipatory thinking are genetically modified food and industrial pesticides. Anticipatory *ethics* is an offshoot of anticipatory governance, focusing on the distinctively ethical implications of emerging technologies. Although anticipatory ethics has received much less attention, several scholars have provided clarifying definitions. According to Johnson (2011, 64), anticipatory ethics has two parts: "(1) engagement with the ethical implications of a technology while the technology is still in the earliest stages of development; and (2) engagement that is targeted to influence the development of the technology". In harmony with this definition but with a somewhat different emphasis, Brey (2012) labels the approach as anticipatory technology ethics (ATE), and defines it as "the study of ethical issues at the R&D and introduction stage of technology development through anticipation of possible future devices, applications, and social consequences".

RRI is another endeavor overlapping with anticipatory governance and ethics that puts the challenge and burden of anticipatory analysis on the researchers and developers who are involved in an emerging technology's development. RRI calls for those who develop new knowledge and new technology to incorporate consideration of social and ethical implications directly into the development process rather than leaving the task to others in separate or later stage activities (von Schomberg 2013).

In this chapter, critical examination of the discourse around IJ and especially the promises and perils of this emerging technology serves as a strategy for anticipating social and ethical implications of IJ and putting this into the discourse that will influence IJ's development.

IJ as an emerging technology with promises and perils

Emerging technologies are those that are believed to be currently in a nascent form of what they will come to be in the future. During the early stages of development, the design, uses, and meaning of new technologies are in flux. Science and technology studies scholars describe this early stage as a state of "interpretive flexibility" (Pinch & Bijker 1987; Orlikowski 1992). During this stage many actors with different interests negotiate, pushing and pulling in different directions about the meaning of what is being developed as well as about designs and uses. Inventors, engineers, and manufacturers work on improvements to the artifacts; those with financial interests make bets and facilitate and constrain certain directions of development; political actors encourage development with funding or express concerns, or threaten regulation; the media inform (and may misinform) the public, shaping attitudes towards what is in the making. The negotiations around new technologies are contingent and multifaceted (Pinch & Bijker 1987). In the case of IJ the actors that are currently negotiating about the design, use, and meaning include, at least, equipment manufacturers, individual entrepreneurial producers (storytellers), potential users such as media companies, journalists and media who tell stories about IJ, academic researchers, and the public.

To say that IJ is an emerging technology is to say both that its current form is nascent and to say that it is a technology (and not just a form of journalism). Framing IJ as a technology acknowledges that artifacts (various types of equipment) are part of IJ but it does not mean that IJ is just equipment. Although it is commonplace to slip into thinking about technology as simply material objects (artifacts), all technologies are ensembles of artifacts, social relationships, social arrangements, and systems of knowledge. Development, adoption, and use of new technologies require engineering new artifacts as well as constituting (or at least reconfiguring) new social relationships, institutional arrangements, social practices, new types of knowledge, and values.

So it is with IJ. Successful development – production, distribution, and use – of immersive stories may involve expensive new equipment as well as new production processes, new forms of financing, new kinds of skills, new organizational arrangements, and new categories of audience. All of these dimensions of IJ are currently in flux and being negotiated. This is reflected in the accumulating body of literature on IJ. Ideas about what it is and its significance for journalism, now and in the future, are being discussed and debated (see the References section of this chapter). Generally, the social negotiations around emerging technologies involve questions about what the new thing is and whether and how it fits into established categories or whether it is unique or even revolutionary. These questions are being raised about IJ. Is it the next step in a long evolution of visual technologies from film to television to video? (Owen 2016). Is it a form of documentary journalism or installation art? (Rose 2018). Is it a form of propaganda? (Kool 2016). Some have even raised the question as to whether there is anything significantly new here (Kool 2016). Recognizing that IJ is an emerging technology allows us to accept that these questions don't have answers yet; the answers are being negotiated. The questions represent the state of interpretative flexibility in which answers are still in the making. Since IJ is not yet a stabilized "thing", the questions are themselves part of the negotiation about what IJ will become.

As already indicated, much of the discourse on IJ features promises or perils, and this is not surprising since emerging technologies and promises and perils are all futuristic. Promises are declarations that something will happen or be done *in the future*. Likewise, perils are harms or losses that may happen *in the future*. Since IJ has not reached a stabilized or mature form, all we can do is anticipate its potential (and potentially disruptive) consequences.

A central feature of emerging technologies is uncertainty about what they will become. It is possible (though this is not a prediction) that IJ will not take hold in journalism even while other uses of VR become highly successful. The point is that whether or not IJ in one form or another takes hold in journalism depends on the discourse that is taking place now.

Empathetic global understanding/manipulation

While the literature on immersive journalism is rife with promises, certain promises receive more attention than others. The idea that IJ will bring audiences closer to real-world situations and thereby help them to empathize with the plights of others has become a focal point of discussion (Sanchez 2017; Shin & Biocca 2017; Rose 2018; Hassan 2019; Sundar, Kang, & Oprean 2017). The global dimension of empathy is more often implicit in the discourse but clearly evident in the subject matter of early IJ productions such as *The Displaced*, *6x9*, and *Clouds Over Sidra*. These stories bring viewers to places that are distant from the typical viewers' geography and circumstances, and the stories focus on people in dire circumstances – war, a refugee camp, traveling to immigrate. The places and topics suggest that the promise of IJ is not just to produce empathic understanding but to produce *global* empathic understanding.

In his 2015 TED talk, Chris Milk used his *Clouds Over Sidra* to explain how virtual reality could change the world. In this talk, he referred to virtual reality as "the ultimate empathy machine". *Clouds Over Sidra* follows the life of a 12-year-old girl living in a Syrian refugee camp in Jordan. Milk explains:

> When you're sitting there in her room, watching her, you're not watching it through a television screen, you're not watching it through a window; you're sitting there with her. When you look down, you're sitting on the same ground that she's sitting on. And because of that, you feel her humanity in a deeper way. You empathize with her in a deeper way.
>
> *Chris Milk, TED Talk 2015*

The promise of IJ that Milk sees here is not just empathy for the sake of empathy; as he explains, "we can change minds with this machine". He showed *Clouds Over Sidra* at the World Economic Forum in Davos, which encouraged him to create other VR stories with the idea of showing his work "to the people that can actually change the lives of the people inside of the films" (Milk 2015).

On the one hand, the promise of empathy has led to discussion and debate and raised questions about what precisely empathy is and what its role in journalism is or should be. The idea of an "empathy machine" has led to an abundance of research that both theorizes what empathy is (Hassan 2019; Sanchez 2017) and tries to empirically document the effects of IJ on viewers (Shin 2018; Sundar, Kang, & Oprean 2017; Kang et al. 2019). Much of this research asks whether the effects of IJ are comparatively more effective than traditional forms of journalism and media.

The emphasis on empathy has generated discourse on an older underlying tension in journalism about the role of emotions. In a 2010 piece co-authored with others, de la Peña, one of the pioneers in the field of IJ, avoids using "empathy" and instead emphasizes emotional involvement. She writes that "An important role of immersive journalism could be to reinstitute the audience's emotional involvement in current events" (298).

New technologies often challenge and reshape prevailing norms and values. Consider, for example, how information technology has changed the value of privacy – the concept as well as attitudes and practices (Johnson 2009). IJ seems to exacerbate the tension in journalism over the proper role of emotions and emotional engagement. On the one hand, journalists are expected to be impartial and objective and, on the other hand, as Baia & Coelho (2018) put it, "one of journalism's basic goals is to create an affective relationship between the public and the news" (1095). Journalists are expected to motivate audiences to care about real-world situations while at the same time maintaining their impartiality and objectivity. This tension is illustrated in the explanation of fairness and impartiality in the Five Core Principles of Journalism issued by the Ethical Journalism Network (EJN).[1] In explanation of the principle of objectivity and impartiality, the document states:

> Most stories have at least two sides. While there is no obligation to present every side in every piece, stories should be balanced and add context. Objectivity is not always possible, and may not always be desirable (in the face for example of brutality or inhumanity), but impartial reporting builds trust and confidence.
>
> *Five Core Principles of Journalism, EJN*

The discourse around IJ seems to heighten and exacerbate this tension.

The promise of motivating audiences to care by generating empathic emotions creates one of the perils of IJ, namely turning journalism into a form of audience manipulation. That is, if IJ producers cross a line – a rather complicated, fuzzy line – in generating emotional responses, they may be accused of manipulating their audiences. This would weaken the credibility of journalists and the trust that audiences place in them.

Manipulation is generally defined as a skillful way of influencing others in an unfair manner. To be sure, journalism is often intended to influence viewers, but the use of the emotional rather than exclusively cognitive material suggests the possibility of "unfair" influence. Presenting viewers with intense visual experiences that generate highly emotional responses which may be hardwired in humans is one factor that creates the peril of IJ being perceived (and actually being) a form of manipulation.

Another element identified in IJ discourse that points to this peril is the absence of any indication of an author (Sanchez 2017; Mabrook & Singer 2019). The concealment of the author within the experience is a recurrent concern. On the one hand, the sense that one is present in a real situation seems to require that viewers not be shown any signs of the author. As Kool (2016) explains: "the erasure of the journalist is only one technique that arguably makes the viewer feel as though the event they are witness to is real and that they are a participant in it" (3). On the other hand, the intentional choice to eliminate the presence of authorship supports the interpretation of IJ as manipulation.

Concealment of authorship is what distinguishes IJ from other forms of journalism such as written text and television and film. In explaining why he thinks that virtual reality is a revolutionary step in the evolutionary progress of delivery mechanisms for journalism, Owen (2016) notes that:

> While the introduction of radio, photography, video, and social media each changed how journalism was framed and how societies produced and consumed media, in each of these previous media, the master's hand was clearer than in virtual reality. With a photo or a video, the audience knows the photographer or videographer is framing the image. There is no pretense that one is seeing everything, and no illusion of actually being there.
>
> *Owen 2016, p. 107*

Kool poses the question: "Is it ethical to erase the mark of the journalist who still has a large stake in the orchestration, construction, and communication of her narrative?" p. 3). Even when the story is told with recordings of real situations, the author has made many important decisions in the "orchestration, construction, and communication of her narrative".

Whether or not and to what extent viewers are unaware that their experience has been authored will be discussed further in the next section. The point here is that one of the perils identified in IJ discourse is that this new journalistic technology would become (and would be seen as) a form of audience manipulation, and this would work against journalistic values of impartiality, objectivity, and credibility.

The peril of manipulation points to another peril of IJ. If IJ has the power to generate emotional responses, empathy, and understanding as claimed by its enthusiasts, then there is nothing that ensures that IJ will always be used for good. In principle, IJ could just as well be used to create empathy and understanding of dangerous causes and heinous people. Sanchez (2017) imagines a dystopian version of IJ "where users are immersed in a world of fake news, their bodies learning to respond automatically and unconsciously with hatred and anger toward the world within and outside virtual reality" (11). So the manipulative potential of IJ creates a peril of IJ being used to present untrue situations and generate hate and anger rather than empathy.

Transparency/opacity

Transparency is generally considered a good thing, and it is an important value in journalism. One of the edicts of the Society of Professional Journalists' Code of Ethics is "Be accountable and transparent".[2] In this context, transparency means journalists should include information about their methods and sources. The SPJ Code specifies that journalists should "explain ethical choices and processes to audiences. Encourage a civil dialogue with the public about journalistic practices, coverage and news content". When readers can see by whom and how information is produced, they are in a better position to evaluate its credibility.

In the discourse on IJ, transparency is sometimes put forward as one of IJ's great promises. Fitzgerald (2016) makes the point unequivocally:

> The reality is that done right, VR has the potential to be more transparent than traditional journalism, traditional documentary filmmaking, because you can see everything. You can't see in traditional filmmaking what's behind the filmmaker's head. [...] In VR, if it's done right, the viewer can see everything the subject can see. I think that has the potential to be pretty radically transparent.
>
> *Fitzgerald 2016*

So transparency is one of the promises of IJ, though it is important to note that the promised transparency is different from the kind of transparency put forward by the SPJ.

Transparency is complicated in IJ. Bringing viewers to real-world situations and allowing them to move around in those situations is a kind of transparency often seen as analogous to looking through glass. One can see through the glass to what is behind it, i.e., to what would be hidden were the glass opaque. IJ is transparent in this sense because it allows viewers to see and experience situations directly, seemingly without mediation. Moreover, glass is not expected to distort what you see when you look through it as other mediums might. So the transparency promised in IJ discourse is to give audiences direct views of the plights of others in far-away places.

This concept of transparency is coherent but it is created, in part at least, by erasing the author from the experience and erasing the constructed nature of the experience, an element of IJ discussed in the previous section. The invisibility of the author and authorship is just the opposite of transparency; it is opacity. Ironically, while hiding authorship is essential to creating presence which is the basis for the claim of transparency, the hiding simultaneously creates opacity with respect to authorship and the constructed nature of the experience. The promise of transparency brings with it the peril of opacity.

The complexity of this discourse on transparency goes further. The concern about erasure of authorship is not quite as justified as it might seem. Rarely in the discourse on IJ is a distinction made between the audience experience *in* a story and the experience of *preparing for and entering* a story. If we focus just on the audience experience in the story, there does seem to be an absence of any signals as to authorship and the constructed nature of the experience. However, if we focus on the experience of audience members as they prepare for the experience, we get a very different picture. Participating in IJ requires cumbersome equipment. Audience members have to "suit up", putting on headsets and other haptic devices. Even before suiting up, audience members have to get access to the requisite equipment; they might do this by purchasing and using it on their own or they may go to a location created by someone else, say, an IJ producer or a media outlet. The process of getting access to and preparing for the experience and later exiting the experience gives participants strong signals that what they experience is something constructed and made available by others. Hence, when the erasure of authorship is claimed either to contribute to the transparency of IJ experiences or to contribute to the opacity of IJ experiences, caution is in order. The extent to which audience members can or do suspend belief is unclear.

Much more attention needs to be paid to the preparation and entry experience since it is part of the overall experience of IJ. Yes, the equipment will likely get better and may become less cumbersome and easier to use, but there will always be a point when a person has to be hooked up to machines – even if it is just putting on glasses or walking into a special room.

This takes us back to acknowledging that IJ is an emerging technology. The contexts of use are still in flux. Issues of how, when, and where IJ will be available is still very uncertain. The form it will take in the future depends on the development of cheaper and more accessible equipment, but it is not just a matter of equipment. A range of decisions about the institutional arrangements, business models, financial models, distribution systems, and public understanding will all shape what IJ comes to be. Much of the current discourse tends to be technologically deterministic and, consequently, the contextual dimension of IJ use – the social practices around its use – has been somewhat neglected.

In traditional media, context signals to audiences what to expect. News reporting is expected to be accurate; social media less so; the opinion section of a newspaper is not expected to be objective; films shown at movie theaters are expected to be entertaining, though documentaries and docudramas are another matter. When Milk showed his IJ story at the World Economic Forum, it was not a surprise to the audience that the production appealed to their empathy. The World Economic Forum is a place known for trying to get people to care. The contextual arrangements that come to constitute the production and distribution of IJ and its users will influence whether and how the promises and perils of IJ are realized.

Just as the promise of empathy leads to the peril of manipulation, the promise of transparency leads to the peril of opacity. Whether or not the erasure of authorship is as serious a peril as the discourse suggests, there is another opacity peril with IJ. The fact that authorship is hidden should lead us to ask what else is hidden. Little attention has been given to the reality that IJ has the potential to facilitate surveillance, two different forms of surveillance. Because IJ experiences involve being hooked up to equipment and much of the equipment is digital, data can easily be collected on audiences. In fact, the equipment for doing this is being developed alongside IJ as researchers are figuring out how to test and quantify audience responses to IJ. Thus, there is the peril that IJ will be used in ways that make audiences subjects of study while they are engaging with IJ stories. Yes, this already happens when online readers/viewers are tracked, but being tracked in a virtual environment when your entire body is hooked up is much more intrusive.

The other kind of surveillance is already present in IJ, and that is surveillance of the subjects of IJ stories. We presume that the subjects of already-made

IJ stories such as *The Displaced* and *Clouds Over Sidra* gave their permission to be filmed, but there is potential in IJ for more expansive intrusions into the lives of IJ subjects. More footage of their lives spread across the world with the intention of improving their situation seems like a good thing, but it nevertheless involves privacy intrusion and the potential for misuse. This is another aspect of IJ that has not been given much attention. How exactly do producers interact with subjects? Will IJ lead to a greater degree of unwanted intrusions in the lives of people in dire circumstances?

Conclusion

Since IJ is still in the early stages of development and we don't know when and what stabilized form it will take, being specific about responsible IJ is somewhat premature. Nevertheless, drawing on the analysis of current discourse just presented and engaging in anticipatory ethics and responsible innovation suggests several areas that need to be monitored and shaped during this early stage. The analysis of touted promises and their correlated perils suggests that the impact of the invisibility of authorship needs to be monitored. Kool's provocative question, "is it ethical to erase the mark of the journalist [...]?", seems to suggest, perhaps, that signs of authorship should be inserted into stories in such a way that participants are reminded of the constructed nature of the IJ story (Kool 2016). However, the analysis here indicates that consideration of the impact of the invisibility of authorship should go beyond the participants' experience in an IJ story and include the preparation and entry phase of an IJ story experience. Indeed, evaluation of the impact should include effects of the broader context in which IJ stories are provided, e.g. institutional arrangements and social practices and what these context features signal to users.

Second, the perils of IJ are threats to the values of journalism. Thus, as IJ evolves, attention should stay focused on maintaining journalistic values such as credibility, transparency in methods, accuracy, and independence. This need not be a conservative activity, that is, it does not have to mean that journalism stays as it always has been. Values are realized in different ways in different modes of journalism. As with any new mode of journalism, it is important to engage with the new possibilities created while at the same time ensuring that the new forms stay true to essential values, even if they are reconfigured. What should be avoided is undermining essential values such as trust and accuracy. Whether or not IJ will undermine or enhance journalistic values is yet to be seen because IJ is still in the making.

Notes

1 The EJN principles are found at: https://ethicaljournalismnetwork.org/who-we-are/5-principles-of-journalism

2 The SPJ Code is available at: www.spj.org/ethicscode.asp

References

Aronson-Rath, R., J. Milward, & T. Owen. 2015. *Virtual Reality Journalism*. New York: Tow Center for Digital Journalism, Columbia University.

Baía Reis, A. & A.F.V.C.C. Coelho. 2018. "Virtual Reality and Journalism: A Gateway to Conceptualizing Immersive Journalism." *Digital Journalism 6*(8): 1090–1100.

Bijker, W.E., T.P. Hughes, & T.J. Pinch (eds). 1987. *The Social Construction of Technological Systems: New Directions in the Sociology and History of Technology*. Cambridge, MA: MIT Press.

Brey, P.A.E. 2012. "Anticipatory Ethics for Emerging Technologies." *NanoEthics 6*(1): 1–13.

de la Peña, N., P. Weil, J. Llobera, E. Giannopoulos, A. Pomés, B. Spanlang, & M. Slater. 2010. "Immersive Journalism: Immersive Virtual Reality for the First-Person Experience of News." *Presence: Teleoperators and Virtual Environments 19*(4): 291–301.

Fitzgerald, M. 2016. "Jake Silverstein: 'Immersing You in Worlds Not Your Own'." *Nieman Storyboard*. http://niemanstoryboard. org/stories/jake-silverstein-immersing-you-in-worlds-not-your-own/

Guston, D.H. 2014. "Understanding 'Anticipatory Governance'." *Social Studies of Science 44*(2): 218–242.

Hassan, R. 2019. "Digitality, Virtual Reality and the 'Empathy Machine'." *Digital Journalism* 1–18.

Johnson, D.G. 2009. *Computer Ethics*. 4th ed. New York: Pearson.

Johnson, D.G. 2011. "Software Agents, Anticipatory Ethics, and Accountability." In: *The Growing Gap Between Emerging Technologies and Legal-Ethical Oversight*. Dordrecht: Springer, pp. 61–76.

Kang, S., E. O'Brien, A. Villarreal, W. Lee, & C. Mahood. 2019. "Immersive Journalism and Telepresence: Does Virtual Reality News Use Affect News Credibility?" *Digital Journalism* 7(2): 294–313.

Kool, H. 2016. "The Ethics of Immersive Journalism: A Rhetorical Analysis of News Storytelling with Virtual Reality Technology." *Intersect: The Stanford Journal of Science, Technology & Society 9*(3): 1–11.

Mabrook, R. & J.B. Singer. 2019. "Virtual Reality, 360-degree Video, and Journalism Studies: Conceptual Approaches to Immersive Technologies." *Journalism Studies 20*(14): 1–17.

Milk, C. 2015. "How Virtual Reality Can Create the Ultimate Empathy Machine." *TED Talk*, March. www.ted.com/talks/chris_milk_how_virtual_reality_can_create_the_ultimate_empathy_machine?utm_campaign1⁄4linkplug&utm_source1⁄4linkplug&utm_medium1⁄4linkplug&u tm_content1⁄4linkplug&utm_term1⁄4linkplug#t-5120 [Accessed 15 March 2020].

Orlikowski, W.J. 1992. "The Duality of Technology: Rethinking The Concept of Technology in Organizations." *Organization Science 3*(3): 398–427.

Owen, T. 2016. "Can Journalism be Virtual?" *Columbia Journalism Review 54*(5): 102–111.

Pinch, T.J. & W.E. Bijker. 1987. "The Social Construction of Facts and Artifacts: Or How the Sociology of Science and the Sociology of Technology Might Benefit each other." In: W.E. Bijker, T.P. Hughes, & T.J. Pinch (eds), *The Social Constructions of Technological Systems: New Directions in the Sociology and History of Technology*. Cambridge, MA: MIT Press, pp. 17–50.

Rose, Mandy. 2018. "The Immersive Turn: Hype and Hope in the Emergence of Virtual Reality as a Nonfiction Platform." *Studies in Documentary Film 12*(2): 132–149.

Sánchez Laws, A.L. 2017. "Can Immersive Journalism Enhance Empathy?" *Digital Journalism*: 1–16.

Shin, D. 2018. "Empathy and embodied experience in virtual environment: To what extent can virtual reality stimulate empathy and embodied experience?" *Computers in Human Behavior 78*: 64–73.

Shin, D. & F. Biocca. 2018. "Exploring Immersive Experience in Journalism." *New Media & Society 20*(8): 2800–2823. doi:10.1177/1461444817733133

Sirkkunen, E., H. Väätäjä, T. Uskali, & P.P. Rezaei. 2016. "Journalism in Virtual Reality: Opportunities and Future Research Challenges." In: *Proceedings of the 20th International Academic MindTrek Conference* (October), New York: ACM, pp. 297–303.

Sundar, S.S., J. Kang, & D. Oprean. 2017. "Being There in the Midst of the Story: How Immersive Journalism Affects Our Perceptions and Cognitions." *Cyberpsychology, Behavior, and Social Networking 20*(11): 672–682.

von Schomberg, R. 2013. "A Vision of Responsible Research and Innovation." In: R. Owen, J.R. Bessant, & M. Heintz (eds), *Responsible Innovation: Managing the Responsible Emergence of Science and Innovation in Society*. Wiley, pp. 51–74.

8

IT'S NOT JUST ABOUT EMPATHY[1]

Going beyond the empathy machine in immersive journalism

Sarah Jones

In November 2015, *The New York Times* released its Virtual Reality (VR) app and distributed cardboard headsets to its 1.2 million subscribers. The app contained an experience called *The Displaced* (dir.: Chris Milk 2015), which told the story of three children who had lost their homes due to war and conflict. The mobile app had more downloads in its first few days than any other *New York Times* app has had at launch; the average time spent within the app was 14.7 minutes; some 92 percent of videos were viewed; and concurrently the videos began trending on social networks (Jaekel 2015). The success of the launch led *Wired* magazine to lead with the headline, "Google Cardboard's *New York Times* Experiment Just Hooked a Generation on VR" (Wohlsen 2015). However, the biggest impact was in the consumer response that *The Displaced* was a transformative experience, something that Milk refers to as an "empathy machine" (Milk 2015). Among the responses online, readers of *The New York Times* said:

> Before today, I never suspected VR would interest me, much less bring tears to my eyes. Incredible. #NYTVR *@jennykutnow*
>
> Never have I been emotionally moved by a new technology. Until just now with my first taste of #NYTVR. Speechless. @google @nytimes *@AmiNahshon*
>
> "Whoaaa, bra! I think I need to sit down." – 10-year-old kid's mind blown by #NYTVR. "Why do we even have wars? We should not have wars." *@lizweil*
>
> Thanks @nytimes, it's been awhile since I've sobbed into a cardboard box. #NYTVR *@tophrrrr*

The emphasis and repeated use of the words "sob", "emotion", and "tears" in the users' descriptions of their experience gives weight to Milk's argument that the technology is a machine that makes people more compassionate, more connected, and more empathetic. This chapter will seek to look beyond this and challenge the argument that VR is an empathy machine. It will argue the proposition that VR as an empathy machine has been a strategic move by the technology industry as a way to humanize the technology. Instead, the technology can effectively be used to enhance emotions through the depiction of a place in a story. This in turn can evoke empathy, but it should not be the driving factor for VR in immersive journalism, as there are limitations that can change the nature of journalism.

Why are we here?

Discussions around media being able to generate empathy are not new. Film critic Roger Ebert, in a speech to accept a star on the *Hollywood Walk of Fame*, stated,

> Movies are the most powerful empathy machine in all the arts. When I go to a great movie, I can live somebody else's life for a while. I can walk in somebody else's shoes. I can see what it feels like to be a member of a different gender, a different race, a different economic class, to live in a different time, to have a different belief.
>
> *Ebert 2005, np.*

The discourse around empathy has been resurrected in discussion around the purpose of VR content, most prominently developed in the work of de la Peña et al. (2010) and Milk's TED talk, "How virtual reality can create the ultimate empathy machine" (Milk 2015). In an analysis of the work of immersive journalism, Sánchez Laws (2017) identified de la Peña's two key notions that give way to immersion and, as a result, empathy:

> The first idea was that being placed in a situation that felt as real as the original news event would heighten engagement. The second idea was that adopting a first-person point of view would lead to a deeper emotional response.
>
> *Sánchez Laws 2017, 2*

Empathy became the gateway for immersive journalism, a reason to bring a new and emerging technology into a new genre.

The drivers for the technology and the emergence of technology companies within the news industry have been covered at length throughout this book. It is important to reiterate that the VR market has largely been dominated by the games industry. To generate the scale of growth and adoption that the technology industry wanted, it needed to reach and secure new audiences. This could only be done by tapping into new markets. Adoption is still a concern, with a survey of developers in 2019 finding that 40 percent of them found this to be the biggest challenge (Fogel 2019). The aim then is to infiltrate a range of industries to ensure wider adoption. Since 2014, a number of industries such as retail, advertising, film, and travel have been experimenting with the technology. Certainly education, healthcare, and training have been using the technology since the second wave in the 1990s.

There is also the realization that games are not enough and for the industry to thrive there needs to be a range of good content. The lessons have been learned from the early days of the internet. Tim Wu's *The Attention Merchants* talks about the notion of "content is king" in discussions with Bill Gates as far back as 1996, where the internet would only succeed if there was good content: "If people are to be expected to put up with turning on a computer to read a screen, they must be rewarded with deep and extremely up-to-date information that they can explore at will" (Wu 2016).

As a result, to generate content and to encourage adoption, technology companies have partnered with news organizations to reach mass audiences, and in particular audiences that weren't traditionally associated with the games industry. Samsung partnered with the *NYTimes* to produce The Daily 360 stories. The project lasted a year and the experiences gained 94 million views on Facebook and 2 million views on YouTube (Willens 2017). This was not the first time the *NYTimes* had partnered with a technology company, as noted in the opening of this chapter and the launch of the cardboard headsets with Google.

Google has also supported a number of organizations to generate VR content: for example, funding to support *Euronews* to integrate 360-degree experiences into their production workflows (Google DNI).

Oculus has been running a Creators Lab with their VR for Good program, and HTC Vive has supported a similar program with VR for Impact. These programs have bought together creators, storytellers, and technologists to produce new content that reaches new and diverse audiences.

It can also be argued that the trend for these VR for Good campaigns has been used to humanize the technology. This is not in the traditional sense of the term, where artificial intelligence is "humanized" to personalize responses, but instead through an accessibility lens. The idea of putting on a VR headset to enter a virtual world could be prohibitive to a wide audience not used to those spaces or technologies. Yet, disguised as a medium to explore a new journalistic narrative or a deeper understanding of a news story, it becomes humanized and is suddenly more accessible. It is this that has driven the use of immersive journalism, as noted at the start through *The New York Times*' VR app and the 1.2 million subscribers holding a cardboard headset to step into another world.

With buy-in from technology companies and the emergence of immersive journalism in a VR form, why then should we stand against empathy as the driver for content?

The limitations of empathy

Zillah Watson has been at the heart of the emerging immersive journalism scene, leading the work for the BBC and developing research and development within this area. She authored one of the most extensive studies on VR in journalism for the Reuters Institute for the Study of Journalism's report *VR for News: The New Reality?* (Watson 2017) where the claim of empathy held little purchase with the creators who were interviewed. One area of concern highlighted in the report was raised by Jason Farkas, VP for Premium Content Video at CNN, where he stressed that, although empathy is an important component of some VR, it isn't the only one. The concern was that in the early days of VR (in this wave), the over-emphasis on empathy may have limited the range of content explored (Watson 2017, 21), something that will be developed later in this chapter.

An in-depth interview with Watson that took place in 2020 has allowed for these topics to be explored further to understand why we should be going beyond the empathy machine when discussing immersive journalism, with the starting point trying to understand how VR came to be almost synonymous with empathy;

> People got so excited by it that this was a unique way to put you in someone else's shoes so you would understand things. People just liked that... It was about the simplicity. All ideas spread when they're ultimately quite simple and it just had a simplicity and beauty to it. Everybody loved the idea that this was going to make us all better people and the world a better place... For some new technology that's actually quite scary, strapping a box on your head, to then believe that it could have this unique superpower to help you deeply understand other people's lives was an incredibly positive thing that I think really helped drive forward interest in it.
>
> *Watson 2020*

With Ebert (2005) likening film to an empathy machine because you could understand things better, it is interesting to understand whether virtual reality is any different to established media forms, or whether the technology itself could drive us to a greater empathetic reaction. For Watson, any chance of empathy lies in the story;

> I see it is all on a continuum from early TV documentaries that showed you very different people's lives and news reports, through to actually being there and seeing it for yourself. But I think ultimately, what was ignored about that early understanding of empathy was just putting it on wasn't enough. Whether it's a novel or whether it's a TV doc or if it's VR, the strength will come from a really beautifully told story, which it will help invoke the empathy.
>
> I've never been that clear that just putting you in a situation to see it necessarily invokes empathy. I mean do we feel empathetic just walking down the

> street and seeing a homeless person? Not always. We often walk past them. Putting on a VR headset isn't any different from that and therefore I've always questioned it. Whereas a good story, told beautifully, certainly can do that.
>
> *Watson 2020*

Clouds Over Sidra (2015), can be used to illustrate this point. It is a piece that is referred to as being one of the leading examples of immersive journalism that creates a sense of empathy, but as Watson identifies, the piece is crafted with a clear narrative and cinematic techniques. In *Clouds Over Sidra*, a 12-year-old girl invites you to experience her life in the Za'atari Refugee Camp in Jordan. The experience allows you to view her school, her makeshift tent, and the football pitch in the camp. Watson refers to the cinematic techniques used, for example the music and a script to evoke "tears and empathy". She suggests it is this combination that is used to evoke emotions. Although you feel as though you are invited into her world by her, through a combination of camera positioning and eye contact (Jones 2017), there is no option to interact with her or take a different journey through her life in the camp.

The limitations of empathy are reflected in the argument put forward by Chun, which proposes that even if you could recreate a perfect sensory match for another's reality, you cannot truly know their experience. As she argues, "if you're walking in someone else's shoes, then you've stolen their shoes" (Chun 2016). The argument is that, when drawing on an empathetic response the other is replaced with the self, so it can only ever be your understanding of what that experience would be like. So, although it can be an invaluable medium to generate reflection and new perspectives, the argument that the experience is of the same value and has the same effect as the contextualized lived experience of the subject is reductive.

Three challenges for empathy in journalism

It is established that a good story and purposeful filming techniques can be used to evoke empathy or enhance an emotional response, but there are three initial concerns for using empathy as a guiding principle for immersive journalism; the first is whether empathy can create long-lasting change, the second is focused around impartiality, and the third is the limitation this has on the development of content.

The discussions around whether VR can create long-lasting change have become more widely discussed in the past few years (Lisetti et al. 2013, Herrera et al. 2018). At Stanford's Human Interaction Lab, "Becoming homeless" gives participants the perspective of being homeless, showing what it would be like to lose their job or their home. This research was developed to understand whether experiences could drive human behavioral change. Two studies took place over a two-month period with more than 560 participants between the ages of 15 and 88, representing eight different ethnicities. One group undertook the experience through virtual reality, the other being shown traditional materials. Researchers found that people who experienced the perspectives in VR developed longer-lasting compassion than those who saw it via other platforms. They were also more likely to sign a petition to support plans for affordable housing. Broken down, 82 percent of participants experiencing being homeless through VR signed the petition, versus 67 percent of the people who read a narrative that asked them to imagine becoming homeless. A lot of criticism for VR as an empathy machine is focused around the idea that you can feel an immediate emotional reaction but that it soon fades; however, in this study, the results were found to be longer-lasting. After four weeks, participants were asked about supporting affordable housing initiatives. Those having had a VR experience still supported the idea, whereas the effect had diminished for those who had experienced it through other means.

A similar impact was demonstrated in a different study (Aitamurto et al. 2018), exploring gender equality in the workplace, which used a technique to split the 360-degree image so that each 180-degree angle would represent a different gender. This study showed an increase in the viewers' feeling of personal responsibility for advancing gender equality in the workplace when they identified themselves with the female perspective.

It was something that Watson found in a study on *We Wait* (2016), a VR experience where you travel across the sea with a Syrian family. This is based on interviews with migrants but was made as an animation. Research analyzed the impact and effect that characters had on the participants and this was assessed based on their sense of presence in the experience (Steed et al. 2018). Further analysis focused on whether participants were sufficiently "moved" to follow up on the story and to seek more information. It was a small study of 32 participants, but the research showed a strong enabler to feeling presence was attributed to whether a character looked directly at you. Twenty-five percent of the participants followed up the experience with a visit to the website, which although seems a low proportion, it was quoted as being significant as only a small number are generally expected to follow up after watching a programme on television. In conclusion to the study, "fostering the sense in the participant that they were 'there' and what was happening was 'real' might be helpful in engendering follow-up and further interest in the news story". (Steed et al. 2018, np). As Watson reflects;

> It was the power of a direct connection with somebody who was explaining their story. However again, it was a beautifully scripted story albeit based entirely on news accounts and interviews and with Matthew Price, a BBC reporter, overseeing the story to make sure it really felt right.
>
> *Watson 2020*

The second criticism relates to impartiality in news, something that Watson has been concerned with when the focus has been on empathy. A story that is focused on generating empathy will be developed to help the audience understand and share feelings in a particular situation. The question is whether this can also be defined as one that is impartial, where both sides of the story need to be presented, to provide information for the audience to make up their own mind;

> News [in VR] is used as far more than empathy and there are plenty of stories that we report and need to report where I don't want to have empathy with the person who's being discussed. It seemed to me to come from a particular view of news, that was kind of a documentary festival view of news, which is "we use these stories to highlight issues about the world", and of course we do that in news but also we have to report about court trials for child murderers. I mean do you want to feel empathy for a murderer? Not particularly but it still is news. It is far more than just feeling empathy.
>
> *Watson 2020*

The changing nature of journalism is often associated with stories of this type, often defined as "advocacy journalism", where objectivity and impartiality are seen as outdated terminology for a media form. In writing for the Independent Media Center in 2004, Berman stated, "If we are ever to create meaningful change, advocacy journalism will be the single most crucial element to enable the necessary organizing" (Berman 2004, in Salas 2018, 34). The approach of advocacy journalism is familiar with supporters using empathy within immersive journalism to call for change, as seen in the early work of RYOT. Established in 2012 with the goal to be "the first news site linking news to action" (Zanger 2017), the first VR/360 projects captured active war zones in Syria and disaster zones in Nepal, often partnering with mainstream organizations such as *The New York Times*, *Huffington Post* and *The Associated Press*. There is a focus on stories that can help raise funds to transform communities and lives. When RYOT released a 360-experience documenting the after-effects of the earthquake in Nepal, the plan was to take users to witness the devastation and to drive donations. Co-founder Bryan Mooser said the technology "is the ultimate fundraising tool" (Streep 2016). This leaves the debate open for what the purpose of journalism is. As a tool for empathy, conditions can be met to achieve longer lasting behavioral change, but this can change the nature and purpose of journalism, where impartiality is no longer a pre-requisite.

Thus, follows the final criticism, that focusing on empathy limits the content production of immersive journalism. The concern was that in the early days of VR (in this wave, post 2010), the over-emphasis on empathy may have limited the range of content explored (Watson 2017, 21). In an early study of content in immersive journalism (Jones and Dawkins 2018), the majority of stories covered were those deemed to be empathy-generating, for example, imagining walking in someone else's shoes in a refugee camp or through a city flattened by bombing, as someone who has been displaced. Developing this further in interview, Watson noted how focusing on empathy limits content production and consequently it can limit the audience;

> It may have prevented audiences developing for early news VR because every story was so miserable and actually one of the things that you want from VR is sometimes a joyful and pleasant experience. Because so many news stories were about bombings and refugees, it was all very bleak content. Particularly if

> you look at content strategies geared towards bringing in younger audiences to news... just bringing misery is not going to work. So I think it led to a distortion, in terms of the sorts of content that might have helped build future audiences, where you want some of it but it needed to be balanced out with some other things that gave slightly more enjoyable experiences as well as being interesting and how people learn about the world.
>
> *Watson 2020*

With the rise in content production of immersive journalism in news organizations, limiting stories to empathy wasn't possible as more content was needed. The *NYTimes* The Daily 360 series produced a range of stories to experiment with understanding what worked for its audience. Watson used the example of *Fukushima, 6 Years On: Empty and Eerie* (2017) as an example where the place was the focus of the experience and it demonstrated a commitment to tackling difficult subjects, without the driving factor being empathy.

Focus on place

The arguments above note that defining immersive journalism by empathy itself is problematic, from the reductive nature through to whether it can effect long-lasting change. There is then the limiting factor it has on the development of immersive journalism if stories are all focused on generating empathy. Earlier in this chapter, it was noted that a diverse range of content was needed in order for the industry to grow, and this is of particular concern in growing audiences for immersive journalism specifically.

One way of diversifying this is creating experiences that focus on place, rather than generating empathy for a specific person. The transportive nature of the technology has long been cited as key to experiences, with the idea that VR allows you to go to another time and place, experiencing that for yourself. This is evident across industries including education (Pantelidis 1993) and travel (Schroeder 2008). The sense of "being there" is something that has dominated research in presence within virtual reality with the idea that as a participant, you would begin to feel that sense of being in the virtual environment that was depicted on the display of the headset (Sanchez-Vives and Slater 2005, Sheridan 1992). Slater (2009) has produced extensive research on "place illusion". By this, it is meant the type of presence that occurs when you feel that you have been transported to another place and are existing, for a time, in that location. As Slater affirms, "It is the strong illusion of being in a place in spite of the sure knowledge that you are not there" (Slater 2009, np). Place illusion is often measured by analyzing the behavior within the environments to assess whether the responses are realistic. Although much immersive journalism content has been developed through 360-degree film, rather than the interactivity of CGI where presence, place, or illusion can be measured and analyzed more easily, the focus on place and how this enables presence in an environment can be developed within the news industry.

Through creating a focus on place, immersive journalism has been able to develop without being underpinned by the empathy epithet. Watson found this in one of the BBC VR experiences, *Damming the Nile* (BBC 2018) where the place became the experience's central character;

> You were showing people places and they could see the scale of something, like the dam being built, and you could visit places you wouldn't be able to go. So, you do get a stronger sense looking around and I think they stay in your memory longer than it would through a television.
>
> *Watson 2020*

This was further demonstrated in another piece produced by the BBC called *Two Sisters, a Mountain Trek and a Wobbly Wire Bridge* (2017). This was a 360-degree experience that took you to a remote village in the Himalayas. As a viewer, you follow the journey of sisters Radhika and Yashoda, who travel up to six hours a day to school and back where they cross rivers and rope bridges. Although it is an experience focused on connecting the audience with the two sisters, for Watson, it is much more about the place, the environment, and the journey than it is about getting into their heads and understanding their plight;

> Does VR get you in someone's head better? I'm not sure but it certainly can take you to a place to see it for yourself and make that sense of geography that helps you understand what's going on somewhere better. That's probably one of its strongest things for news.
>
> *Watson 2020*

With a shift in focus from empathy-generating to understanding a place and the environment, it opens up new content and opportunities to develop immersive journalism. It allows you to hand the role of the reporter to the audience to let them see and understand a place, rather than the emotions of the people in that environment. This is evident from the BBC audience research, a study in 2019 that ran in 160 libraries in the UK. Out of more than 1,700 responses, 96 percent found the content enjoyable and 91 percent found it immersive (BBC 2019, 28). More than half of the users were experiencing VR for the first time. What was important within this audience study was the type of stories that had the most impact, and it was place that drove that engagement, not the stories that were perceived to be popular, like *Doctor Who*. One response in the study said, "I never thought I'd end up in the Congo when visiting the library" (BBC 2019, 29). As Watson said, they were "totally unprepared" for the response to the Congo piece. The Congo experience also evidences how experiences focused on place can encourage deeper engagement with the subject, with 83 percent of participants who watched the experience saying that they would then go on to watch a full-length documentary about the country (BBC 2019, 28).

This shift in focus to place changes the role of the journalist, rather than the role of journalism. The arguments for immersive journalism still hold true – that it offers new perspectives to a story. By taking the journalist out of the frame and allowing the user to enter into the world, it means that the viewer feels as though the event they are witnessing is real and they are a real participant in it (Kool 2016). This remains true whether the experience is designed to evoke an emotional state or is, more critically, unbiased reportage of a current news event. It is for the audience to experience the location and develop an understanding of the place that will determine any response they have, rather than that being the intention of the journalist. Research has found how the perception of the story can take on different meanings when the audience becomes the "actor" in the environment, through managing the information in a different way, whether that be through a filmed 360-degree environment or a recreated reality in CGI (Seijo 2017).

There are much greater opportunities when attention is turned to the concept of storyliving, as opposed to empathy. Since 2017, industry publications have been defining some forms of immersive storytelling as "storyliving". Aside from the practice of immersive media, it is growing as terminology within cultural and commercial circles, with *The Drum* stating: "brands need to do more than just tell a story. They need to live them", and that people "demand experiences that truly matter" (*The Drum* 2017).

Camille Cellucci, head of production at immersive studio The Void, said:

> What we're really moving into in this new world is "story-living". We're creating spaces and worlds where people have a chance to live out their own stories within a framework that we design.
>
> *Rolling Stone 2018*

Maschio and Baumann (2017) argued that the distinctive nature of journalism within virtual reality was that an audience lives the story, as opposed to being told it. Through an approach of storyliving, it would expand perspectives and the audience would be left with a powerful emotional experience. Critical to the understanding of storyliving and a non-directed narrative where audiences can take away different experiences is Walser's idea of the "spacemaker" (Walser 1991). The "spacemaker" is represented as a "magician" that creates a cyberspace where different realities can emerge.

If we begin to explore these ideas for immersive journalism, new narratives can be formed and new experiences realized. Emotionally charged experiences will remain and there will always be experiences that evoke or form pro-social behaviors, but this should not be the only way that immersive journalism is defined.

Conclusion

There is no denying that the promotion of empathy-driven immersive experiences has enabled new audiences to experience virtual reality and increased adoption rates, away from a gaming audience. However, the argument that is put across is that the dominance of the "empathy machine" epithet limits the opportunities that the technology brings and challenges the traditional notions of what journalism should be. Empathy may have been the gateway to opening up news organizations to creating immersive journalism experiences, but it is also what has limited the development of content.

Virtual reality pioneer Jaron Lanier has written extensively about the need to use VR as a way to transform new thoughts and ideas, with cyberdelics, improvising reality, and shared lucid dreaming (Lanier 2017). However, he notes that "Virtual reality is the ultimate lack of class or race distinctions or any other forms of pretense since all form is variable" (Lanier 1988, np). The consequence of this is that it can be an extraordinary tool for increasing empathy. The critical argument, though, remains the same:

> VR is certainly capable of facilitating new experiences of subjectivity, perception, and sociality, but to call all these phenomenon [sic] "empathy" limits the potential of the medium.
>
> *Sutherland, nd*

What this chapter does is to present the critiques to the argument that VR is an empathy machine. It acknowledges the arguments that are made against empathy and the concerns of using this as an umbrella term for all immersive journalism content. What it hasn't done is address the ethical concerns of using VR as an empathy term, an area that needs further research, especially in relation to donations to causes and how experiences could distort the mind and one's viewpoint.

It is evident that, through using the empathy line, more content has been formed. It has allowed those who may not have been engaged in VR previously to watch experiences and be transported to places to understand stories better. This has great impact for immersive journalism as a concept and a tool for deepening perspectives. However, immersive journalism can, and needs to, be much more that. It needs to focus on storyliving, allowing people to develop their own understanding themselves, being free to form a narrative to live an experience, rather than being told it through a journalistic lens. This is a challenge to traditional journalistic narratives, but it offers something new and a potentially new area for the news industry to thrive.

Interview

With thanks to Zillah Watson for an in-depth interview on empathy in immersive journalism, conducted in July 2020. Zillah was the Commissioning Editor for Virtual Reality at the BBC, leading the BBC VR Hub. She is executive producer of a number of VR experiences for the BBC including *Damming the Nile*, *Make Noise*, and *Nothing to be Written*.

Note

1 This chapter was revised in July 2020.

Immersive experiences and organizations

Clouds Over Sidra. 2015. [immersive experience] Directed by G. Arora and B. Pousman. *VRSE*.

Damming the Nile. 2018. [immersive experience] BBC. https://www.bbc.co.uk/news/world-africa-43117710. [Accessed 15 January 2020].

Fukushima, 6 Years On: Empty and Eerie. 2017. [immersive experience] Directed by V. Shastri, M. Rich and J. Thomas. *The New York Times*. https://www.youtube.com/watch?v=ThP3HsuWKU4. [Accessed 15 January 2020].

Google Digital News Initiative: https://newsinitiative.withgoogle.com/dnifund/ [Accessed 15 January 2020].

HTC Vive: https://vrforimpact.com [Accessed 15 January 2020]. Oculus VR for Good: www.oculus.com/vr-for-good/application/?locale=en_US

The Displaced. 2015. [immersive experience] Directed by B. Solomon, I. Ismail, C. Milk, & J. Silverstein. *The New York Times*.

The Machine to be Another. 2019. *The Machine to be Another*. www.themachinetobeanother.org [Accessed 18 January 2019].

Two Sisters, a Mountain Trek and a Wobbly Wire Bridge. 2017. [immersive experience] BBC. https://www.bbc.co.uk/news/world-41527080 [Accessed 15 January 2020].

We Wait. 2016. [immersive experience]. Aardman and BBC. https://www.oculus.com/experiences/rift/1248924088498899/?locale=en_GB [Accessed 15 January 2020].

References

Aitamurto, T., S. Zhou, S. Sakshuwong, J. Saldivar, Y. Sadeghi, & A. Tran. 2018. "Sense of presence, attitude change, perspective-taking and usability in first-person split-sphere 360 video". In: *Proceedings of the 2018 CHI Conference on Human Factors in Computing Systems*. New York: ACM, p. 545.

BBC. 2019. "Storytelling and audience insights 2019". https://downloads.bbc.co.uk/aboutthebbc/internetblog/bbc_vr_storytelling.pdf [Accessed 15 January 2020].

Chun, W. 2016. "WEIRD REALITY: Head-mounted art && code: Wendy Hui Kyong Chun". *Vimeo*. https://vimeo.com/214713185 [Accessed 13 October 2018].

de la Peña, N. 2017. "Towards behavioural realism: Experiments in immersive journalism". In: J. Aston, S. Gaudenzi, & M. Rose (eds), *i-Docs: The Evolving Practices of Interactive Documentary*. New York: Columbia University Press, pp. 206–222.

de la Peña, N., P. Weil, J. Llobera, E. Giannopoulos, A. Pomés, B. Spanlang, D. Friedman, M. V. Sanchez-Vives & M. Slater. 2010. "Immersive journalism: Immersive virtual reality for the first-person experience of news". *Presence: Teleoperators and Virtual Environments 19*(4): 291–301.

Drum, The. 2017. "Moving from storytelling to story living". www.thedrum.com/industryinsights/2017/03/21/moving-storytelling-story-living-0 [Accessed 15 January 2020].

Ebert, R. (2005). "Ebert's Walk of Fame remarks". https://www.rogerebert.com/roger-ebert/eberts-walk-of-fame-remarks [Accessed 15 January 2020].

Fogel, S. 2019. "VR developers say audience adoption is their biggest challenge". https://variety.com/2019/gaming/news/htc-vive-vr-developer-survey-1203197302/ [Accessed 15 January 2020].

Herrera, F., J. Bailenson, E. Weisz, E Ogle, & J. Zaki. 2018. "Building long-term empathy: a large-scale comparison of traditional and virtual reality perspective-taking". *PloS one, 13*(10), e0204494.

Jaekel, B. 2015. "NY Times? VR play is publisher's most successful app launch". *Mobile Marketer*. www.mobilemarketer.com/ex/mobilemarketer/cms/news/video/21676.html [Accessed 15 January 2020].

Jones, S. 2017. "Disrupting the narrative: Immersive journalism in virtual reality". *Journal of Media Practice 18*(2–3): 171–185.

Jones, S. & Dawkins, S. 2018. "Walking in someone else's shoes: Creating empathy in the practice of immersive film". *Media Practice and Education 19*(3): 298–312.

Kool, H. 2016. "The ethics of immersive journalism: A rhetorical analysis of news storytelling with virtual reality technology". *Intersect: The Stanford Journal of Science, Technology & Society 9*(3): 1–11.

Lanier, J. 1988. A Vintage Virtual Reality Interview. http://www.jaronlanier.com/vrint.html [Accessed 15 January 2020].

Lanier, J. 2017. *Dawn of the New Everything: Encounters with Reality and Virtual Reality*. New York: Henry Holt and Co.

Lisetti, C., R. Amini, U. Yasavur, & N. Rishe. 2013. "I can help you change! An empathic virtual agent delivers behavior change health interventions". *ACM Transactions on Management Information Systems (TMIS)*, *4*(4): 1–28.

Maschio, T. & K. Baumann. 2017. *Storyliving: An Ethnographic Study of how Audiences Experience VR and What That Means for Journalists*. Google News Lab.

Milk, C. 2015. "How virtual reality can create the ultimate empathy machine." *TED Talk*, March 2015. www.ted.com/talks/chris_milk_how_virtual_reality_can_create_the_ultimate_ empathy_machine [Accessed 2 September 2018].

Pantelidis, V. S. 1993. "Virtual reality in the classroom". *Educational Technology 33*(4), 23–27.

Salas, B. (2018). *Basic Concept of Journalism*. UK: Scientific e-Resources.

Sanchez-Vives, M.V. & M. Slater. 2005. "From presence to consciousness through virtual reality". *Nat. Rev. Neurosci.* 6: 332–339. (doi:10.1038/nrn1651).

Sánchez Laws, A.L. 2017. "Can immersive journalism enhance empathy?" *Digital Journalism*. doi:10.1080/21670811.2017.1389286

Schroeder, R. 2008. "Defining virtual worlds and virtual environments". *Journal For Virtual Worlds Research*, *1*(1).

Seijo, S.P. 2017. "Immersive journalism: From audience to first-person experience of news". *Media and Metamedia Management*. Springer, Cham. 113–119. https://doi.org/10.1007/978-3-319-46068-0_14

Sheridan T.B. 1992. "Musings on telepresence and virtual presence". *Presence: Teleop. Virtual Environ.* 1: 120–126.

Slater, M. 2009. "Place illusion and plausibility can lead to realistic behaviour in immersive virtual environments". *Philosophical Transactions of the Royal Society of London. Series B, Biological Sciences*, *364*(1535): 3549–3557. https://doi.org/10.1098/rstb.2009.0138

Steed, A., Y. Pan, Z. Watson, & M. Slater. 2018. "'We wait'—the impact of character responsiveness and self embodiment on presence and interest in an immersive news experience". *Frontiers in Robotics and AI*, *5*, p. 112.

Streep, A. 2016. "Crisis and opportunity: How one VR startup is capturing the 360-degree reality of the world's most vulnerable people". *Wired.com*. www.wired.com/2016/07/ryot-darg-mooser-disaster-vr/ [Accessed 15 January 2020].

Sutherland, A. n.d. "The limits of virtual reality: Debugging the empathy machine". *Docubase*. https://docubase.mit.edu/lab/case-studies/the-limits-of-virtual-reality-debugging-the-empathy-machine/ [Accessed 15 January 2020].

Valdes, Giancarlo. "Lucasfilm: The Future of VR Is 'Story-Living' and Cross-Platform Play." Rolling Stone, 23 Mar. 2018.

Walser, R. 1991. "The emerging technology of cyberspace". In: S.K. Helsel & J. Roth (eds), *Virtual Reality: Theory, Practice, and Promise*. Westport, CT: Meckler.

Watson, Z. 2017. *VR for News: The New Reality?* Digital News Project. Oxford, UK: Reuters Institute for the Study of Journalism, University of Oxford. https://reutersinstitute.politics.ox.ac.uk/sites/default/files/research/files/VR%2520for%2520news%2520-%2520the%2520new%2520reality.pdf [Accessed 15 January 2020].

Willens, M. 2017. "One year in: What The New York Times learned from its 360-degree video project, The Daily 360". *Digiday*. https://digiday.com/media/one-year-new-york-times-learned-360-degree-video-project-daily-360/ [Accessed 15 January 2020].

Wohlsen, M. 2015. "Google Cardboard's New York Times experiment just hooked a generation on VR". *Wired.com*. www.wired.com/2015/11/google-cardboards-new-york-times-experiment-just-hooked-a-generation-on-vr/ [Accessed 15 January 2020].

Wu, T. 2016. *The Attention Merchants: The Epic Scramble to Get Inside Our Heads*. New York: Vintage Books.

Zanger, D. 2017. "'None of it made sense at times': RYOT CMO on what makes a great story". *The Drum*. www.thedrum.com/news/2017/11/16/none-it-made-sense-times-ryot-cmo-what-makes-great-story [Accessed 15 January 2020].

PART III

Production and design

9

PLACE-BASED JOURNALISM, AESTHETICS, AND BRANDING

David O. Dowling

The debut of *Bear 71* at the Sundance Film Festival in 2012 established a major milestone in the evolution of interactive cinema. Five years later, the film's reformatting and re-release in 2017 as a virtual reality (VR) experience viewed through head-mounted displays (HMDs) signaled the future of immersive journalism (Jardine 2017). In it, the viewer tracks the movement and behavior of a female grizzly bear in Canada's Banff National Park, which provides the setting for this poignant piece revealing the human impact on wildlife. The VR edition enabled the large-scale setting of the wilderness to take on the powerful intimacy of an immersive news experience of the sort showcased in Nonny de la Peña's pioneering *Hunger in L.A.*, which also debuted at Sundance in 2012. As with *Bear 71*, *Hunger in L.A.* offered a moving human encounter rather than "cold facts and figures", in its case "by taking a small scale drama and turning it into an emotional confrontation with the everyday reality of hunger in one of the richest countries in the world" (van der Haak 2014). Despite being only seven minutes in length, the work left a deep impression on audiences. "Viewers of the piece tried to touch the nonexistent characters and many cried at the conclusion", according to de la Peña (as quoted in van der Haak 2014). Roughly three times the length, *Bear 71*'s 2017 VR edition expanded the template for the virtual news experience into a more distinctly cinematic, longform mode of storytelling, extending the reach of the medium's already considerable empathic powers.

This chapter examines interactive documentary's evolution since 2012, particularly visible in the emergence of VR/360 journalism. 360- degree video (in spherical rather than flat formatting) viewed through the "magic window" on mobile devices or with HMDs in the more fully immersive VR format have propelled documentary journalism to new technological and narrative heights, achievements attained in part through alternative brand economies, industrial logics and marketing strategies. News organizations, researchers, and tech companies have begun to explore cost-efficient ways of bringing immersive video to a mainstream audience. As Watson (2017) notes, 360- degree videos have "made [VR] more accessible to consumers" despite not providing "the immersive experience delivered by a high-end (and more expensive) headset". For journalists, the new VR technology presents one of the most potent storytelling tools in all media, one that demands a thorough reconsideration of editing methods, which have radically destabilized ethical principles of production. Out of this early experimental phase an uneven and highly contested set of best practices has begun to take shape, bearing distinct advantages in spatial storytelling, while diminishing the importance of the cut as a vital editorial tool and means of expression. Interactive video's function as place-based journalism is discussed in the following section. Case studies then examine Google's *Beyond the Map*, *Sports Illustrated*'s *Capturing Everest*, and the National Film Board of Canada's *Bear 71*, immersive documentaries that reflect the industrial protocols of their respective production companies and demonstrate corporate synergies converging into promotional media.

VR documentary as place-based journalism

The latest phase in the evolution of digital journalism has expanded beyond the linear presentation of facts for passive consumption. Now longer-branching narrative formats within expansive virtual environments situate subjects in their social, political, and economic contexts, which are embodied and dramatized through their geographical surroundings. Subjects of such situated documentaries are thus "more contextualized and placed within a broader environment of events, trends, and issues" (Pavlik & Bridges 2013, 22). The analytic and ethnographic approach scholars call for as a means of producing more accurate journalism (Neveu 2014; Davis 2016) can be realized in interactive documentary.

Unlike the highly distracting interface of conventional online news, digital journalism produced as interactive documentary provides an immersive app-like environment that eliminates distraction from having multiple windows open in addition to banner and pop-up advertising (Hernandez & Rue 2016, 105). This highly engaging and interactive design functions as a cognitive container, as the viewer's attention remains in the space of the story world and its embedded multimedia elements without being scattered onto the open web via hyperlinks (Dowling 2017, 103). Although interactive documentaries deploy a wide spectrum of diverse digital designs, most create a sense "of embarking on an experience similar to a video game or movie" within a unified and self-contained story world (Hernandez & Rue 2016, 103).

Interactive documentaries are linked to VR in important ways that bear on narrative content as well as user understanding. Aston, Gaudenzi, and Rose (2017) note that interactive documentaries, or "i-docs", include a vast array of projects such as "transmedia documentaries, serious games, locative docs, interactive community media, docu-games", as well as nonfictional VR and live performance documentary. Each of these shares innovation in "documenting away from the lineage of documentary film" (2). The cases examined in this chapter provide an interactive experience, one featuring a radical diversity of genre conventions across media akin to Wagner's concept of the *Gesamtkunstwerk*, an artwork synthesizing a variety of different forms (Aston 2017a). Cases examined here hybridize conventions from documentary film to journalistic data visualization and video games, in the process re-mediating reporting and writing associated with older forms of print longform journalism, particularly investigative and profile feature storytelling. By breaking down the "fourth wall", as Aston (2017a) explains, new "forms of audience engagement and participation [go] beyond the 'point and click' interactivity to screen-based work" (224). Of particular interest here is the effect of works that create "both experiential and readerly ways into documentary content" specifically to challenge the user to "make things feel a little more difficult", as in interactive theater's capacity to "make the hairs stand up on the back of peoples' necks, and to make them feel 'alive'" (Aston 2017a, 224–225). Each case underscores the affirmation that "the future of storytelling is absolutely about placing the audience at the heart of the experience", as Aston (2017a) notes of interactive theater (225).

By navigating data-rich maps, users can experience interactive documentaries on the most intimate level, while also seeing the full expanse of the virtual environment from the seemingly omniscient perspective of 360-degree footage. In this sense, the genre resonates with twenty-first-century place-based literacies and the rise of spatial journalism (Schmitz Weiss 2015). According to Murray (2011), the affordances of digital media are procedural (a set of rules), participatory (inviting action and manipulation of the virtual environment), encyclopedic (the presence of large amounts of data presented in various forms), and spatial (that allows for navigation throughout an information repository and/or virtual environment) (as cited in Aston 2017b). Immersive media – particularly the interactive documentary and multimedia feature – have evolved in such a way as to bring a spatial orientation to the other three major affordances of digital media. Indeed, the spatial dimension of interactive documentary storytelling, as this chapter demonstrates, subsumes procedural, participatory, and encyclopedic affordances. Prior to the emergence of immersive storytelling such as 360- degree video and VR, each of these four affordances was more evenly represented in digital publications, precisely because they lacked the capacity to represent three-dimensional space with such fidelity to the real world, and to plunge the viewer into it so deeply (Aston 2017b).

Interactive documentary encourages a process that in effect "engages a citizenry increasingly disengaged from traditional news" (Pavlik & Bridges 2013). New media's potential for increased user engagement is particularly evident in 360-degree video, which intensifies immediacy through fictional techniques used to capture nonfictional lived events and subjects rather than escapist fantasies (Atkins, McLean, & Canter 2017). In VR stories viewed through HMDs, imagery plays a crucial role in the effects of narrative transportation (Green & Brock 2002). There are significant differences, however, between the effects of VR stories, 360-degree video (without HMD), and text on presence, memory, credibility, empathy, and sharing (Sundar et al. 2017).

This new medium builds on the longstanding principle of nonfiction film as "the art of *re*-presentation" responsive to "immediate moments" and therefore "rooted in a cultural context that should be studied" (Barsam 1979, 583). Like its pre-digital forbears, the interactive documentary "is usually filmed without sets, costumes, written dialogue, or created sound effects", with the ostensible aim of recreating the sense of "being there" with as much veracity as the situation allows (Barsam 1979, 583). Just as nonfiction film evolved toward increasingly immersive forms in the late 1960s and early 1970s, interactive documentaries have begun expanding toward longer templates, as seen in *Capturing Everest*.

Prior to HMD and 360 VR technology associated with spherical film, the narrative complexity and emotional import of documentary shot in traditional flat formats steadily increased from the late 1960s to the early 2000s (Bondebjerg 2014). Documentarians have experimented with surreal representations of psychological interiority as in the Japanese film *The Man Who Skied Down Everest* (1975 Academy Award Winner), dramatic character-based multi-plot narratives as in the critically acclaimed *Hoop Dreams* (1994), and scientific data visualization as in Al Gore's *An Inconvenient Truth* (2006 Academy Award Winner). In such cases, "emotional layers in documentaries appear through narrative structures, through character identification, and through audio-visual effects", techniques also used in fiction films. "But they are also directly connected to content and themes with links to real life" in documentary films, and crucially, "to our decisions to act directly or indirectly when confronted with social problems" (Bondebjerg 2014, 21).

Branching narrative and the Google brand: "beyond the map"

Google has drawn recognition as an industry leader in mobile digital mapping. To appeal to the coveted mobile audience, 90% of whom are constantly using location-based services (Anderson 2016), the company has differentiated its maps from the competition by emphasizing place in comparison to more navigation-oriented products such as Apple's AR Flyover for iOS 11. Google's augmentation of map locations has advanced beyond visitor reviews and popular times to include contextualizing images and material designed to encourage deeper exploration of communities and cultures. Immersive geographic storytelling is not an end in itself, but a means of inspiring the user to move beyond the map and into the world.

Until recently, the favelas of Brazil's Rio de Janeiro existed outside the reach of online cartographers. *Beyond the Map* fulfills Google's presumed social mission to bridge the digital divide by mapping this uncharted terrain, and thus give presence and significance to the favelas, most of which were unmapped on Google Maps at the time. The highly sharable series was designed precisely to leverage 2016 Olympic coverage of Rio undertaken by all major media outlets of the world, given the magnitude of the event. This local color of the host city was told through branching or ergotic narrative, as Hernandez and Rue (2016) describe film that allows the viewer to choose their own path through the story (103). Those paths follow several denizens of the favelas. In all cases the narrative avoids soliciting the subjects as objects of sentimentality, but instead humanizes them through authentic moving portraits.

A unifying motif connecting each of the figures profiled in *Beyond the Map* is digital technology, which for one aspiring performance artist takes the form of a video game dance simulator essential to his professional development. Another profile delves into the story of a young woman who seeks a career in computer science, a story directly linked to Google's brand and its theme of bridging the digital divide. A third segment profiles a middle-aged entrepreneur of many stripes who had run a business launching hot air balloons in celebration of prison releases, spectacular shows of freedom financed by family and friends of the released inmate. Google mapping technology in his case improved his business ventures by making him more visible to customers, especially in support of his most recent company specializing in surfing and wind-surfing lessons. Aspiration is a common element connecting their stories, and Google's digital technology plays a central role in each.

According to the film's promotional and branding logics, digital mapping technology is vital to the individual and collective welfare of Brazil's and, by extension, the world's most impoverished populations. Navigation, for example, is crucial to the travel of the young dancer to the academy, and to the entrepreneur in attracting customers through a visible web presence. The film itself, produced in a spherical format, embodies this vision of liberation through technology, as VR/360 and drone cameras joined the cast of characters. Interactive 360-degree shots taken on a motorcycle speeding through the favelas are not mere displays of technological prowess, but help drive the narration of its cartographic theme.

Digital cartography is thus a process of cultural geography, according to the thematic import of *Beyond the Map*. The work's spatial conception of subjects and styles strongly suggests the formation, however embryonic, of interactive documentary's first genre convention of emphasizing people and place. This spatial orientation reflects "emplacement", defined by Aston (2017) as "the creation, manipulation and sharing of meaning through engaged interaction, bringing our bodies and minds into direct interplay with the wider environment" (233). The viewer never encounters a conventional map; space is represented through spherical filmed footage (as in Google Earth or Satellite) for immersion in the lived ecosystem of the favela communities. This controlling metaphor of cartography – as organizing principle for the film's subject, branding strategies, and user experience – is a self-reflexive iteration of the "third meaning" Barthes (1977, 52) describes in film, one that lies just beyond denotation and connotation. The "excess", which constitutes "elements that escape unifying impulses", in this case actually serves the film's unifying principle (as quoted in Bordwell 1985, 53). While the viewer can savor random color, shapes, and sounds on screen not immediately linked to the figure being profiled, such details point to Google's uncanny capacity to evoke a place, and thus support the film's unifying principle of digital technology's role in the cultural geography of developing communities. The third meaning of *Beyond the Map* is thus industrially and culturally instantiated in the story.

Interactive documentary editing plays into the viewer's innate desire to assemble a story of the content. According to Sergei Eisenstein, the staging of action is a representational act, "a pattern which the perceivers of narratives create through assumptions and inference". The details behind that pattern, David Bordwell (1985) explains, constitute the data with which "the viewer builds the fabula on the basis of prototype schemata (identifiable types of personas, actions, locales, etc.), template schemata (principally the 'canonic' story), and procedural schemata (a search for appropriate motivations and relations of causality, time and space)", all processes that are intersubjective (49). The interactive documentary has reconfigured the gestural, connotative quality of film by enabling thorough and autonomous exploration of the range of vision of any given shot. What brings unifying meaning to interactive documentary now lies as much in "what is materially present on the screen or soundtrack" as in what is implied beyond it (Bordwell 1985, 49). VR/360 technology enables viewers to connect eye-line matches themselves in what is essentially a cut-free experience on the level of the scene.

A major departure from traditional film in interactive documentary lies in the sequencing of events. The viewer of *Beyond the Map*, for example, is invited to explore the narrative profiles of the figures featured in the film in any order they wish, beginning atop a hill above the sprawling narrow streets of the favelas. In the presence of the narrator the viewer can choose their path in this virtual world as in a video game, thus becoming the architect of their own string of experiences. Useful in understanding the aesthetic and narrative structure of this effect is Roman Jakobson's concept of stylistic composition via paradigmatic groupings based on "the principle of equivalence from the axis of selection to the axis of combination" (quoted in Bordwell 1985, 277). The profile features, for example, are similarly produced in terms of shots, pacing, and duration, each rearranging documentary narration into "paradigmatic groups basic to its construction" (Bordwell 1985, 277). *Beyond the Map* offers a typology of aspiration as a deep dive into the lives of Rio's inhabitants, told through the immersion of the viewer. The viewer can shift between each profile at will, yet within a virtual environment emphasizing similarities of paradigmatic categories of race, social class, connectivity, privilege, and, ultimately, technology's role in each. (That technological role, of course, bears the Google brand.) As Bordwell describes of film narrative, "any sequence of units – phonological, syntactic, semantic – strives to build an equality with the others, creating designs" within the larger work (quoted in Bordwell 1985, 277).

Re-branding *Sports Illustrated*'s longform legacy for the digital age: *Capturing Everest*

Just as Google sought uncharted territory in Rio to stake its claim in the new media ecosystem of immersive online storytelling, *Sports Illustrated* set its sights on the iconic summit of Mount Everest. Capitalizing on spatial journalism's unique appeal to audiences' place-based knowledge (Schmitz Weiss 2015), *SI*'s *Capturing Everest* reprises the cartographic theme common to immersive media. Profile feature storytelling augments the significance of the main narrative covering the dramatic journey to the summit. Brent Bishop serves as veteran guide and son of Barry Bishop, a member of the first American team to reach Everest's summit in 1963. He is joined by Lisa Thompson, breast cancer survivor, and Jeff Glasbrenner, who lost his right leg just below the knee at the age of 12 in a farming accident. Glasbrenner became the first amputee to reach the top of Everest on an expedition that also made media history as the first-ever bottom-to-top ascent of Everest filmed spherically in 360- degree.

Capturing Everest distinguished itself for its length and format consisting of four eight-minute episodes, significantly extending the standard 3–5 minutes for VR. The film functions differently on a narrative level from the highly interactive, data-driven *Bear 71*. Rather than presenting a map challenging users to decide where to enter the environment, *Capturing Everest* unfolds in the manner of an on-demand TV docuseries. The sense of immersion is immediate, as the user is treated to an experience previously only available in IMAX theaters. Episode 1 opens during a training session in preparation for Everest. On the high cliff wall, surround footage is at its most compelling. Any distinction between action in front of and behind the camera vanishes in contiguous angles that all contribute vital material to the *mise-en-scène*. The shot effectively places the viewer on the wall with the climbers, thus breaking down the arbitrary divisions between directed/non-directed action. Non-diegetic narration allows the visuals to dominate. The interactivity here lies not in selecting data caches and scanning maps to navigate the virtual environment as in *Bear 71*, but in the seemingly omniscient power to scan all angles of every shot. Like Emerson's transparent eyeball in the forest, the user sees all but is nothing, disembodied, and emptied of self precisely to achieve a visceral nearness to nature and humanity.

Cliff-hanger endings, recap openings, and an icon in the upper right of the screen indicating progress toward completion all draw on on-demand television series conventions for the digital design of *Capturing Everest*. Each episode, however, is packaged to stand alone as an autonomous piece in order to increase spreadability on social media. The film's transmediation extends to *SI*'s print magazine, where readers can use their mobile device to scan the AR box on the cover featuring Glasbrenner. Although HMDs provide the optimal experience, panning or simply swiping a finger on the screen in any direction allows views of the surrounding field of vision. Pictured in action on the mountain, Glasbrenner's prosthesis is prominently displayed on this *SI* cover.

Rather than relying on voice-of-God narration often used in traditional documentaries, extra-diegetic narrative is supplied through the commentary of the three subjects. The lack of omniscient audio narration allows for a more cinematic viewing experience, precisely because the film instead focuses on "strong central characters doing something filmable directly related to their story", which is the expedition itself, rather than shots of them describing a past accomplishment (Tu 2015, 74). Real-time live events are the staple of televisual sports journalism. To maintain that feel, no *SI* reporters and production crew appear in the main film's audio or visual content. Journalistic control is evident in the explanatory text superimposed on the screen, which is strategically positioned at intervals around the perimeter (rather than clustered in one spot) to encourage exploration of the full panorama. Between action and climbing sequences, characters thus narrate their own stories – providing the color commentary, as it were – through responses to interview questions left off the soundtrack.

SI self-consciously highlighted its legacy in longform journalism, which it had done in its first digital features for its "Going Deep" department established in 2012 just after the publication of *Snow Fall* (Dowling & Vogan 2015). To promote *Capturing Everest*, *SI* emphasized its brand as legacy longform through Bishop's father's 1963 achievement as a member of the first American team to summit the famous peak. But one decade earlier, *SI* published the most thorough coverage in the news media at the time on the 1953 first-ever ascent by Sir Edmond Hillary. As with Google's brand-building through digital cartography and ground-breaking exploration by which geographical terrain becomes a trope for technological advancement, *SI* invoked the space race of the mid-twentieth century as technology and exploration converged "long before the moon landing" when "mankind made its first terrestrial leap" (Stone 2017).

Emerging editorial norms and the 2017 VR edition of *Bear 71*

Traditional editorial techniques less reliant on the cut to establish continuity are far more compelling when deployed in 360- degree. The long tracking shot and pan, for example, have become staples of the new medium because it allows the viewer to experience travel and motion with a full range of vision. Hence travel, distance, and movement remain core components of the spatially oriented narratives that have come to define the genre, as seen in *Beyond the Map* and *Capturing Everest*. Interestingly, since it is already built into every shot, 360- degree automates panning by in effect placing the camera in the hands of the viewer. 360- degree is ideally suited to journalistic documentary's dedication to verisimilitude by virtue of its reliance on storytelling through spatial narrative emphasizing *mise-en-scène* rather than through cuts emphasizing time. "The cut is more manipulative" because it "interrupts and remodels reality". By contrast, "the pan is the more realistic [...] since it preserves the integrity of space" (Monaco 1981, 143–144). Andre Bazin observed connections between realism and *mise-en-scène*, and impressionism and montage, a point useful in explaining 360- degree's predilection toward nonfiction storytelling. What "montage simply did in time is what mise-en-scène does in space", as Jean-Luc Godard noted (cited in Monaco 1981, 145). Journalistic documentary in this sense shares the spatial storytelling staple of *mise-en-scène* with realistic fiction films. With its space-driven narrative more thickly layered with more *mise-en-scène* than ever, spherical 360- degree technology uses movement – both the filmmaker's and the viewer's – through the virtual environment to dictate tempo.

Despite the loss of quick cutting and montage as engines driving visual storytelling, producers of VR journalism can maintain narrative control in graphic and video overlays as well as direction of subjects before the camera. The technology may be highly automated, but it does not establish the course of the narrative journey nor plot the thematic interconnections between its branches and detours users may choose to pursue. "Audiences will be able to choose different story paths as they freely explore the virtual space", a process akin to open-world gaming, only in a nonfictional context of a "'choose your own adventure' version of journalism", according to a 2017 Associated Press study (Marconi & Nakagawa 2017).

The viewer of *Bear 71* is similarly immersed in a potentially overwhelming amount of data, yet non-diegetic narration maintains focus for the spatial storytelling preferences and place-based knowledge of today's online audience (Schmitz Weiss 2015). Beginning with moving footage of the capture, radio tagging, and release of a three-year-old female grizzly bear in Banff National Park, the piece then releases the viewer to explore the behaviors and travels of the animal – along with some wandering humans mounted with audio and video recording devices – through surveillance clips taken by cameras rigged throughout the wilderness. The viewer can navigate the terrain autonomously, as non-linear serendipitous exploration is balanced by Mia Kirschner's narrative voiceover from the perspective of *Bear 71*, tethering attention to the arc of story that follows the bear's life for the next five years until the dramatic closing scene. While audio maintains narrative trajectory, open-world design encourages autonomous exploration through hundreds of thousands of pictures, clips, and images captured by motion-detector webcams revealing how other tagged animals and humans encroach on the bear's territory and affect her life. In the process of blurring the lines between "story structure, database information, surveillance, and the complex interrelationship between humans and animals", the piece relies on an intense place-based interactive experience (Hernandez & Rue 2016, 145).

A telling sign of the tech industry's centrality to the evolution of the interactive documentary appeared in *Bear 71*'s 2017 re-release, five years after its original debut, as a virtual reality work designed for viewing with Google Daydream and the more affordable Google Cardboard, headsets designed for use with smartphones. Neither Google, nor any other brand, tech or otherwise, had a stake in the original 2012 production of *Bear 71*, initially a public media project via the Canadian National Film Board (NFB) and the Canadian National Park system. This corporate partnership arguably may not undermine the conservation message, as the technology of Google Daydream enhances the immersive effect of the medium, and thus its power to move viewers to action (Aitken 2013; Perse & Lambe 2016) on behalf of wildlife protection.

A key factor distinguishing *Bear 71*'s process of production from those of interactive documentaries by Google and *Sports Illustrated* lies in its partnerships with both the National Film Board of Canada, for digital architecture and construction, and the Canadian National Park system, for its raw data. Indeed, the piece demanded no independent development of data-gathering devices, methods, or even immersive reportage in a remote location. Instead, a vast untapped data cache of thousands of hours of wildlife footage taken by motion-activated cameras for surveillance of Banff National Park was repurposed as the raw material for place-based journalism. Rose (2017) identifies such collaboration as "co-creation", an arrangement that draws subjects, and those close to them, into the process of production, one that enables an activist agenda aiming beyond representation toward social change (51). Leanne Allison originally proposed the project as a traditional documentary to the NFB, who suggested instead an interactive format. The project made novel use of already available technology and resources for the purpose of interactive spatial journalism (Schmitz Weiss 2015). Wired with cameras for conservation and law enforcement purposes, the thoroughly documented Canadian wilderness of Banff was repurposed as an ideal journalistic digital archive. In this sense, the film is the product not of corporate partnerships or branding strategies, but of new video surveillance technology funded by Canadian taxpayers. The automated recordings brought a windfall of data simplifying the information-gathering portion of the reporting process. Thus the film's conservation message traces back to that of the publicly funded data-gathering of Banff National Park, which in turn was shaped into the interactive narrative by the NFB, yet another nonprofit entity charged with serving the public interest rather than marketing its brand.

Unlike the production process for traditional documentary dedicated to shooting extensive original footage and culling a fraction of it for the final cut, the most labor-intensive and time-consuming aspect of *Bear 71* was in curating the park's endless low-resolution images and footage. Since Allison shot none of the wildlife footage herself, her task was essentially editorial, yet in ways totally distinct from conventional documentary production, which would have left thousands of hours of footage on the cutting-room floor. The digital archive of *Bear 71* lends itself well to VR, as outdoor settings continue to set the standard for interactive web documentaries. The personal connection with subjects in the film, which builds on documentary cinema's increasing use of emotional appeals and literary techniques (Bondebjerg 2014; Parisi & Holcornb 1994), is enhanced by VR.

Conclusion

Capturing Everest capitalized on the empathic power of the form when it became the first feature-length film shot in VR released on the internet. The compassion for the climbers, whom the viewer joins in the ascent of the world's most iconic mountain, intensifies in proportion to the film's immersive quality much in the manner of Google's *Beyond the Map*. Google's partnership in the re-release of *Bear 71* by virtue of enabling viewing through Google Daydream and Google Cardboard carries important implications for the role of large tech corporations in the evolution of interactive documentary. News organizations have played a key role in the development of the genre, infusing it with journalistic research, reporting, and writing that remediates print narrative longform genres such as profile, historical, investigative, embedded, and trend feature stories. The interactive documentary thrives on industrial shifts that have given rise to partnerships tracing back to Samsung's underwriting of *The New York Times*' 360- degree experimentation that spawned NYTVR.

Tension in merging journalism and documentary tends to center on filmmakers' reluctance to be shackled by the expectation of reportorial objectivity. In speaking about working with *The New York Times* on the production of *A Short History of the High Rise*, for example, NFB producer Gerry Flahive noted that "Journalism is not a term we ever used at NFB in regards to our documentary work. It implies that a point of view is a bad thing, when for documentary filmmakers it is central to the creative act" (Uricchio et al. 2015, 79). Certainly daily breaking news producers can be characterized as resisting point of view and subjectivity. Yet a long and rich tradition of literary journalism featuring the reporter as narrator and/or key character shaping the story is evident in the 1960s New Journalism movement spearheaded by Tom Wolfe. Without eschewing traditional journalism's truth-telling covenants, interactive documentaries also embrace point of view as central to the creative act. The pursuit of rigorous reporting according to the journalistic principle of verification is indeed consonant with the truth claim at the core of documentary filmmaking.

Journalism and documentary combine in cinematic VR for powerfully affective narrative emphasizing felt detail and intimacy with subjects through a heightened sense of embodied presence in a specific place. The centrality of point of view in interactive documentary is evident in the form's genetic blueprint, which traces back to MIT's OpenDocLab that inspired *The New York Times*' 2012 launch of Op-Docs, the first video opinion documentary as a news form. The interactive longform documentary similarly foregrounds the point of view of its creators, yet moves beyond unsupported editorializing into narrative buttressed with rigorous research and reporting, as evident in *Beyond the Map*, *Sports Illustrated*'s *Capturing Everest*, and the National Film Board of Canada's *Bear 71*. Documentary's long dedication to the truth claim as its source of rhetorical power is indeed well suited to journalism's foundational principles of accuracy and verification. VR and media hybridity allows for more fluid definitions of documentary that embraces journalism, a category whose literary forebears align it with, rather than against, "openly rhetorical filmmaking" (Corner 2008, 23). Technological innovations toward increasingly immersive formats now enable documentaries to function both as a subset of journalism and a form as personal as fiction filmmaking that bears the stamp of those who made them, producers ranging from tech companies and legacy media to university labs and national film boards (Bruzzi 2006).

References

Aitken, Ian. 2013. *Form and Reform: John Grierson and the Documentary Film Movement*. New York: Routledge.

Anderson, M. 2016. "More Americans Using Smartphones for Getting Directions, Streaming TV." Pew Research Center, 29 January. www.pewresearch.org/fact-tank/2016/01/29/us-smartphone-use/ [Accessed 15 March 2020].

Aston, Judith. 2017a. "Interactive Documentary and Live Performance: From Embodied to Emplaced Interaction." In: Judith Aston, Sandra Gaudenzi, & Mandy Rose (eds), *i-Docs: The Evolving Practices of Interactive Documentaries*. London: Wallflower Press, pp. 222–231.

Aston, Judith. 2017b. "Interactive Documentary: What Does it Mean and Why Does it Matter?" *i-Docs*. http://i-docs.org/2016/03/27/interactive-documentary-what-does-it-mean-and-why-does-it-matter/ [Accessed 13 October 2019].

Aston, Judith, Sandra Gaudenzi, & Mandy Rose. 2017. "Introduction." In: Judith Aston, Sandra Gaudenzi, & Mandy Rose (eds), *i-Docs: The Evolving Practices of Interactive Documentaries*. London: Wallflower Press, pp. 1–3.

Atkins, A., D. McLean, & W. Canter, 2017. "Narrative Transportation, News, 360 Video and Virtual Reality." Poster presented at the American Educators of Journalism and Mass Communication (AEJMC) Conference, Chicago, IL, 6–10 August.

Barsam, Richard Meran. 1979. "Nonfiction Film: The Realist Impulse." In: Gerald Mast & Marshall Cohen (eds), *Film Theory and Criticism: Introductory Readings*. New York: Oxford University Press, pp. 580–593.

Barthes, Roland. 1977. *Image, Music, Text*. Trans. S. Heath. New York: Hill and Wang.

Bondebjerg, I. 2014. "Documentary and Cognitive Theory: Narrative, Emotion, and Memory." *Media and Communication 2*(1): 13–22.

Bordwell, D. 1985. *Narration in the Fiction Film*. Madison, WI: University of Wisconsin Press.

Bruzzi, Stella. 2006. *New Documentary*. 2nd ed. New York: Routledge.

Corner, John. 2008. "Documentary Studies: Dimensions of Transition and Continuity." In: Thomas Austin & Wilma de Jong (eds), *Rethinking Documentary: New Perspectives, New Practices*. Berkshire, UK: Open University Press, pp. 13–28.

Davis, S. 2016. "Slowing Down Media Coverage on the US-Mexico Border: News as Sociological Critique in Borderland." *Digital Journalism 4*(4): 462–477.

Dowling, D. 2017. "Toward a New Aesthetic of Digital Literary Journalism: Charting the Fierce Evolution of the 'Supreme Nonfiction.'" *Literary Journalism Studies 9*(1): 100–116.

Dowling, D. & T. Vogan. 2015. "Can we 'Snowfall' This? Digital Longform and the Race for the Tablet Market. *Digital Journalism 3*(2): 209–224.

Eisenstein, Sergei. 2010. "Towards a Theory of Montage.". In: Michael A. Glenny & Richard Taylor (eds), trans. Michael Glenny), *Sergei Eisenstein, Selected Works 2*. New York: I.B. Tauris.

Green, Melanie C. & Timothy C. Brock. 2002. "In the Mind's Eye: Transportation-Imagery Model of Narrative Persuasion." In: Melanie C. Green, Jeffrey J. Strange, & Timothy C. Brock (eds), *Narrative Impact: Social and Cognitive Foundations*. Mahwah, NJ: Lawrence Erlbaum, pp. 161–176.

Hernandez, Richard Kosi & Jeremy Rue. 2016. *Principles of Multimedia Journalism: Packaging Digital News*. New York: Routledge.

Jardine, A. 2017. "Award-Winning Interactive Film 'Bear 71' Gets a Virtual Reality Makeover." *AdAge*, 1 March. https://adage.com/creativity/work/bear-71-vr-version/51125 [Accessed 15 March 2020].

Marconi, F. & T. Nakagawa. 2017. "'Choose Your Own Adventure': VR Journalism Gives Audience Control." *Columbia Journalism Review*, 3 October. www.cjr.org/tow_center/virtual-reality-study-engagement.php [Accessed 15 March 2020].

Monaco, James. 1981. *How to Read a Film: The Art, Technology, Language, History, and Theory of Film and Media*. New York: Oxford.

Murray, Janet H. 2011. *Inventing the Medium: Principles of Interactive Design as a Cultural Practice*. Boston: MIT Press.

Neveu, E. 2014. "Revisiting Narrative Journalism as One of the Futures of Journalism." *Journalism Studies 15*(5): 533–542.

Parisi, P. & B. Holcornb. 1994. "Symbolizing place: Journalistic narratives of the city." *Urban Geography 15*(4): 376–394.

Pavlik, John V. & Frank Bridges. 2013. "The Emergence of Augmented Reality (AR) as a Storytelling Medium in Journalism." *Journalism & Communication Monographs 15*(1): 4–59.

Perse, Elizabeth & Jennifer Lambe. 2016. *Media Effects and Society*. New York: Routledge.

Rose, Mandy. 2017. "Not Media About, but Media With: Co-creation for Activism." In: Judith Aston, Sandra Gaudenzi, & Mandy Rose (eds), *i-Docs: The Evolving Practices of Interactive Documentaries*. London: Wallflower Press, pp. 49–65.

Schmitz Weiss, A. 2015. "Place-based Knowledge in the Twenty-First Century: The Creation of Spatial Journalism." *Digital Journalism 3*(1): 116–131.

Stone, C. 2017. "Editor's Note: Experience a Climb to the Top of the World with SI's Capturing Everest." *Sports Illustrated*, May. www.si.com/more-sports/2017/capturing-everest-editors-note-sports-illustrated-virtual-reality [Accessed 15 March 2020].

Sundar, S.S., J. Kang, & D. Oprean. 2017. "Being There in the Midst of the Story: How immersive Journalism Affects Our Perceptions and Cognitions." *Cyberpsychology, Behavior, and Social Networking 20*(11): 672–682.

Tu, Duy Linh. 2015. *Feature and Narrative Storytelling for Multimedia Journalists*. New York: Focal Press.

Uricchio, William, S. Wolozin, L. Bui, et al. 2015. *Mapping the Intersection of Two Cultures: Interactive Documentary and Digital Journalism*. Boston: MIT Open Documentary Lab, MacArthur Foundation.

van der Haak, B. 2014. "Hunger in L.A." *Multiple Journalism*. www.multiplejournalism.org/case/hunger-in-la [Accessed 15 March 2020].

Watson, Zillah. 2017. *VR for News: The New Reality*? Digital News Project. Oxford, UK: Reuters Institute for the Study of Journalism, University of Oxford. https://reutersinstitute.politics.ox.ac.uk/our-research/vr-news-new-reality [Accessed 15 March 2020].

10

CASE STUDY

Creating a business value in immersive journalism

Ilona Ilvonen, Joel Vanhalakka, and Nina Helander

The litmus test for all new gadgets and technologies is the market: whether, or not, consumers buy and use them. A meaningful innovation is really created only along market success. In all immersive technologies the path from the early steps of the technology to success in the market has been slow in coming. There is anticipation of a revolution in how entertainment and media content are delivered and consumed (Watson 2017), but the revolution has yet to come.

The value of immersive technology to journalism is clear, as it provides means for creating more engaging experiences as well as the possibility to create more engaging content. More engagement with the users or the "audience" means more business opportunities in a market that is as a whole changing in terms of value creation and business logics (Dowling 2016). However, to provide sustainable business opportunities, immersive journalism needs a critical mass of users along with an understanding of the variety of value the technology helps create (Cook & Sirkkunen 2013; Dowling 2016; Watson 2017). The whole financing scheme of journalism is changing (Küng 2017), and the emergence of immersive technologies can facilitate this change, or at least benefit from the changes already taking place.

The mass markets can be reached by mobile VR applications. The limited technological capabilities, however, limit the business potential of the mobile VR for immersive journalism. On the other hand, high-quality production that takes into account these limitations already has much potential, but is often still very expensive. Therefore, immersive journalism needs to find a balance between the content production costs and content quality. One example of how to handle this balance comes from *The New York Times* (NYT) and their VR application NYTVR, which mainly consists of branded content, i.e., VR advertisements in a journalistic storytelling form. This content is paid for by NYT's enterprise customers. However, at the same time it works as a learning platform for journalistic VR content and offers more engaging content for their subscribers.

This chapter explains the business value aspects of immersive journalism production with a case study of NYTVR. It analyzes how journalistic enterprises can create, deliver, and capture value with immersive journalism, and what novel business opportunities the technologies and their interactive nature can enable. The chapter also explores what business partners, activities, and resources exist that could be used to leverage immersive technology-related business models in journalism. The chapter concludes by suggesting business models for immersive journalism such as subscription fees for special content, customized Virtual Reality advertising, and sponsored content/content marketing. In addition, it discusses what supporting activities journalistic enterprises should undertake to ensure successful immersive productization.

Value creation viewpoints to digitalization

A classical value creation process is a flow where the need for a product is identified, then the product is purchased, implemented, and thus utilized (Helander & Vuori 2017). In the field of media industry the customer has traditionally been quite passive in this process. The media content creators have taken care of identifying needs (deciding what the readers/viewers are likely to be interested in) and, even in the cases where the consumers themselves paid for the content, they did that by long-term subscriptions. Purchase was thus not done for individual products, but for the general collection of products the media creator offered. Although the modern media consumer also pays through subscriptions, the duration of the subscription may heavily depend on individual content on offer (such as HBO subscriptions plummeting between the second-to-last and last seasons of the streaming series *Game of Thrones*, despite the amount of other content available; consumers were not prepared to pay the monthly fee for over a year while waiting for the next season to start). In the case of traditional media products, the implementation phase is not really relevant; a traditional newspaper, for example, is a ready-to-use product without the need of actual implementation or installation. Usage is also a fairly short phase in the value creation process: once the paper is read, it is discarded.

Another classical way to look at value is to examine different value functions. The most often recognized value functions are the direct ones: profit, volume, and safeguard (Walter et al. 2001). It is good to note that these describe how the customer creates value for the creator. When a customer gets the product, they are willing to pay for it, so the provider makes financial profit. The provider strives to increase the volume of business both in terms of the number of customers as well as the amount of revenue from each customer. Lastly the provider aims to safeguard business with a commitment from the customer to keep on doing business with them, i.e., so that the provider will have a positive publication circulation.

New digital technologies change where the profit to content creators comes from. Advertiser-funded media content as a dominant finance logic is giving way to a subscription-based way of operation and it also builds the grounds for view-based advertising in online media (Stroud et al. 2016). One motivation for media content subscriptions (such as Spotify, and various tv-streaming service providers such as Ruutu+ in Finland) is to let people avoid advertisements. The user thus pays for the opportunity to not be distracted. This option is visible also in gaming, where gamers can opt to play for free and see ads, or pay for the game and avoid the ads. The flow of money is thus changing from coming from advertisers and long-time subscribers to short-time subscribers who make their buying decisions based on currently available content and additional attractions such as fan events, as well as targeted advertisement income (Küng 2017). Wide, and fairly steady, streams of income are thus transforming into many smaller trickles, which are more difficult to predict. In value creation terms, the safeguard that value creators receive is decreasing. This is why new forms of financing, for example crowdfunding (Aitamurto 2015), have entered into the field. One challenge thus is to locate the parties that are willing to pay for the creation of the immersive content (Westlund 2015). Because the immersive technologies naturally create a loosely coupled network of technology providers, network providers, content creators, and supporting actors, it is necessary to understand that the revenue may come from multiple sources in the complex network. There may be multiple motivations to participate in content co-creation and surprising sources of income.

The content can be co-created, which brings more actors into the picture of the network. Good immersive content requires not only journalism and storytelling skills, but technological and audiovisual skills as well. Thus the creation is most likely done in collaboration by multiple actors of different professions who have their individual motivations for entering the network. While some may strive for increasing direct profits, others may be after other kinds of benefits altogether. This is why, in addition to the direct value functions, also indirect ones should be discussed. These functions are, for example, innovation, market, access, and scout (Walter et al. 2001). These functions enable the creation of new innovations or innovative ways of operation, or creation of possible new market opportunities. An indirect value can also take the form of access to new potential customers or an opportunity to gain new information by scouting, for example, consumer behaviors. Although their worth is difficult to measure in direct monetary terms, they can be immensely valuable for business in the long term, even if immediate monetary profit is not gained. In the case of immersive journalism, since high production costs make it difficult for the content creator to gain direct profit from the content, identifying as many indirect value opportunities as possible is important.

To understand value creation in the setting of immersive journalism, one can look at value creation in fields that rely on digital technologies in general. The emergence of digital technologies is transforming business and value creation processes in many fields. Often the technology provides, for example, cost and time savings, and transforms the way end-users experience various products (Nelson & Ryan 2017). The entry of immersive technologies to journalism is certainly transforming the way consumers experience journalism content, but one key obstacle in the way of success is that it is not doing that by decreasing costs from the point of view of the journalism content creator. This is why a wider view of the value network around the technologies is needed to analyze the business value potential created by the technologies.

Digitalization also changes the way in which the end-value that the consumer receives is created. The consumer is no longer a passive end-receiver of the product (Lewis & Westlund 2015; Lee & Hsiang 2014); instead, they are an active participant (Grönroos & Voima 2013). This is especially true in the case of immersive technologies, where the immersion is partly caused by the fact that the consumer can be active and interact with the content, or, at least, they can make decisions of where to look and in what order to take in things. The experience of consuming the media content is thus partly created by the consumer. It also poses challenges for the way the content is created, since the content needs to be constructed from modules that are not dependent on their order of appearance.

One challenge that digitalization poses for news and other journalism products is the pace of communication. Because a bulk of the income in the journalism field comes from advertising, gaining as much visibility and as quick visibility as possible is vital for beating competition (Newman 2016). The emphasis on a fast pace of communication and the "publish first and then dig for more information" (ING 2014) mindset runs contrary to the demands of creating high-quality immersive content, which takes time.

In addition to the value process and function perspectives, we can summarize the business value of immersive technologies by dividing it into four different themes: 1) engagement and experiences, 2) eliminated complexity and improved user experience, 3) reduced costs, and 4) better communication and collaboration (Vanhalakka 2018). We can identify how these themes also apply in immersive journalism and to tools already in use, such as 360-degree videos. 360-degree videos can connect audiences from their homes to the other side of the world, providing more realistic and more engaging journalistic scenes than traditional mediums (Prat 2018). With a headset, the 360-degree view can easily be controlled by natural movements such as gestures of the hand or moving the head, therefore making experiences such as navigating in a landscape easier than on a surface display of a webpage. While the technology is still suffering from some limitations, with enough raw material 360-degree can be a very cost-efficient way to reproduce physical environments. It's also in some contexts a better way to communicate with audiences due to its realistic nature.

Although the value of immersive technology is becoming better understood every year, the technologies have not yet made a substantial breakthrough in the field of journalism. Immersive journalistic solutions are still mostly explorative (Watson 2017). Creating high-quality content can be expensive and, while it's possible to create immersive experiences more affordably, compromising quality for costs can often lead to bad experiences, such as simulator sickness, which can turn away users from the mobileVR (Habig 2016). However, despite its challenges, major investments into the technologies by large news agencies such as *The New York Times*, *USA Today Network*, *Die Welt*, *Blick*, *Dagens Nyheter*, ARTE, *The Guardian*, Sky, and *Euronews* (Watson 2017), and the formation of the more recent journalistic consortiums such as Journalism 360 (Medium.com 2018) signal a strong belief in the technologies' large potential to become the next journalistic medium. While these investments and consortiums do not prove that VR/AR (virtual reality/augmented reality) will definitely become the next big thing in journalism, there are some success stories such as NYTVR that prove it is possible to both explore the technologies of VR/AR and create profit, despite the costs of high-quality production.

Case of NYTVR

The New York Times' NYTVR was one of the first journalistic applications on the VR/360-degree market (Watson 2017). It's a platform for high-quality VR/360-degree experiences for mobile VR headset audiences. What makes the NYTVR case interesting is that, when many other news mediums were still only exploring the technologies without considering profits, NYTVR had a clear business plan from the start: to monetize their high-quality VR/360-degree content creation in NYTVR using branded content (i.e., advertisements) (Hall 2016).

In this chapter we use the business model canvas (BMC) (Osterwalder & Pigneur 2010) to analyze and illustrate the complex elements of value in the chosen case of NYTVR. The canvas model is usually drawn as a graphical illustration of different value fields. These fields are: *Value propositions*, *Customer relationships*, *Channels*, *Customer segments*, *Revenue streams*, *Key activities*, *Key resources, Key partners*, and *Cost structure*. In the illustration the customer-related elements are grouped to the right-hand side and the partner-related elements to the left-hand side of the canvas, with the driving element, the value proposition, shown in the middle. The business model of NYTVR is presented below in Figure 10.1 with the help of the BMC canvas. In the following some of the value elements have been grouped together for ease of following the analysis.

Value propositions and customer segments: In the case of NYTVR two value propositions can be identified. The first value proposition of the NYTVR business model is high-quality immersive VR/360-degree content for mobile devices. High quality in this case means best possible technical quality and high production value. Since value is subjective, it is good to link to a specific customer segment. With this value proposition, the customer segment is all mobile VR users; to visualize the connection, all blocks related to this specific value proposition and customer segment are colored white.

The second value proposition of NYTVR is the ability to engage audiences, which refers to offering an engaging interactive platform for content delivery that attracts audiences. This is directed toward *The New York Times*' corporate customers, i.e., companies/enterprises with global brands. This value proposition is represented by gray blocks.

Channels: the main channel for delivering the first value proposition (white blocks) is *The New York Times*' NYTVR application. Other ways to access the

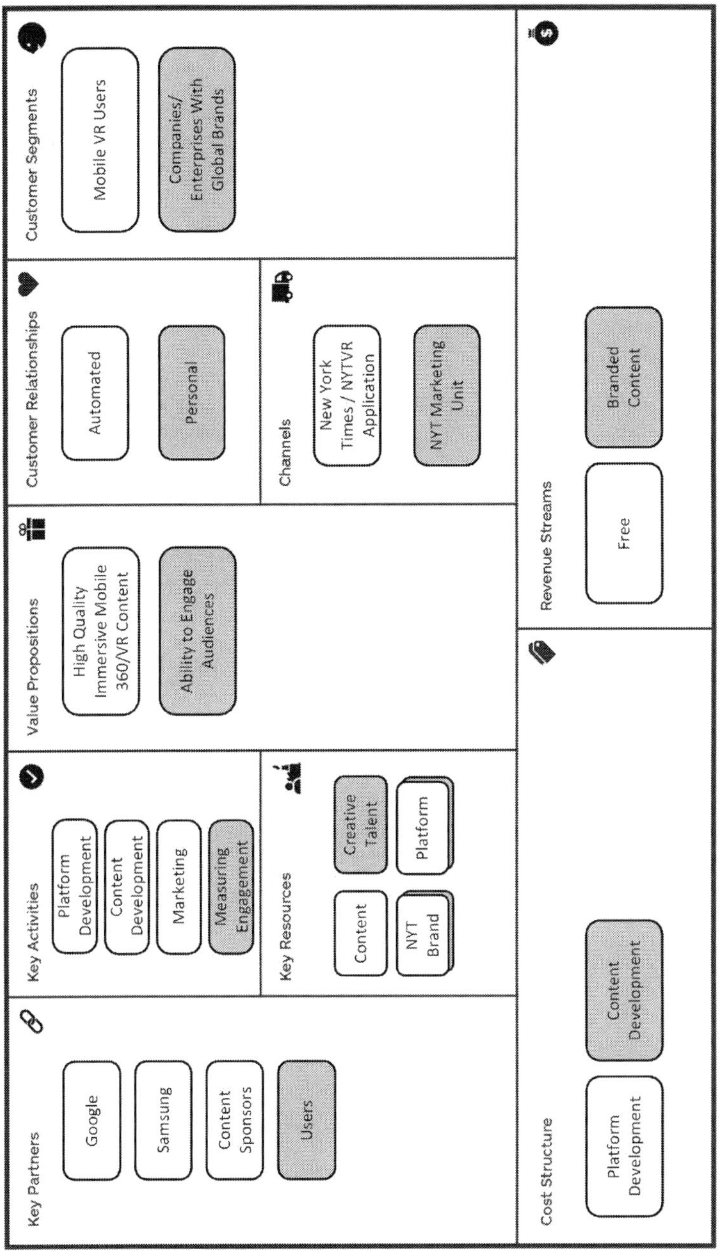

FIGURE 10.1 NYTVR Business Model (adapted from Vanhalakka 2018 and based on the model by Strategyzer 2018, image template used under CC 3.0 license).

content are through Youtube or Samsung VR applications. It is important to note that in order to fully experience NYTVR, a mobile VR headset is required. When NYTVR was initially launched, *The New York Times* partnered with Google and gave their subscribers free Google Cardboard headsets (Robertson 2016), thereby creating more users and hype for their platform. More recently mobile headsets have become more common and there are even specialized phones for mobile VR.

The second value proposition (grey blocks) is delivered by *The New York Times*' marketing unit, T Brand Studio, that uses *The New York Times*' branded journalistic approach, multidisciplinary knowledge, and new technologies to create branded content/advertisements for their corporate customers (T Brand 2017).

Customer relationships: NYTVR is a mobile application, therefore the relationship between the content consumers (white blocks) is mostly automated. The relationship between *The New York Times*' corporate customers (grey blocks) is more personal, since the content is created as a collaborative effort between *The New York Times* and their client companies.

Revenue streams: the NYTVR application is free to use, therefore the content consumers do not provide direct revenue. The platform is monetized through its content; almost all production inside the NYTVR application is branded content, i.e., advertisements with an element of journalistic storytelling, that have been created together with NYTVR's corporate customers (grey blocks), and thus the revenue comes from them as advertisement payments. The potential of NYTVR to attract new NYT subscribers is acknowledged with a dashed white block, which indicates potential future revenue for NYT as a whole, or a motivation for a person to stay as a subscriber.

Key partners: for the first value proposition (white blocks) there are three key partners: Google, Samsung, and content sponsors. The partners enable NYTVR to reach potential consumers, as well as provide Google and Samsung with a way to offer more content for their appliances. The third key partners for the first value proposition are the content sponsors as they sponsor more content for the platform, making it more compelling for users, and mostly cover the content development costs.

For the second value proposition the key partners are the users of the platform, since they are the audience for the branded content. Due to the engaging nature of VR/360-degree production, the users are more prone to sharing their experiences (Habig 2016) and thus become a key partner for the content sponsors in increasing awareness of the advertised brands.

Key activities: key activities for the first value proposition (white blocks) are platform development, content development, and marketing. The platform needs to develop simultaneously with the devices and software. At the same time, NYTVR needs to continue developing content, in order to retain or bring users back to their platform by offering them new enticing content. The final key activity for the first value proposition is marketing, since by attracting more users *The New York Times* makes their platform also more attractive for enterprises and companies.

For the second value proposition (grey blocks) the most important activity is measuring engagement, i.e., collecting metrics. These metrics can provide proof of concept about the different aspects of VR/360: for example, whether the videos attract more engagement than the more traditional methods of branded content.

Key resources: the most important key resource for the first value proposition (white blocks) is the content. The content is required to attract an audience. The most important key resource for the second value proposition (gray blocks) is the creative talent, i.e., content creators. *The New York Times*' marketing unit consists of multidisciplinary teams, combining the same talents who are responsible for their news content with marketing specialists (T Brand Studio 2017). This enables them to combine journalistic storytelling with branded content. The shared resources (white blocks overlapping with gray blocks) between both value propositions are NYT Brand and the NYTVR platform. *The New York Times* brand is known for high-quality branded content (Main 2017) and, as such, brings in customers for both value propositions. The NYTVR platform is a key resource, as it enables both value propositions and, from it, the company can collect metrics about the success of their content.

Cost structure: the main costs for the first value proposition (white blocks) come from the platform development. As mentioned before, the way mobile VR should be utilized is still exploratory, so the platform needs to be developed as the industry evolves. The main costs for the second value proposition come from the content development. It could be argued that the content development costs are a shared cost for both value propositions; however, in this case they is linked to the second value proposition for a reason. While the technologies of VR/360 have large potential for use in a journalistic context (Watson 2017), the problem is that creating high-quality VR/360 content is expensive. Instead of only exploring how to use this technology in The Daily 360 (the journalistic VR/360 channel of *The New York Times*), *The New York Times* is exploring this in their branded content too. This means that their clients, the global brands, are paying for the content development and at the same time *The New York Times* learns about the technology and also attracts more customers to its own platforms.

Key findings: the most important finding from the business model is the synergy NYTVR offers to *The New York Times*. Media companies often have advertisement-based business models. *The New York Times*, on the other hand, has a subscription-based business model and, for them, advertisements are low-margin (NYT 2020 Group Report 2017). To get subscribers, *The New York Times* needs to offer engaging content. The technologies of VR/360 offer a new possible platform for media, but the technologies are still at an exploratory stage and, as such, the methods still require resource-greedy development (Watson 2017). *The New York Times* is exploring how to use these new methods in creating their branded content, delegating the production costs to their corporate customers. While exploring and learning how to use the technology in their own journalistic context, they are creating more engaging content for their subscribers and potentially attracting new subscribers.

The BMC model offers an at-a-glance canvas that communicates the value creation elements. The two distinct value propositions presented in this analysis also well identify the two-directional nature of value creation: while the content consumers are receiving entertainment value from the content they are viewing, they are part of the value proposition to other actors present in the canvas. With multiple value propositions and multiple revenue streams, it becomes easier to identify the path for financial gains in the immersive technology field. The value functions introduced in the previous section can be useful in identifying the multiple value propositions and the key partners and activities of value creation. The BMC visualization is thus a way to highlight and summarize the value function analysis, which otherwise may sometimes be a little difficult to communicate.

Implications

The opportunities for new kinds of ways to experience journalism that the immersive technologies offer have also a potential to create business value. However, the capture of this value in terms of financial profits is not straightforward. Immersive technologies often offer cost savings as a substantial value proposition in different industries. Identifying different value functions and elements on the BMC helps to communicate the value that is created with the immersive journalism approach, and is a step toward identifying the financial gains from it. Content creation is expensive, and thus the avenue for direct cost savings is not viable in the field of journalism. The value function and BMC analysis tools help to identify other reasons why investing resources to create immersive content might be viable.

Examples from the field of digital journalism show that the overwhelmingly hectic pace of communication in news media has created a counter-movement in slow journalism (Dowling 2016). Immersive journalism has similar elements to the slow movement, with the emphasis on high-quality and thought-through development processes. A broad understanding of value reduces the significance of publication pace as an element of value.

Value analysis also helps journalism organizations to view consumers as key partners in the value creation process. Instead of being a mere recipient, the consumer becomes an active participant in the process of viewing the immersive content. This role can be further emphasized by engaging the consumers as ideators, promoters, and even creators of the immersive content. The role of the media company changes from content creator to content production coordinator, and at the same time the possibilities of value creation and monetization become more varied. Indirect value functions such as market, access, and scout can be important to point out, and lead the immersive branded content creation from being thought of as only marketing or advertising toward co-innovation with different actors.

References

Aitamurto, T. 2015. "The Role of Crowdfunding as a Business Model in Journalism: A Five-Layered Model of Value Creation." In: B. Chin, L. Bennett, & B. Jones (eds), *Crowdfunding the Future.* New York: Peter Lang, pp. 189–205.

Cook, C. & E. Sirkkunen. 2013. "What's in a Niche? Exploring the Business Model of Online Journalism." *Journal of Media Business Studies 10*(4): 63–82.

Dowling, D. 2016. "The Business of Slow Journalism." *Digital Journalism 4*(4): 530–546.

Grönroos, C. & P. Voima. 2013. "Critical Service Logic: Making Sense of Value Creation and Co-creation." *Journal of the Academy of Marketing Science 41*(2): 133–150.

Habig, J. 2016. "Is 360 Video Worth It?" *Thinkwithgoogle.com.* www.thinkwithgoogle.com/advertising-channels/video/360-video-advertising/ [Accessed 23 September 2019].

Hall, S. 2016. "The New York Times' VR Experimentation Is Making Money." *Fipp.com.* www.fipp.com/news/features/nyt-vr-experimentation-is-making-money [Accessed 23 September 2019].

Helander, N. & V. Vuori. 2017. "Value Co-Creation Analysis in Customer-Supplier Network Relationships." In: J. Vesalainen, K. Valkokari, & M. Hellström (eds), *Practices for Network Management: In Search of Collaborative Advantage.* London: Palgrave Macmillan, pp. 251–262.

ING. 2014. "2014 Study Impact of Social Media on News: More Crowd-Checking, Less Fact-Checking." *Ing.com.* www.ing.com/Newsroom/All-news/NW/2014-Study-impact-of-Social-Media-on-News-more-crowdchecking-less-factchecking.htm [Accessed 23 September 2019].

Küng, L. 2017. *Going Digital: A Roadmap for Organisational Transformation.* Oxford, UK: Reuters Institute for the Study of Journalism with the support of Google and the Digital News Initiative.

Lee, A. & I. Hsiang. 2014. "When Newsworthy is not Noteworthy: Examining the Value of News from the Audience's Perspective." *Journalism Studies 15*(6): 807–820.

Lewis, S. C. & O. Westlund. 2015. "Actors, Actants, Audiences, and Activities in Cross-media News Work." *Digital Journalism 3*(1): pp. 19–37.

Medium.com. 2018. "Journalism360." *Medium.com.* https://medium.com/journalism360 [Accessed 23 September 2019].

Nelson, J. & F. Ryan. 2017. "The Effect of Digital Platforms on News Audience Behavior." *Digital Journalism 5*(6): 609–633.

Newman, N. 2016. *News Alerts and the Battle for the Lockscreen.* Oxford, UK: Reuters Institute for the Study of Journalism, Oxford University. *Apo.org.* https://apo.org.au/node/71073 [Accessed 23 September 2019].

Osterwalder, A. & Y. Pigneur. 2010. *Business Model Generation: A Handbook for Visionaries, Game Changers, and Challengers.* Hoboken, NJ: John Wiley & Sons.

Prat, C. 2018. "How 360 Video Can Add Value to Journalism." *Medium.com.* https://medium.com/journalism360/how-360-video-can-add-value-to-journalism-227c461b9aca [Accessed 23 September 2019].

Robertson, A. 2016. "The New York Times is Sending Out a Second Round of Google Cardboards." *The Verge.* www.theverge.com/2016/4/28/11504932/new-york-times-vr-google-cardboard-seeking-plutos-frigid-heart [Accessed 23 September 2019].

Strategyzer. 2018. BMC template. www.creatlr.com/template/UOLHsfqGrLzugzVVttoi1e/business-model-canvas/ [Accessed 23 September 2019].

Stroud, N., C. Peacock, & A. Curry. 2016. "Mobile News Notifications. Engaging News Project." Austin, TX: Center of Media Engagement, Moody College of Communication, University of Texas. https://mediaengagement.org/research/mobile-news-notifications/ [Accessed 23 September 2019].

T Brand Studio. 2017. Home Page. www.tbrandstudio.com/about-us/ [Accessed 23 September 2019].

Vanhalakka, J. 2018. "Value Creation in Virtual and Augmented Reality." Master's thesis. Finland: Tampere University of Technology.

Walter, A., T. Ritter, & H. Gemunden. 2001. "Value-Creation in Buyer-Seller Relationships: Theoretical Considerations and Empirical Results from a Supplier's Perspective." *Industrial Marketing Management 30*: 365–377.

Watson, Z. 2017. "VR for News: the New Reality?" Digital News Project. www.digitalnewsreport.org/publications/2017/vr-news-new-reality/#a-news-vr-proposition-to-win-tomorrows-audience [Accessed 23 September 2019].

Westlund, Oscar. 2015. "News Consumption in an Age of Mobile Media: Patterns, People, Place, and Participation." *Mobile Media & Communication 3*(2): 151 159.

11

THE HIERARCHY OF NEEDS FOR USER EXPERIENCES IN VIRTUAL REALITY

Chelsea Kelling, Heli Väätäjä, Otto Kauhanen, Jussi Karhu, Markku Turunen, Vesa Lindqvist, and Pasi Ikonen

Virtual reality (VR) is rapidly becoming more widely adopted by various industries, and virtual content is just as rapidly becoming available for consumers. However, there is a lack of guidelines and standards for VR content to be held to in terms of experiential design. Because VR is a relatively new media form for consumers, there is a high risk of user attrition due to the novelty of the service. Therefore, if the first experience of the technology is with poorly made content, users will be much less likely to use VR again. Therefore, as various industries and organizations digitalize and adopt emerging technology such as VR, great care should be given to the way the virtual content and experiences are created. This chapter discusses the key experiential elements of users' experiences with immersive journalism (IJ), particularly in the case of a virtual museum application. We present a user study of this application and introduce a model based on the results that details the most crucial user experience components for designing VR content.

Immersive journalism presents a story from a first-person perspective that fosters a connection by allowing users to actually experience the events themselves (de la Peña et al. 2010). Therefore, storytelling is an integral piece to creating an engaging and memorable experience of immersive content. In this research we focus more specifically on cultural journalism, which concerns the arts and creative work, and on individuals and institutions working in the area. In our case study of an omnidirectional (360-degree) application, we aimed to tell the story of a piece of art and the artist behind the work. As shown by others, cultural journalism can be greatly enhanced with elements of immersive storytelling, adding new ways to appreciate and connect with the art (Hürst et al. 2016). To create this connection with and foster interest in the content, storytelling elements were used to create an application that explores the work of a Finnish artist with a journey from a museum to a cultural site where the art is featured.

Immersive journalism encapsulates a promise of special experiences beyond the existing. However, knowledge of the user experience of VR and IJ is still evolving, and research has yet to catch up with the needs of content creators and journalists (Shin & Biocca 2017). With the results of our user study, we present a model of user experience components that outlines the elements that affect users' experiences with VR content. The model can be used by practitioners when creating experiences for immersive journalism and by academics to study the experiences. Inspired by Jordan's Hierarchy of User Needs (Jordan 1997) for pleasurable experiences, ours is a hierarchical model for the components of user experience (UX) in immersive journalism. The model incorporates the influence of five UX elements (physical comfort, usability, audiovisual quality, storytelling, and satisfaction), along with the effects of immersion and presence, that build upon each other in the creation of a positive VR experience. The model aims to aid not only immersive journalists, but also VR researchers, designers, and, more widely, content creators in other industries.

Background

As VR becomes a more widely used medium for learning and experiencing, new VR use cases are being explored more and more. Virtual reality can transport users to new worlds and adventures regardless of where they are physically in the real world. This opens new opportunities in many different domains and institutions, as is the case in immersive journalism. Readers can experience news in a more exciting way, immersing themselves in stories that feel more realistic than ever. Immersive journalism presents a chance for a more impactful, empathy-inducing news format. Similarly, virtual cultural experiences offer a possibility to learn and explore the past and present in a deeply engaging way. In normal, everyday life, if a person would like to see an art exhibition, they must leave their home or workplace and travel to the museum or location. In the case of virtual experiences, though, users can view works of art at any time, without the trouble of traveling or interrupting their day. However, the ins and outs of creating these virtual environments can make or break the experience; journalists and other virtual content creators need to understand their users in order to create a positive and memorable experience. Through the art of storytelling, immersive content, and engaging user experience elements, creators can bring their stories to life in an impactful and extraordinary way.

Immersive cultural experiences

VR opens the possibilities for both experts and non-experts to experience art and culture (Bellini et al. 2018). The immersive experience can bring new perspectives to both, allowing museum-goers to see the art in ways that they could not in reality. Furthermore, VR can offer an interactive and more "hands-on" experience for cultural exhibits than would be possible otherwise; most cultural artifacts are displayed behind barriers and cannot be touched or examined too closely. Science museums, for example, provide many opportunities to learn by doing that intrigue, captivate, and stimulate the minds of visitors (Carrozzino & Bergamasco 2010). VR holds the potential to bring these types of experiences to more traditional museums, allowing visitors to enjoy the art in new ways without endangering the pieces of art themselves.

Virtual exhibitions in museums are not an entirely new concept (Lepouras & Vassilakis 2004; Styliani et al. 2009; Wojciechowski et al. 2004), but with the increasing availability and decreasing cost of VR systems there is currently a need for further investigation of what exactly the technology can provide. Beyond the obvious uses of virtual museums, such as replicating a museum or its items in 3D, lie other less explored opportunities. An interesting use of VR for museums is in supplementing the museum experience and adding new ways to appreciate and connect with the exhibits. This topic was explored in a study by Hürst et al. (Hürst et al. 2016) where Van Gogh's *Starry Night* was expanded from beyond the picture frame and onto surrounding walls in a virtual environment. Participants wearing a head-mounted display (HMD) navigated a virtual museum with three differently designed rooms displaying *Starry Night*, two with artistic effects around the painting, and one with only the painting on a blank wall. The study found that participants enjoyed the rooms with the artistic effects over the blank room. Interestingly, participants expressed that this preference was only for the virtual environment and that, in a real museum, the supplementary effects would distract too much from the actual work of art (ibid.). Participants wanted that extra element in the virtual world to experience something more than what was normally experienced in reality; although a museum setting is familiar, the unfamiliar element of the morphing paintings creates a whole new perspective (Bosworth & Sarah 2019). This point is important for VR designers and content creators in that they should carefully examine whether the experience is unique or if it is too much like everyday life.

User experience

As outlined by Shin and Biocca (2018), knowledge of the user experience of VR and immersive journalism is still evolving, and research has yet to catch up with the needs of content creators and journalists. Although well-known news organizations such as *The New York Times* have been producing increasingly more immersive 360-degree content over the past few years, much of the content is still largely experimental (Sirkkunen et al. 2016). Further, a lack of unified guidelines and models that creators can follow to craft positive experiences for users presents a challenge to those in the field of immersive journalism (Shin & Biocca 2018). Although research on these experiences is growing, there is still a large amount of uncertainty as to what a "good" experience is, what a "bad" experience is, and how this can be generalized across the population of varied users and use cases. The visual quality and realism are constantly evolving; however, the quality of experience and acceptance of the quality are dependent not only on the capturing and viewing technology, but also on other vital aspects such as the content or story, context of use, and even the quality of the audio (Jumisko-Pyykkö 2011). Immersive journalism could therefore benefit by further understanding the various UX elements of VR, as well as how they apply specifically to immersive journalism and storytelling in VR.

To create a truly immersive and engaging experience, elements of storytelling are vital. Storytelling has been utilized in the entertainment and gaming industries and is an obvious companion for immersive journalism and VR experiences, but it is not yet clear exactly how storytelling affects users' experiences in VR. However, there are promising results that highlight the additional engagement that immersive storytelling brings. Journalism in itself is a form a storytelling, a means for the public to not only receive news but also to feel involved and engrossed in the story and information presented. With immersive journalism, the public can feel that they are actually a part of the story, whether through direct participation or passive observation (Lugrin et al. 2010). This deep sense of involvement is largely due to feeling immersed and present in the story. Although immersion is given many different definitions, it is most widely defined as the sense of being in the virtual environment that is enabled by the technology, hardware, and objective qualities of the VR system (Slater 2003). Presence, on the other hand, is the subjective experience of "being there" that is derived from an individual's perception of immersion (Slater 2003). These qualities of immersive storytelling can transform traditionally extrinsic emotions into more personal, intrinsic feelings (de la Peña et al. 2010).

In addition to storytelling, there are many other elements that influence VR experiences that can be understood from the perspective of the field of UX. The Components of User Experience (CUE) model by Thüring and Mahlke (2007) has proven to be useful in examining virtual experiences (Wienrich et al. 2018; Kelling et al. 2017). The CUE model focuses on how users perceive three areas of UX when interacting with a system: instrumental qualities, non-instrumental qualities, and emotional reactions (Thüring & Mahlke 2007). The user then experiences these characteristics in a unique way and forms a certain emotional reaction, and this combination results in the user's overall experience of the system. From a somewhat different perspective, Hassenzahl (2005) approaches experience with an emphasis on the pragmatic and hedonic characteristics of a product or system. Pragmatic attributes satisfy the utility or usability of a product or system, while hedonic attributes include the functions or elements that produce pleasure or positive psychological stimulation (Hassenzahl 2005). Although the CUE model and Hassenzahl's approach serve as a solid foundation on which user experience can be studied with technology in general, they do not specifically address the experience of immersive technologies such as VR. Somewhat more specifically relevant, Jumisko-Pyykkö (2011) has extensively studied quality of user experience in the case of mobile television, taking into account the content and media as part of the system characteristics, in addition to the characteristics of the user and the context contributing to the experience. Jumisko-Pyykkö's work is closest to ours in terms of theoretical framing of user experience. Our aim here is to add to the knowledge of what the components of user experience are in immersive cultural journalism in the case of 360-degree videos.

Hugo Simberg VR: a virtual experience of cultural journalism

We created an interactive omnidirectional (360) video prototype as part of a project examining the user experience of immersive technologies and their application in journalistic contexts (Kauhanen et al. 2017). The aim of the application was to utilize aspects of immersive journalism with respect to a piece of cultural heritage. The prototype focused on the work of Finnish artist Hugo Simberg and introduced users to his works and a piece of the story behind them. In the prototype, the user first finds themselves in front of stairs leading up to an exhibition in a room of the Finnish National Gallery's art museum, Ateneum. The user can move around the room in the museum using interactive icons, one of which leads to Simberg's famous painting, *Wounded Angel*. By looking at the painting, the user unlocks access to a different location, a cathedral in Tampere, Finland, where another version of the *Wounded Angel* is painted as a fresco on the wall of the cathedral. The user first stands in front of the fresco and can then explore several spots in the cathedral and return to the museum if they so wish (Kauhanen et al. 2017).

The application was implemented with a Unity-based editing software developed at Tampere University that allows the user to set either omnidirectional videos or images as scenes (Saarinen et al. 2017). Three-dimensional objects and two-dimensional images can be placed in the scene with a gaze interaction functionality, which allows the triggering of audio files, appearance of text, or transition between scenes. The icons leading to the transition were positioned in the direction of another scene, or the position of the next transition. The application's scenes were created with omnidirectional images captured at the museum and cathedral with a Nikon Keymission 360-degree camera (resolution: 7744x3872). The images were edited with Adobe Photoshop to reduce stitching errors. Simple two-dimensional icons were used for moving from spot to spot. Once gazed at, the icons start expanding, and after two seconds the user is transported to the next scene or viewing location. The application was intended for free exploration in any order in the two environments, with audio narration at scenes of Simberg's works.

In a previous evaluation of the initial prototype, several issues with the experience of the application were identified, including issues with navigation, poor image quality, and lack of engagement (Kauhanen et al. 2017). In further iterations of the prototype, these issues were addressed and improved, especially so with the addition of audio and narration (Kelling et al. 2018). The current study further examines the effectiveness of the improvements and also dives deeper into the complexities of the immersive experience in an attempt to provide insight for researchers and content creators to utilize and build upon.

User study

A total of 21 participants (eight male, twelve female, one other) aged between 20 and 57 were recruited via social media and email and given a cinema ticket for their participation. Nine of the participants worked in the information and communication technology sector, eight in journalism/media, and four stated a variety of professions. In self-reporting of their attitude towards technology (Jumisko-Pyykkö & Häkkinen 2008), ten participants were late adopters, five early majority and six late majority. Most of the participants had no experience with VR, or had tried it only once or twice (six and twelve, respectively), while two had used a VR device 3–5 times within the last month, and one had used VR devices 3–5 times a week during the last month.

The study was conducted in a laboratory setting in a small room free from outside disturbances. While using the application, the participants sat on a swiveling chair in the middle of the room and wore over-the-ear headphones for the narration and background music. The devices used included a Samsung Gear VR, which used a Samsung Galaxy S7 smartphone as the main device.

The post-test questionnaire administered after the experience aimed to examine participant reactions to several different aspects of the experience, such as the emotional (Thüring & Mahlke 2007), story presence (Schubert & Regenbrecht 2002), and the virtual environment itself (Witmer & Singer 1998). The post-test interview was semi-structured, consisting of two pre-set questions: "Are you feeling nauseous?" and "What feelings, thoughts, and ideas arose when using the application?" (Jumisko-Pyykkö & Utriainen 2011). The first question was used as an indicator as to whether the participant was able to continue, while the second was aimed as an open-ended interview starter, where further questions were based on the topics brought up by participants.

The testing procedure lasted 30 minutes at maximum. After signing the consent form, the participants were shown how the VR headset and headphones should be worn. The participants were asked to follow the think-aloud protocol while using the application. The application advised participants how to use the application at the start of the experience. After the participants finished using the application, a short open-ended interview was conducted, after which the participants filled in a post-test questionnaire. The participants were then asked if they had any questions regarding the study or the project, and were given a cinema ticket for their participation.

Results

Two types of data were gathered from the study. The first was quantitative and comprised of the answers to the post-test questionnaire. The second was qualitative and comprised of the participant comments during the application usage and the post-test interview.

Post-test questionnaire

The questionnaire had a total of 21 items. The statements and their responses can be seen in Figure 11.1. The responses are shown as percentages of the corresponding five-point Likert scale value (completely agree, somewhat agree, neither disagree nor agree, somewhat disagree, and completely disagree).

All participants agreed to some degree that they are interested in art, reflecting that they would be in the real-case user group for the application. Most participants agreed that the experience was pleasant (86%) and that using the application was easy (91%), and 81% agreed that they would recommend the experience to their friends or loved ones. Moving from one spot to another via the icons was reported as mostly logical (76% agreed), 67% of the participants agreed to some degree that the consequences of their actions resulted as expected, and 62% of the participants agreed that the transition from the museum to the cathedral felt natural. In contrast, the item that was received most negatively was about the image quality: only 19% agreed that the quality was good, while 71% disagreed to some extent.

The answers to the items pertaining to presence (questions 6 and 7) were somewhat more divided, with 67% reporting that they felt like they were there in the virtual space and 19% disagreeing. Just under half (47%) felt aware of their outside surroundings while in the virtual experience, 33% did not feel aware, and about 19% neither agreed nor disagreed. Similarly, the feeling of being immersed in the story was also split, with 52% agreeing, 14% neutral, and 33% disagreeing to some extent. When asked where participants would like to use a similar VR application, the items with the largest agreement were, first, in an educational establishment; next, at home; then, at a museum; and lastly, at a public café. Most of the participants agreed that they would like to know more in-depth details about the story (76%) and that they would like to get to know other artists and their work in a similar way (86%). Three-quarters of the participants (76%) agreed that the music was pleasant, and that the narration was interesting. Nearly all the participants (95%) felt that the environments they visited left an impression. Finally, none of the participants reported feeling nauseous during or after use of the application.

Think-aloud comments and post-test interview results

In this section, we present the analysis results based on the comments made by the participants during and after application use. All of the comments were transcribed from the experiment recordings. Each statement was extracted into single comments so that they could be reviewed and grouped, totaling 434 comments. The comments were analyzed in a cyclical manner (Saldaña 2009), which allowed for examination of the data in several iterations. Participant comments were first transcribed, validated, and then coded according to their subject matter. The codes were then sorted into groups so that similar comments were together in one group. The initial transcription and validation was conducted by one researcher and

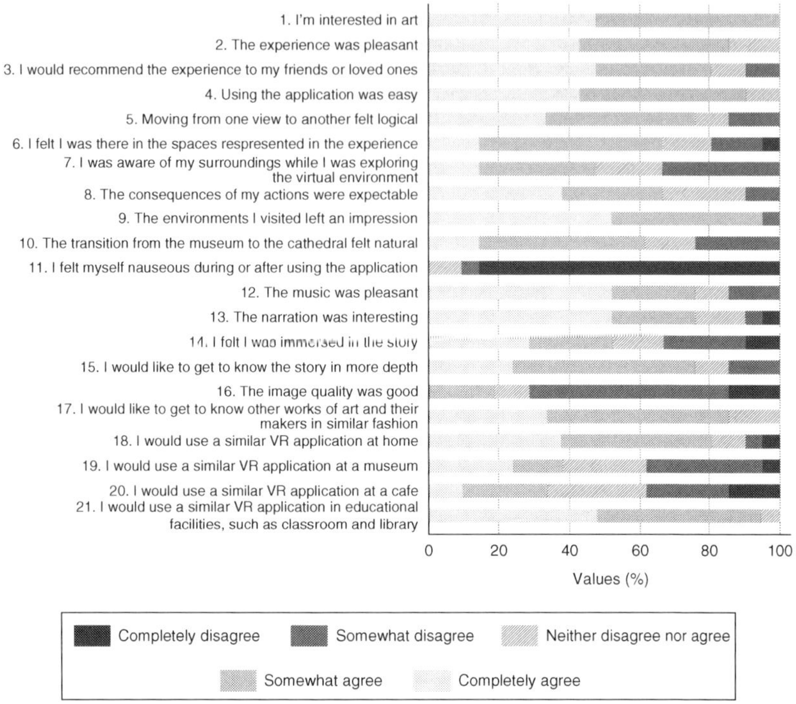

FIGURE 11.1 Post-test questionnaire results.

reviewed by a second researcher, while the coding and grouping was conducted by two researchers in an affinity wall type of setting, then further reviewed by a third researcher to increase accuracy and validity. The results of this process can be seen in Table 11.1. In the table, the main groupings are in bold on the left, subcategories in the middle, and further descriptions on the right. The number of comments is in parenthesis next to the main groupings and subcategories.

As Table 11.1 shows, the majority of the comments made by the participants was about the usability of the application (19 out of 21 participants). While 20/75 of these comments stated that the application was generally easy to use, most (55/75) of the category's comments concentrated on low affordability and difficulties activating the icons used to traverse the virtual environments. This somewhat contradicts the results of the questionnaire, where three-quarters of the participants agreed that the movement from one spot to another was logical. Exploration was also commented on by most of the participants (19/21) during or after using the application. The comments from this category were grouped into six subcategories representing different attributes, such as interest towards exploration, "I still have to check this [icon] out" (transl.) and elements the participants wanted to see and learn from textual and visual information in the environment, "[...] I would've wanted to go read those texts, but they were so far you couldn't see them [...]" (transl.).

TABLE 11.1 The categories that resulted from the analysis of the post-test interview data. The categories are listed from most frequently mentioned to least frequently mentioned.

USABILITY	**(75)**	*Icon Activation*	*(38)*	*Icon responsiveness*
Degree of functionality and interactivity of application elements		Ease of Use	(20)	*Level of ease perceived by participants*
		Icon Affordances	(17)	*Ability to recognize & understand icons*
EXPLORATION	**(56)**	Interest in Exploration	(23)	*Desire to look around further*
Desire to explore and facilitation of exploration		Interest in Textual Information	(7)	*Wishing to read more about artworks*
		Ease of Virtual Visit	(7)	*Facilitation of virtual tours*
		Free Exploration	(6)	*Independence in examining the VE*
		Desire to Learn More	(8)	*Minting to obtain addition or re-hear information*
		Lack of Fine Details	(5)	*Minting to see closer details of artworks*
VISUAL QUALITY	**(53)**	Visual Execution	(15)	*Technical aspects of 36D photography*
Level of acceptance of visual elements		Image Accuracy	(10)	*Lack of Visual Precision*
		Expectation of Graphical Representation	(10)	*Visual quality of artwork did not meet expectations*
		Image Quality	(9)	*Elements of general image quality*
		Resolution	(9)	*Pixilation and blurriness*
STORYTELLING	**(43)**	Interest in Narration	(17)	*Degree to which narration appealed to participants*
Influence of story and narration on overall experience		Supplementing the Museum Atmosphere	(15)	*Impact of narration on museum atmosphere*
		Unclear Topic	(11)	*Inability to discern narration subject*
AUDIO	**(37)**	Narrator and Music Imbalance	(14)	*Inability to hear narrator over music*
Significance of music and narrator on virtual experience		Impact of Music	(14)	*Effect of music on general atmosphere*
		Voice of Narrator	(9)	*Inability to hear narrator over music*

(continued)

TABLE 11.1 (Cont.)

PHYSICAL COMFORT	**(37)**	Body Disassociation	(14)	*Adverse reactions to lack of body in the VE*
Bodily response to virtual environment and device		Nausea	(10)	*Feelings of nausea*
		Nausea Susceptibility	(7)	*Reflections on sensitivity to VR-induced arousal*
		Vertigo	(4)	*Reactions to perceived height in the VE*
		Physical Symptoms	(2)	*Discomfort caused by head-mounted display*
ENJOYABILITY	**(36)**	Pleasantness	(12)	*Feeling pleasant, comfortable or easy*
Emotional valence and degree of interest towards the experience		Fun	(7)	*Having fun in the experience*
		Cool	(6)	*Feeling amazed and intrigued*
		Impressive	(6)	*Feeling impressed*
		Interesting	(5)	*Showing general interest*
IMMERSION	**(26)**	Realism	(17)	*Extent to which the experience felt realistic*
Loss of reality and degree of absorption in the VE		Detachment from Real World	(6)	*Loss of presence in reality*
		Captivation	(3)	*Becoming engrossed in the VE*
MOVING IN VR	**(22)**	Transition	(16)	*Attitudes towards transitions within the environments*
Movement within and between an environment		Transition Between Environments	(6)	*Attitudes towards transitions between environments*
CONFUSION	**(18)**	Disorientation	(14)	*Loss of sense of location in the VE*
Feeling disoriented and uncertain		Uncertainty	(4)	*Obscure purpose and questioning of expected actions*
PRESENCE	**(16)**			
The extent of presence in the VE		Feeling Present	(16)	*The sense of "being there"*
RECOGNITION & RECOLLECTION	**(15)**	Familiarity	(11)	*Relating virtual environments/ elements to their real counterparts*
Reactions based on personal memories and knowledge		Similarity to Guided Tours	(4)	*Associating experience with real-world museum behaviors*

Visual quality received mentions from 18/21 of the participants. These comments were concentrated on how the participants perceived the experience and the issues with it, such as remarks on visual flaws, insufficient image accuracy, and blurriness. The storytelling elements received comments from 16/21 of the participants. The comments were grouped into three subcategories: *Interest in Narration, Supplementing the Museum Atmosphere*, and *Unclear Topic*. The second subcategory discusses how the narration felt suitable in the museum atmosphere and how in turn that affected the experience positively, such as, "It made me feel that I wasn't in a hurry anywhere" (transl.). Participants also made comments on the narration being unclear, as the narration started automatically when entering a scene with narration, without warning.

The category of Audio received comments from 12/21 participants that concentrated on the quality of the audio, including the voice of the narrator and the background music, and how the music affected the experience. One participant mentioned that the background music in the cathedral, "Was very peaceful and surely an effective way to escape the mundane" (transl.). Finally, 17/21 participants made comments regarding their Physical Comfort during and after using the application. A combined total of 18 comments by eight participants noted feelings of vertigo or body disassociation, such as, "It's strange since I can't see my arm" (transl.).

Although the previous study (Kauhanen et al. 2017) and the current study are not directly comparable because of differences in the questionnaires, there appear to be many improvements with the addition of the storytelling elements and other added features. In the previous study, 58/288 (20%) comments described feeling disoriented while in the virtual environment. Comments from the current study related to disorientation and confusion amounted to only 18/434, or 4% of the total comments, resulting in a clear decrease in disorientation. Similarly, comments related to immersion also increased from 1/288 (0.3%) to 26/434 (6%), suggesting that participants in this study were somewhat more engrossed in the viewing experience.

Discussion and conclusions

The results of this study revealed numerous experiential elements that arose from stepping inside the virtual application. Upon a more holistic analysis of both the questionnaire and interview data, we found that there were many facets of the experience that could not come to fruition unless other specific aspects had already been fulfilled. Jordan (1997) introduced a model called the Hierarchy of User Needs, where functionality was placed at the bottom of the pyramid, followed by usability, and pleasure resting at the top. This model is often referred to when showing the hierarchy for the experience-related aspects. The base needs should be met before the next level of needs in the pyramid can be met. Functionality and usability are sometimes therefore referred to as "hygiene" factors in this model. Therefore, the data from our study made sense from a bottom-up approach: to be able to enjoy the more hedonic aspects of the experience, the more practical aspects must be satisfied first. Thus, we present a model for the Hierarchy of User Experience Components in Immersive Journalism, shown in Figure 11.2.

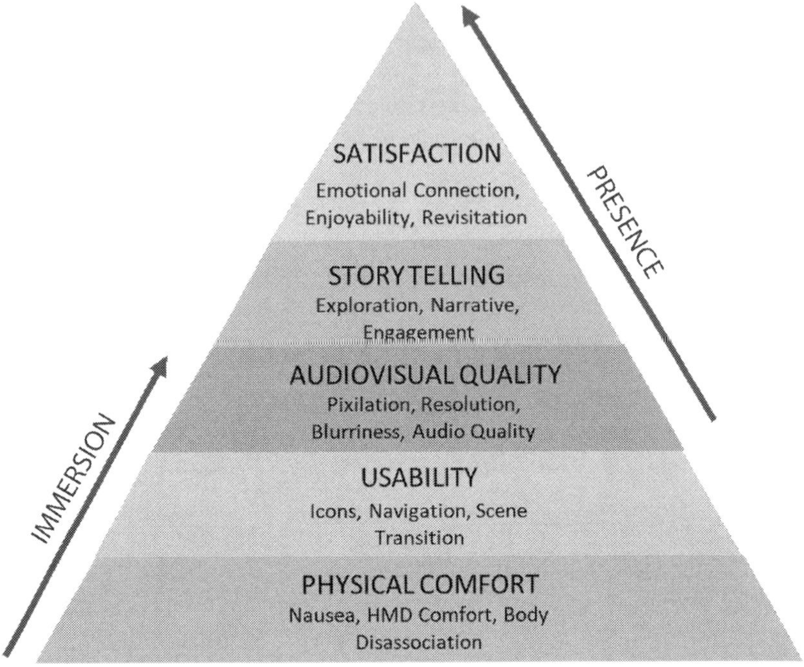

FIGURE 11.2 Hierarchy of User Experience Components in Immersive Journalism.

At the base of our model are the basic physical characteristics of the technology that can affect the VR experience. If motion sickness results from use or if the headset itself is uncomfortable, the user will be distracted from all other elements of the experience. In the next tier, the elements pertaining to usability can be found, such as issues with navigation or spatial understanding and the quality of the audio and images. Pixilation of the viewing content can be highly distracting and cause annoyance, and is therefore on one of the bottom tiers of the model. These are the basic elements that need to be of high quality for the user to be able to focus on other aspects of the experience. Storytelling sits next in the pyramid, and includes the core elements that will connect the viewer with the content, encouraging exploration and fostering engagement. As explained, storytelling is an integral piece of journalistic VR and, if the basic experiential components are first fulfilled, the story is what will grip viewers and pull them deeper into the experience and on to the top tier of the model: Satisfaction. For a user to be fully satisfied with an immersive experience, they will have most likely connected emotionally with the content and story and will be more motivated to try a similar VR experience. They will feel fulfilled and content after the experience, likely to form positive memories related to it. In addition to the elements within the pyramid, our model also integrates the influence of immersion and presence. Related to the more practical qualities of the experience, immersion increases as the bottom tiers are fulfilled. Similarly, presence increases as the more subjective needs are met in the higher tiers.

Based on previous research in the field and our own experimental observations, the Hierarchy of User Experience Components in Immersive Journalism offers journalists, researchers, and designers a basis on which to create positive VR experiences. It is also possible that these results could be applied to VR content in other fields and industries, at least when it comes to building memorable experiences and engaging UX. The novelty of VR will not last forever, and content creators can no longer rely on rollercoaster gimmicks or 360-degree content too blurry to even recognize. Users are looking for well-crafted adventures and immersive experiences that pull them away from the binds of day-to-day life. We hope our model introduces the most important experiential elements of VR that will allow journalists and other content creators to impact each viewer in a memorable way, aiding in the next level of VR creation and experiences. Future work should build upon the current model to better understand the specific elements within the tiers and discover further elements that might be missing, such as the effect of the context of use and possible differences between individual preferences and current creation standards.

References

Bellini, Nicola, Massimo Bergamasco, Rémi Brehonnet, Marcello Carrozzino, & Joëlle Lagier. 2018. "Virtual cultural experiences: the drivers of satisfaction." *Symphonya: Emerging Issues in Management 2*: 52–65.

Bosworth, Melissa & Lakshmi Sarah. 2019. *Crafting Stories for Virtual Reality*. Abingdon-on-Thames, UK: Routledge.

Carrozzino, Marcello & Massimo Bergamasco. 2010. "Beyond virtual museums: Experiencing immersive virtual reality in real museums." *Journal of Cultural Heritage 11*(4): 452–458.

de la Peña, Nonny, Peggy Weil, Joan Llobera, Elias Giannopoulos, Ausiàs Pomés, Bernhard Spanlang, Doron Friedman, Maria V. Sanchez-Vives, & Mel Slater. 2010. "Immersive journalism: Immersive virtual reality for the first-person experience of news." *Presence: Teleoperators and Virtual Environments 19*(4): 291–301.

Hassenzahl, M. 2005. "The quality of interactive products: Hedonic needs, emotions and experience". In: C. Ghaoui (ed), *Encyclopedia of Human Computer Interaction*. Hershey, PA: Idea Group, pp. 652–660.

Hürst, Wolfgang, Bibi de Boer, Wouter Florijn, & Xhi Jia Tan. 2016. "Creating new museum experiences for virtual reality." In: *2016 IEEE International Conference on Multimedia & Expo Workshops (ICMEW)*. IEEE, pp. 1–6.

Jordan, Patrick W. 1997. "Pleasure with Products: Human Factors for Body, Mind and Soul." In: Green, William S. & Patrick W. Jordan. *Human Factors in Product Design. Current Practise and Future Trends*. London: Taylor & Francis, pp. 206–207.

Jumisko-Pyykkö, Satu. 2011. "User-centered quality of experience and its evaluation methods for mobile television." Finland: Tampere University of Technology: *12*.

Jumisko-Pyykkö, Satu & Jukka Häkkinen. 2008. "Profiles of the evaluators: Impact of psychographic variables on the consumer-oriented quality assessment of mobile television." In: *Multimedia on Mobile Devices 2008, 68210*L. International Society for Optics and Photonics.

Jumisko-Pyykkö, Satu & Timo Utriainen. 2011. "A hybrid method for quality evaluation in the context of use for mobile (3D) television." *Multimedia Tools and Applications 55*(2): 185–225.

Kauhanen, O., H. Väätäjä, M. Turunen, T. Keskinen, E. Sirkkunen, T. Uskali, & J. Karhu. 2017. "Assisting immersive virtual reality development with user experience design approach." In: *Proceedings of the 21st International Academic Mindtrek Conference*. New York: ACM, pp. 127–136.

Kelling, Chelsea, Heli Väätäjä, & Otto Kauhanen. 2017. "Impact of device, context of use, and content on viewing experience of 360-degree tourism video." In: *Proceedings of the 16th International Conference on Mobile and Ubiquitous Multimedia*. New York: ACM, pp. 211–222.

Kelling, Chelsea, Otto Kauhanen, Heli Väätäjä, Jussi Karhu, Markku Turunen, & Vesa Lindqvist. 2018. "Implications of Audio and Narration in the User Experience Design of Virtual Reality." In: *Proceedings of the 22nd International Academic Mindtrek Conference*. New York: ACM, pp. 258–261.

Lepouras, George & Costas Vassilakis. 2004. "Virtual museums for all: employing game technology for edutainment." *Virtual Reality 8*(2): 96–106.

Lugrin, Jean-Luc, Marc Cavazza, David Pizzi, Thurid Vogt, & Elisabeth André. 2010. "Exploring the usability of immersive interactive storytelling." In: *Proceedings of the 17th ACM Symposium on Virtual Reality Software and Technology*. New York: ACM, pp. 103–110.

Saarinen, Santeri, Ville Mäkelä, Pekka Kallioniemi, Jaakko Hakulinen, & Markku Turunen. 2017. "Guidelines for designing interactive omnidirectional video applications." In: *IFIP Conference on Human-Computer Interaction*. Cham, Switzerland: Springer, pp. 263–272.

Saldaña, Johnny. 2009. *The Coding Manual for Qualitative Researchers*. SAGE *45*: 66–70 & 74–77.

Schubert, Thomas & Regenbrecht, Holger 2002. "Real and illusory interactions enhance presence in virtual environments." *Presence: Teleoperators & Virtual Environments 11*(4): 425–434.

Shin, D., & F. Biocca. 2018. "Exploring immersive experience in journalism." *New Media & Society 20*(8): 2800–2823. doi:10.1177/1461444817733133

Sirkkunen, Esa, Heli Väätäjä, Turo Uskali, & Parisa Pour Rezaei. 2016. "Journalism in virtual reality: Opportunities and future research challenges." In: *Proceedings of the 20th International Academic Mindtrek Conference*, New York: ACM, pp. 297–303.

Slater, Mel. 2003. "A note on presence terminology." *Presence Connect 3*(3): 1–5.

Styliani, Sylaiou, Liarokapis Fotis, Kotsakis Kostas, & Patias Petros. 2009. "Virtual museums, a survey and some issues for consideration." *Journal of Cultural Heritage 10*(4): 520–528.

Thüring, Manfred & Sascha Mahlke. 2007. "Usability, aesthetics and emotions in human–technology interaction." *International Journal of Psychology 42*(4): 253–264.

Wienrich, Carolin, Nina Döllinger, Simon Kock, Kristina Schindler, & Ole Traupe. 2018. "Assessing user experience in virtual reality: A comparison of different measurements." In: *International Conference of Design, User Experience, and Usability*, pp. 573–589. Cham, Switzerland: Springer.

Witmer, Bob G. & Michael J. Singer. 1998. "Measuring presence in virtual environments: A presence questionnaire." *Presence* 7(3): 225–240.

Wojciechowski, Rafal, Krzysztof Walczak, Martin White, & Wojciech Cellary. 2004. "Building virtual and augmented reality museum exhibitions." In: *Proceedings of the Ninth International Conference on 3D Web Technology*, New York: ACM, pp. 135–144.

12

IMMERSIVE GAMING AS JOURNALISM

Jonne Arjoranta, Raine Koskimaa, and Marko Siitonen

As a field, journalism constantly strives to connect with its audiences and find ways to utilize emerging media technologies in its operations. Sometimes this is done simply to reach audiences that have ceased to use traditional media, or to invite new audiences in, but often it is also a matter of perceived benefits related to using the affordances of certain technological solutions. One recent example is the interest surrounding the concept of *immersion*. For example, recent research has explored the question of whether there is a connection between the immersiveness of a technology and the users' empathetic responses (Archer & Finger 2018; Herrera et al. 2018). While some of these explorations are done specifically within the context of journalism, there is a considerable amount of overlap between different fields of interest, warranting a broader look at how the concept of immersion has been theorized.

This chapter discusses immersion and how it may be applied to journalism. In order to do so, we start by unraveling the concept of immersion itself as a reminder that it is not only connected to virtual reality (VR) or augmented reality (AR) technologies, but rather that it is a multifaceted concept that may be understood in many ways. Here, we turn specifically to the theorizing done in the context of digital games research, where immersion and some related concepts have been explored in detail over the last decades. This theorizing helps us see how immersion can be understood and in what way the concept may be problematic. The chapter maps out some of the historical precedents for immersion, discusses alternative and related concepts (such as presence), and how this understanding may be used to inform discussions of immersive journalism.

The magic circle of immersion

Immersion is a recurring concept when discussing video games and the way that players engage with them. It is often seen as a given that players immerse themselves in the game when playing. The roots of the concept of immersion related to play can be traced back to the classic *Homo Ludens* (1971[1938]) by Johan Huizinga. He never used the word "immersion", but his concept of the "magic circle" can be seen as the precursor for most game immersion discourse. According to Huizinga, a player is transferred from the everyday reality to the realm of game for the duration of play. While within the magic circle, the rules of play replace the everyday setting, and the strong sensation of the game space characterizes play: "[...] in this intensity, this absorption, this power of maddening, lies the very essence, the primordial quality of play" (Huizinga 1971[1938], 2).

The concept of the magic circle has been adopted by most of the game and play theorists since Huizinga, but, as there is not a very systematic definition of the concept in *Homo Ludens*, it has received numerous interpretations. For many game scholars today, the concept of the magic circle actually refers primarily to Katie Salen and Eric Zimmerman's characterization, which owes to Huizinga but cannot be fully reduced to it. They use the concept as a "shorthand for the idea of a special place in time and space created by a game" and to describe "where the game takes place" (Salen & Zimmerman 2004, 95).

Jaakko Stenros (2014) has gone through the history and uses of the magic circle, and found three main interpretations: 1) spatial or "arena", 2) social contract, and 3) psychological bubble. Of these three, the psychological bubble, "the 'protective frame' that surrounds a person in a playful state of mind", is most directly related to immersion. Drawing from Michael J. Apter's (1991, 14–15) reversal theory of personality, motivation and emotion, which recognizes opposite metamotivational states of "serious" and "playful", Stenros concludes that when a player is within the psychological bubble, "[t]here is a 'border' around her experience that guides her interpretation of the situation" (2014, 173–174).

Another influence on conceptualizing immersion in games comes from Janet Murray's book *Hamlet in the Holodeck* (1997), even though the book itself focused on issues related to virtual reality and future narrative forms. Murray has a different approach than Huizinga, who was focusing on the characteristics of play as a specific type of activity. Murray starts from the power of narration to transfer the audience to another world created by the narrative. She sees online and virtual worlds as the latest phase in the development of narrative media, and replaces such concepts as "make-believe" and "willing suspension of disbelief", more familiar in literary studies, with the concept of immersion adopted in the then-novel field of computer-based virtual worlds:

> Immersion is a metaphorical term derived from the physical experience of being submerged in water. We seek the same feeling from a psychologically immersive experience [...] the sensation of being surrounded by a completely other reality [...] that takes over all of our attention, our whole perceptual apparatus.
>
> *Murray 1997, 98*

François Laramée, when writing on game design principles, neatly illustrates this kind of approach to immersion, and promotes it as the highest priority of all entertainment: "All forms of entertainment strive to create suspension of disbelief, a state in which the player's mind forgets that it is being subjected to entertainment and instead accepts what is perceived as reality" (Laramée 2002, according to Salen & Zimmerman 2004, 450). It is, however, quite problematic to assume immersion requires the "forgetting of the reality". Instead, the phenomenological concept of *bracketing*, temporarily setting aside the assumed objective reality, would be a more accurate expression here. Other examples of immersion-characterized video game theory can be found from James Newman, "videogames may be characterized by a sense of 'being there'" (2004, 17), or from Nick Yee (2002), who identified one of the core factors for MMORPGs' (massively multiplayer online role-playing games') holding power as being "the immersive nature of these virtual environments" (9).

Expanding the concept of immersion

The way Murray (1997) conceptualizes immersion emphasizes fictional content in the process. When applied to games and play, this is problematic in two obvious ways: 1) there are games, also highly popular ones, without fictional world or narrative content, and 2) games and game play involve other aspects than the fictional game world, also in those cases where such a world exists. A player of *Tetris*, for example, may be clearly "immersed" in the game *action*, even if there is not an apparent fictional world to speak of. It is necessary to distinguish the two levels of videogame play: the represented world or *diegetic* level (which may be a narrative-based fictional world, or an abstract world) and the real-life player action, *non-diegetic level*, in which the player operates the game controller and devises her strategies. Alison McMahan (2003) has noted how immersion may take place in regards to both of these levels. For McMahan, immersion refers both to how the player may be "caught up in the world of the game's story", but also to her "love of the game and the strategy that goes into it" (2003, 68).

According to McMahan (2003), the use of immersion in game studies has suffered from serious confusion, partly caused by the borrowing of terms from the fields of virtual reality and interface design. She proposes *presence* as a more general, and in many cases more accurate, term than immersion. McMahan defines presence as "the artificial sense that a user has in a virtual environment that the environment is unmediated". Sense of presence is a complex phenomenon involving a set of dimensions: quality of social interaction, realism in the environment, the effect of "transportation", immersiveness generated by the interface, the user's ability to accomplish significant actions within the environment, and users responding to the computer as an intelligent, social agent. The environments and experiences vary greatly depending on the presence or absence of, and interplay between, these dimensions, but all of the six dimensions share the perceptual illusion of nonmediation (McMahan 72–73, referring to Lombard & Ditton).

Immersion and engagement are both aspects of presence in McMahan's framework. Immersion relates to presence on a diegetic level, whereas engagement relates to presence on a non-diegetic level, including such actions as gaining points and devising a winning strategy, etc. (McMahan 2003, 69, 79). In this framework, immersion is just one dimension of presence, and much of immersion talk actually relates to presence instead.

For example, in the game *1979 Revolution: Black Friday* (iNK Stories 2016) the player adopts the role of Reza Shirazi, a photojournalist present in the 1979 Iranian revolution. One of the central ways of interacting with the game is taking pictures of the events happening around Reza. The photos taken by the player are then contrasted with historical pictures taken by Michel Setboun, showing what the events looked like outside of the game. This necessarily reminds the player of events beyond the game, lessening the player's immersion – but the reminder that the events they are witnessing are based on historical events may also enhance their sense of engagement with the game. From a journalistic point of view, the inclusion of authentic photos is easier to defend than using only imaginary examples. Therefore, at least in this case, pursuing immersion alone would not lead to the optimal outcome.

Salen and Zimmerman's (2004) interpretation of the possibility of *shifting frames* is especially valuable in that it is able to explain how frequent shifts between immersion in the game world and engagement in the game play may take place so smoothly, by their both being encapsulated within the magic circle (ibid., 455). The presence in the magic circle does not break, despite movement between the states of immersion and engagement. It is, for example, quite common for the person involved in the game play to momentarily acknowledge also the space outside the magic circle, be it one's own living room, an eSports arena, or a public transportation vehicle, so that the periods of deep immersion and engagement may be relatively short, but also returning to the magic circle may happen quickly again. Of course, in the case of virtual reality specifically, it may be that the technology-related issues such as physical visors and earphones, or long loading times for software, prohibit such behavior, and push users towards spending a longer time within the VR experience.

Finally, game theorists have tried to adopt the concept of immersion to better suit interactive media. Calleja (2011, 1) argues that the concepts of presence and immersion both assume that the relation between a user and a system is unidirectional, from a physical reality into a virtual one, or a "dive of human subjectivity into a containing vessel". This metaphor does not work in media where the user can affect their surroundings, because it does not sufficiently take into account the medium's role. He suggests that, instead, a better metaphor would be *incorporation*, the absorption of a virtual environment into consciousness, yielding a sense of habitation, which is supported by the systemically upheld embodiment of the player in a single location represented by the avatar.

This goes beyond immersion, since it includes how the system acknowledges the player's existence. This does not automatically mean that incorporation is a better concept for understanding immersive experiences, but it is a useful reminder that virtual realities can have varying amounts of interactivity with the users.

Sensory immersion and VR technology

A somewhat different take on immersion is provided by Frans Mäyrä, who brings the choice of visual perspective into the game as an additional factor. Strong sensory immersion is provided, especially by the first-person view in games played on screen, and even more so with VR headsets. Freedom of moving around and instantaneous feedback from the game environment give rise to immersion in actions of play, which can be called a "challenge-based form of immersion into games" (2008, 107–108.) This approximately resembles McMahan's engagement, but also comes close to Mihaly Csikszentmihalyi's (Csikszentmihalyi & Csikszentmihalyi 1975) concept of *flow*. Mäyrä also recognizes immersion in the game world, describing it as absorption: "[…] another kind of immersion involved, as the player becomes emotionally as well as intellectually absorbed in the game world. […] we can call it imaginative immersion" (ibid., 109). If we compare McMahan and Mäyrä with each other, the models are quite compatible, with the exception that sensory immersion is of a different conceptual level than presence. Sensory immersion is clearly one way of creating a sense of presence, but not the only one available; we can find immersion and engagement, for example, in interactive fiction (text-based adventure games).

When looking at VR immersion specifically, there are certain aspects of the presented world which contribute to immersion, in addition to the sensory apparatus. The first-person perspective fosters immersion, but what Newman (2004) has called "first-hand participation" may be an even more significant factor, meaning active agency in the game world. First-hand participation is not reliant upon first-person perspective, but may appear independently and can "engender a degree of interactive connection with the gameworld that goes far beyond the abstracted 'use' of a system or vicarious identification with and manipulation of an iconic character or world" (2004, 142). It is important here that first-hand participation is conceptually separated from the game character (avatar), as they are usually strongly limited in gestural affordances when compared to degrees of freedom when using one's own body.

The oft-cited early example of building VR immersion is *Hunger in Los Angeles* (2012), a VR experiment recreating a crisis in a food bank line in Los Angeles. The experiment, which combined a 3D-modeled environment with an audio recording of the actual incident, aimed at recreating the feeling of "being there", according to the head developer Nonny de la Peña. While the technology of the time consisted of prototypes, there was a clear intention by the designers to recreate reality as faithfully as possible. The characters, the world, and especially the audio track point to a "real" reality which is experienced via a first-person perspective. However, there is little real first-hand participation, due to the fact that the player is represented by a bodiless floating "ghost", and the event will play out the same way regardless of their actions.

Similarly, in CNN's *An ordinary day in North Korea*, the camera is placed so high as to break the illusion of human viewpoint. In other typical cases, such as the BBC's story on weapons-training in Polish schools, the focus of the story is on a specific person, who presents a focal point, but here again the reader finds themselves in the role of a faceless observer without any other agency than to turn around. This might be an intentional design choice: by limiting the user's agency, CNN and the BBC have tighter editorial control on what their VR experiences convey to their users. Most likely it also speaks of the technical limitations of the camera setups used to construct most VR journalistic pieces: after all, the procedure of recording VR footage often includes using static camera(s) and trying to make sure the camera crew are not visible in the captured footage.

Whatever the reasons may be, it is clear that most contemporary examples of VR journalism have emphasized audiovisual fidelity or sensory immersion. From a game studies point of view this appears problematic. In a somewhat polemical fashion, Katie Salen and Eric Zimmerman (2004) call the over-emphasis of sensory immersion "the immersive fallacy":

> [...] the idea that the pleasure of a media experience lies in its ability to sensually transport the participant into an illusory, simulated reality. [...] Although the immersive fallacy has taken hold in many fields, it is particularly prevalent in the digital game industry.
>
> *Salen & Zimmerman 2004, 450–451*

The mistake behind immersive fallacy is to focus solely on the representational aspect and neglect the interface issues and play activity itself. As Marie-Laure Ryan has noted, in many fields over the past decades immersion has become less important and self-referentiality rendering the medium visible has gained more ground (Ryan 2001, 349). Thanks to this cultural movement, other media are largely avoiding the immersive fallacy, whereas, according to Salen and Zimmerman, "within the digital game industry, belief in the immersive fallacy remains alive and well" (2004, 451). The immersive fallacy does not mean that there would not be immersion related to games and other media at all, but rather that immersion usually appears as an element within a complex process of mediation. It is prudent to ask whether there is a distinct risk that the field of journalism, in the pursuit of exploring emerging technologies' affordances, is also in danger of falling into the trap of immersive fallacy by considering immersion in too narrow a way?

A gameful approach to immersive journalism

What would it mean in practice if there were to be more interaction and more intense gamification added to VR journalism? What kind of consequences would it entail in journalistic terms, and what would it be like as an audience experience? It is hard to avoid the notion that interactivity and gamification will definitely make things more complicated. The main challenge that all interactive storytelling faces is finding a balance between a scripted story, designed in advance, and the user's freedom of choice and first-hand participation. The more freedom is granted to the user, the more difficult it is to deliver a specific message with a fixed perspective. Game designers, however, have come up with several techniques to accomplish this feat. Often the trick involves making the player believe they have more freedom of choice in the game world than they actually possess. Since there is a lack of truly interactive, gamified pieces of VR journalism to date, we will next use newsgames as examples of journalistic content where game design principles emphasizing first-hand participation and immediate feedback are employed, giving rise to immersive and engaging experiences.

For example, *The Uber Game* (*Financial Times* 2017) sees the player take on the role of an Uber driver. The player has to choose how to approach the job, highlighting choices such as which kind of car to get (Uber drivers have to provide their own cars) and whether to get a business license or not. The game shows that the question of whether one can make it in the "gig economy" is often a matter of chance and that it may involve sacrificing other, valuable things, such as family time, in order to chase the elusive bonuses offered by the company. The picture portrayed by the game is very different from the one advertised by the company, which highlights the drivers' freedom to work as they see fit. A game system like *The Uber Game* is well fit to portray systemic phenomena, such as the complex reality of handling a job in the gig economy. To an extent, other journalistic media can also portray experiences of precariousness, but games are perhaps uniquely positioned to reflect on the relation between choice and chance, freedom and uncertainty. Players can try to inhabit the position portrayed by the game themselves, gaining at least some insight into the uncertainty of the situation.

If the goal is to create gameful journalism, there are new issues that must be taken into account. The tools to create these experiences are quite developed, but far from trivial to use. Designing gameful journalism takes a skillset that may not necessarily be obtained by doing traditional journalism. Even if gameful journalism promises to be able to do some things better than some other journalistic approaches, this only applies if the approach is used successfully. This takes resources, skills, and reflection on the ethical dimensions.

Conclusion

If we apply these lessons from how game studies have approached immersion to how immersion may be pursued or utilized in the field of journalism, we can see some suggestions for what to focus on and what to avoid. First, it is necessary to begin with a reminder that there is no one sense of immersion. Rather, the word has been used in different ways in different contexts. They are all more or less compatible, but highlight different aspects of the experience. Here we have drawn, for example, from McMahan (2003), who proposed a distinction between *presence*, *engagement*, and *immersion*, where presence operates as an umbrella term under which a more content-driven immersion and a more user-action-centered engagement are situated. This kind of division is useful as it reminds us that while speaking about immersion it may actually be engagement that technologically oriented developers are after – and that, if this division is not clear, it may lead to misunderstanding the available affordances, as well as their possible effects. It also reminds us that one does not necessarily need high-quality graphics or realistic virtual environments to be immersed in journalistic storytelling.

It should be clear by now that different applications, be they virtual worlds or games, induce different types of immersion (Ermi & Mäyrä 2005). It is also worth noting that different types of immersion may give rise to different ethical requirements (Mäyrä 2008, 125). For example, the question of whether or not to include the "shadow of a leggy tripod with a spherical camera head" in the VR recording becomes not only technical but also ethical when one considers the repercussions of "hiding" authorship and the constructed nature of VR news stories (Kool 2016, 9). Indeed, for a few years now there have been calls for increased transparency regarding VR journalism. As Tom Kent put it in his essay, "Viewers need to know how VR producers expect their work to be perceived, what's been done to guarantee authenticity and what part of a production may be, frankly, supposition" (2015 n.p.).

As the question of immersion is closely tied to technological affordances, it is also worthwhile to keep a close eye on developments that take place outside of and parallel to VR. The concept of Augmented or Added Reality, AR, is often used together with VR, and they are considered as close relatives. In some aspects this is true, but it is especially in regards to immersion that their premises should be closely scrutinized. AR applications posit features on top of the physical surroundings. This may take the form of extra information layers on the perceived environment, and the power of AR lies in incorporating the familiar physical environment into the partially crafted experience. Presence, then, would rely on such characteristics of the situation as the embodied experience and the environment's responsiveness, which is closer to engagement than immersion. AR journalism would serve well in providing a new perspective in familiar surroundings, as many players of *Pokémon Go*, for example, have reported to have noticed. This is quite a different road than much of the VR applications have taken, and points towards approaches complementary to VR journalism, focusing on the local and specific sites. It may well be that there are lessons to be learned in how AR will be utilized in journalism, and how applications using AR will affect audience expectations and perceptions.

Finally, perhaps the most important lesson that game studies have for journalism is to avoid the immersive fallacy, or at least become aware of its dangers. Focusing on feeling the "reality" of the events, or the feeling of "being there" (de la Peña et al. 2010) is but one way of approaching the question of immersion (or presence). Immersion may be a part of experiencing mediated environments, but it is only a part of that experience and, depending on the context, not necessarily the most important one. Instead, it can be used strategically, either to pull a user into an experience or push them out of it, when it is more useful, for example, that they should be reflecting on their experience. There is no one way to be immersed, so choosing what type of immersion to aim for and when is a design choice when building immersive experiences. In contexts like journalism, reflection may sometimes be more valuable than immersion.

References

Apter, Michael J. 1991. "A structural-phenomenology of play." In: J.H. Kerr & M.J. Apter (eds), *Adult Play: A Reversal Theory Approach*. Amsterdam: Swets & Zeitlinger.

Archer, D. & K. Finger. 2018. "Walking in another's virtual shoes: Do 360-degree video news stories generate empathy in viewers?" Academic Commons, Tow Center for Digital Journalism, Columbia University. https://academiccommons.columbia.edu/doi/10.7916/D8669W5C [Accessed 28 May 2019].

Calleja, G. 2011. "Incorporation: A renewed understanding of presence and immersion in digital games." In: *DiGRA 2011: Think Design Play, 2011*. Netherlands: Utrecht School of the Arts.

Csikszentmihalyi, M. & I. Csikszentmihalyi. 1975. *Beyond Boredom and Anxiety: The Experience of Play in Work and Games*. San Francisco, CA: Jossey-Bass Publishers.

de la Peña, N., P. Weil, J. Llobera, E. Giannopoulos, A. Pomes, B. Spanlang, D. Friedman, M.V. Sanchez-Vives, & M. Slater. 2010. "Immersive journalism: Immersive virtual reality for the first-person experience of news." *Presence 19*(4): 291–301.

Ermi, L. & F. Mäyrä. 2005. "Fundamental components of the gameplay experience: Analysing immersion." In: *DiGRA 2005 Conference: Changing Views – Worlds in Play, 2005*. Netherlands: Utrecht School of the Arts. www.digra.org/dl/db/06276.41516.pdf [Accessed 15 March 2020].

Financial Times. 2017. "The Uber game." https://ig.ft.com/uber-game/ [Accessed 15 March 2020].

Herrera, F., J. Bailenson, E. Weisz, E. Ogle, & J. Zaki. 2018. "Building long-term empathy: A large-scale comparison of traditional and virtual reality perspective-taking." *PLOS ONE 13*(10): e0204494. https://doi.org/10.1371/journal.pone.0204494.

Huizinga, Johan. 1971[1938]. *Homo Ludens: A Study of the Play-Element in Culture*. Boston: Beacon Press.

Hunger in L.A. [Hunger in Los Angeles]. 2012. VR documentary by Nonny de la Peña. https://emblematicgroup.com/experiences/hunger-in-la/ [Accessed 15 March 2020].

iNK Stories. 2016. *1979 Revolution: Black Friday*. New York: iNK Stories.

Kent, T. 2015. "An ethical reality check for virtual reality journalism." https://medium.com/@tjrkent/an-ethical-reality-check-for-virtual-reality-journalism-8e5230673507 [Accessed 15 March 2020].

Kool, H. 2016. "The ethics of immersive journalism: A rhetorical analysis of news storytelling with virtual reality technology." *Intersect: The Stanford Journal of Science, Technology, and Society 9*(3): 1–11.

Mäyrä, Frans. 2008. *Introduction to Game Studies: Games in Culture*. London; New York: SAGE.

McMahan, A. 2003. "Immersion, engagement and presence." In: M.J.P. Wolf & B. Perron (eds), *The Video Game Theory Reader*. New York: Routledge, p. 86.

Murray, Janet H. 1997. *Hamlet on the Holodeck: The Future of Narrative in Cyberspace.* New York: Free Press.

Newman, James. 2004. *Videogames.* London: Routledge.

Ryan, Marie-Laure. 2001. *Narrative as Virtual Reality: Immersion and Interactivity in Literature and Interactive Media.* Baltimore; London: The Johns Hopkins University Press.

Salen, K. & E. Zimmerman. 2004. *Rules of Play: Game Design Fundamentals.* Cambridge, MA: MIT Press.

Stenros, J. 2014. "In defence of a magic circle: The social, mental and cultural boundaries of play." *Transactions of the Digital Games Research Association 1*(2): 147–185.

Yee, Nicholas. 2002. "Ariadne: Understanding MMORPG addiction." Available online: www.nickyee.com/hub/addiction/addiction.pdf [Accessed 15 March 2020].

13

AUGMENTED REALITY AS NEWS

Pasi Ikonen and Turo Uskali

> If you are building complex, expensive VR today for the limited number of people, who get VR headsets, and [are] willing to scratch up on their heads to have the experience, experimentation is great, nice, but [...] I think augmented reality is actually more interesting and has more potential for news.
>
> *A manager of a big tech company 2016*

This quotation is from an expert interviewed during the Global Editors Network's summit in Vienna in June 2016. A management-level employee of a big tech company, who asked for anonymity, criticized the hype around virtual reality (VR) and predicted that actually augmented reality might serve journalism better than VR. Indeed, following the VR chapters in this volume, it is time to direct our attention to the implications of augmented reality (AR). In this chapter we introduce the AR concept, provide a brief history, and finally focus on the use of AR in journalism and other productions.

In AR, virtual information or objects are added to the otherwise real environment. Comparing VR, AR, and mixed reality displays, Milgram and Kishino (1994, 4) defined AR as "any case in which an otherwise real environment is 'augmented' by means of virtual (computer graphic) objects". Ronald Azuma added the attribute of real time to the definition, requiring that AR combines real and virtual, is interactive in real time, and is registered in three dimensions (Azuma 1997).

AR history goes way beyond Snapchat filters from 2015 and the worldwide success of *Pokémon Go* in 2016. One groundbreaking experiment in the field included "The Sword of Damocles" from 1968, the first-known head-mounted display (HMD), created by Ivan Sutherland and Bob Sproull (Kipper & Rampolla 2013). The history of AR research in the United States (US) also stretches back to the 1970s and 1980s (Feiner 2002).

In 1990 Boeing engineers Tom Caudell and David Mizell designed an HMD system that provided wiring instructions for airplanes (Berryman 2012). More importantly, they later coined the term Augmented Reality in a 1992 conference paper (Caudell & Mizell 1992).

By 1997 AR had been applied or tested at least in medical visualization, maintenance and repair, annotation, robot path-planning, entertainment, and military aircraft navigation and targeting (Azuma 1997). Furthermore, by 2012, Kipper and Rampolla (2013) also listed advertising, task support, navigation, home, industry, art, sightseeing, gaming, social networking, education, and translation as areas of use for AR.

The superimposed virtual elements can be viewed and interacted with 1) wearable HMDs such as AR glasses, 2) a smartphone, tablet, or personal computer with a webcam, or 3) via a spatial display such as a window, projector, or a specially designed room (Kipper & Rampolla 2013). AR applications can either add more information to the user's perception of the current physical reality (e.g. cafeteria recommendations when walking in the city) or create an artificial environment where the user is (e.g. virtual furniture in the user's home). AR can base its tracking on markers, such as shapes and images, or a location, e.g. the Global Positioning System (GPS) (Kipper & Rampolla 2013).

The technology: smartphones, smart glasses, and authoring tools

> The user of one of today's visual displays can easily make solid objects transparent – he can "see through matter!"
>
> *Ivan Sutherland 1965*

Currently in 2019 smartphones are by far the most popular means of using AR, although AR was not originally designed for mobile phone use (Pavlik & Bridges 2013). HMD and smart glasses also have AR storytelling potential.

The first AR product to generate massive hype was Google Glass, prototyped in 2013 and publicly released in 2014. The sales of the much-criticized glasses were halted in 2015 (Langley 2018). In other words, it flopped. There were particularly serious privacy concerns (Cave 2015; Levy 2017). Since 2017, the company X (a subsidiary of Alphabet Inc.) has been selling Glass Enterprise Edition for its partners (Kothari 2017). Microsoft released HoloLens in 2016 and HoloLens 2 in 2019 (Bohn 2019). Many other companies are introducing their own products (see e.g. eMacula 2019; Heaney 2019; Statt 2019). For example, since August 2018, consumers have been able to acquire the much-hyped Magic Leap One glasses (Swider & Fitzsimmons 2019). In recent years smart glasses' prices have come down, and one can acquire the cheapest ones for a few hundred US dollars, whereas the enterprise version of HoloLens 2 was priced at around $3,500 in 2019 (Bohn 2019).

Producers need an authoring tool to create AR applications. Tools are made for both programmers and non-programmers (Schmalstieg, Langlotz & Billinghurst 2011). Wikitude, the first web browser for AR, was launched in 2008 (Hauser

2010). Early AR tools used by media companies included Junaio (later purchased by Apple) and Aurasma (Pavlik & Bridges 2013). Both Google (ARCore) and Apple (ARKit) released their own platforms for building AR experiences in 2017 (Allum et al. 2018), and they are being used, for example, by *The New York Times* (*The New York Times* 2019). Facebook has its own AR platform called Spark AR (previously Camera Effects Platform) that helps developers build apps for the social networking platform (Spark AR 2018).

The evolution of AR in journalism

Azuma (2015) sees storytelling as one of the most important ways to utilize augmented and mixed reality. John Pavlik and Frank Bridges see AR as serving the same function as news: "it augments the user's experience with the real-world, natural environment" (Pavlik & Bridges 2013, 6).

One can argue that sports broadcasts paved the way for AR in journalism. AR has been used in sports at least since 1998, when Sportvision broadcast the first virtual yellow first down marker during a live American football National Football League (NFL) game (Augment.com 2016). These real-time virtual lines, visible to TV audiences, have been used since then in many other sports events, such as athletics and swimming, to indicate record times or target levels.

Newsrooms started experimenting around 2010 with AR technology using printed paper extensions and Quick Response (QR) codes. *Esquire* magazine created a cover and a few articles for their November 2009 issue that could be augmented with a mobile app (*Esquire* magazine 2009; Pavlik & Bridges 2013). In a similar vein, augmenting *Süddeutsche Zeitung*'s *SZ* magazine in 2010, users could watch videos using the mobile app Metaio (O'Hear 2010). *The New York Times Magazine* used a QR code on its 10th anniversary special cover in 2010 to link users to short video clips (Pavlik & Bridges 2013). Some early examples were various companies that targeted children (*The Hamilton Spectator* 2016; Baluja 2013), experimented with AR advertising (*The Guardian* 2012), and created a location-based experience (Valcarce, Bolós, & Recio 2017). Similar extensions to print products have been produced around the world. Table 13.1 lists early print AR extensions from different countries.

Smaller news outlets have rarely tried out AR. In a 2017 survey for local newsrooms in the US, none of the respondents reported using AR (Radcliffe, Ali & Donald 2017), despite the fact that researchers had found some evidence of AR productions. For example, *The Herald and News* in Klamath Falls, Oregon, has experimented with AR since 2015 (Radcliffe, Ali & Donald 2017). The same report hinted at newsrooms' modest interest in learning about AR technology.

From 2016 onwards, AR journalism applications have mostly used 3D models, location-based stories, and augmented studios. Big media outlets in the US have led this development. In some rare cases, smart glasses have been utilized, and AR has occasionally been also used as a reporting tool. We now look at some of the most prominent examples.

TABLE 13.1 Examples of printed paper AR extensions from different countries.

Country	*Publisher/magazine/newspaper & year of publication*	*Reference*
Canada	*Glacier Media*: 12 newspapers in 2013 *Toronto Star* 2013 *Winnipeg Free Press* 2013 *The Hamilton Spectator* 2016	(Layar 2013) (Emrich 2013; Baluja 2013) (*Hamilton Spectator* 2016)
Germany	*SZ* magazine 2010 *Stern* 2011 *Welt der Wunder* 2011 *Auto Bild* 2015 *Rheinische Post* 2015	(O'Hear 2010) (Raso et al. 2016)
India	*Mid-Day*: QR code 2010 *Times of India* 2012 *Dainik Bhaskar* 2016	(Pahwa 2010) (Chaudhary 2012) (Goyal 2016)
Japan	*Tokyo Shimbun* 2013	(Baluja 2013)
Malaysia	*The Star*: iSnap 2012	(Mahpar & Mahalingam 2012)
Spain	*Fotogramas* magazine: QR code 2010	(Valcarce, Bolós & Recio 2017)
United Kingdom	*The Guardian*: AR advertising 2012 *The Times* 2013 *The Telegraph* 2013 *The Independent* 2013 *Talk About Local* 2013	(*The Guardian* 2012) (Witkin 2013) (*Press Gazette* 2013)
United States	*Esquire* magazine 2009 *The New York Times Magazine*: QR code 2010 *Boston Globe Winter Arts Guide* 2011	(*Esquire* magazine 2009) (Pavlik & Bridges 2013) (Kieslow 2011)

When using 3D models for AR, graphics are superimposed over the user's real environment via a smartphone app. *The Washington Post* first used AR in May 2016, when they published a story on the arrest and death of Freddie Gray in Baltimore, using narrated scenes with 3D models for their app (*WashPostPR* 2016). They continued with a series on architecture (Moses 2017). Quartz updated their iPhone app with AR capabilities in September 2017, bringing to life, for example, the Cassini-Huygens spacecraft, the Roland TR-808 drum machine and the Berlin Wall (Southern 2017). *The New York Times* released their first AR production for mobile phone in February 2018, centered on the PyeongChang Winter Olympics and sponsored by Ralph Lauren (Branch 2018). A different perspective was given by the Tham Luang Cave story, also at *The New York Times*: it brought to the user's environment models of the small openings of the cave where 13 members of a youth soccer team were trapped in 2018 (Beech 2018). Australian Broadcasting Company (ABC) introduced a Space Discovery app in May 2018 (Bazley 2018).

Applications for AR glasses remain rare, as the technology has not yet become more common. CNN (Roettgers 2019) and Cheddar (Strange 2018) have released news applications for the Magic Leap One AR glasses, allowing users to pin regular 2D news videos to the walls and ceilings of their real environment.

Similarly to how sports broadcasts have employed AR, television studios can be augmented too. In May 2018, ABC News in the United States produced an augmented news report on air about the British royal wedding with 3D models brought to the studio (ABC News 2018), and they had an AR studio for the US midterm elections (Jacobson 2018). Al Jazeera has also built AR studios to cover the Winter Olympics 2018 (Hill 2018a) and provide a tour of Jerusalem (Hill 2018b), among other topics.

One of the most active news outlets to augment studios has been The Weather Channel (together with the Future Group). They have used AR in weather forecasts since summer 2018 (LaForme 2018). The company has planned to produce 80 percent of its programming using AR and VR by 2020, according to their Director of Weather Presentation in a *Washington Post* interview (Cappucci 2018). Their weather forecasts from 2018 and 2019 have portrayed a tornado that also seems to enter the studio and break it apart, a hurricane with rising water levels with the meteorologist standing next to the flood, and an ice storm that causes a bus to almost crash into the meteorologist situated in the middle of the scene.

These fact-based but obviously made-up animations bring about some ethical considerations. It should be considered how the forceful visualizations affect attention and whether they interfere with or direct viewers' attention toward the storms' facts and impacts. In addition, the relation between factual information and visual speculation calls for ethical discussion.

Besides speculative animations, AR does raise more general ethical issues in journalism. Fundamental public values, such as privacy (e.g. issues related to recording, face-recognition technology, and ownership of AR information) and balance of power (who sets the standards for technology?) touch upon AR (Royakkers et al. 2018). The physical appearance of technology can affect social situations, and sensor-based reality has an effect on privacy, security, and trust. Ethics should therefore be considered in the design and applied to the possible interventions needed, researchers argue (Mann et al. 2018). Use of smart glasses creates concerns about privacy, identity, autonomy, and ownership (Wolf, Grodzinsky, & Miller 2016). AR also poses legal challenges (Lemley & Voloch 2017) that relate to privacy, marketing, intellectual property, real property, torts, personal injury, and criminal acts (Wassom 2014). Another ethical consideration is what topics are even suitable for AR (Kunova 2019).

What about harnessing AR technology as a reporting tool? The *Hindustan Times* employed Snapchat filters when Yusuf Omar interviewed underage survivors of rape. The filters, used during the interviews, helped to create anonymity and give a sense of security to the interviewees on the extremely sensitive topic (Scott 2016).

AR could also be used for crowdsourcing. One research paper found that AR could be applied in crowdsourcing processes to support its planning and crowdworkers' activity and for sharing and consuming location-based user-generated content (Väätäjä et al. 2013).

News organizations continue experimenting with AR. Google News Initiative, the Knight Foundation and the Online Journalism Association gave out Journalism 360 Awards in December 2018. Three of the 11 winners included AR in their project descriptions: these relate to 3D assets, a spatialized audio editor, and AR prototypes for health and science news (Knight Foundation 2018).

Future inspiration: other kinds of AR stories

Overall, a huge selection of AR experiences and applications exists for devices accessible by ordinary consumers. As the examples in this chapter show, the technology itself holds many unexplored options for journalistic use. Creating location-based features, crowdsourcing, and utilizing social networking in AR remain as such possibilities (Pavlik & Bridges 2013).

Interestingly, research on user experiences of AR storytelling is still almost non-existent. In one example, Fedorovskaya and Yu (2015) studied the preferences of 32 participants reading a short story (print or digital) with or without video augmentation. In their study, AR was found to enhance the overall experience. Overall, AR user experience has been studied in many contexts, however (see e.g. Dirin & Laine 2018; Ko, Chang, & Ji 2013; Siriborvornratanakul 2018; Zhou 2018).

Experimenting with augmenting another medium, Billinghurst, Kato, and Poupyrev introduced the augmented book, *MagicBook*, in 2000 (Billinghurst, Kato, & Poupyrev 2001). It was a combined AR and VR experience, with the users holding a hand-held display, allowing for a simultaneous multi-user experience. Many augmented books have been seen since, for example the graphic novel *Priya's Shakti* from 2004 (Bosworth & Sarah 2018).

The 2019 book by Melissa Bosworth and Lakshmi Sarah offers an excellent review of VR, mixed reality, and AR storytelling cases from recent years (Bosworth & Sarah 2018). In addition, the Optimist issue of *Time* magazine in 2018 was augmented with videos, infographics, and animations, including narration from Bono and Bill Gates. Outthink Hidden, a production of *The New York Times*' T Brand Studio, offered location-based stories of remarkable but relatively unknown scientists. The user could place virtual statues in ten cities around the US and learn about the scientists' stories. Three of the experiences mentioned in Bosworth and Sarah's book were based on an exact location. "Hello, We're from the Internet" was an independent "guerilla" AR museum experience in 2018. Users could point their phones at paintings in the Museum of Modern Art in New York to see other artworks. "New Dimensions in Testimony" at Illinois Holocaust Museum (2017) is a very ambitious project in which holocaust survivors answered around 1,250 pre-recorded questions. Viewers who see a hologram of the survivor in the museum theater can ask them any questions, while a natural-language processing system determines which answer the hologram will use. In "Terminal 3" (2018), created by Asad Malik, users put on Microsoft's HoloLens and saw an airport interview of a person selected based on racial screening. When finishing this experience, the users were instructed to go to the next room, where they met in real life the person they had just seen virtually (Bosworth & Sarah 2018).

Robert Azuma has stressed the utility of location-based experiences, observing that they could make users view the world in a different way (Azuma 2015). Some early situated experiences offered an opportunity to experience narratives from different points of view. "Three Angry Men" from 2003 did this in a fictional setting, whereas "You Get Me" from 2008 used authentic stories of real people in London, and it was playable at the Royal Opera House in London. In "MR Sea Creatures" from 2005, a museum interior was transformed to be underneath the sea, with virtual ancient sea creatures brought to life. "The Westwood Experience" from 2010 combined a variety of MR effects with live actors and an authentic environment related to the story (Azuma 2015).

AR storytelling types for journalism

By reading through the AR academic literature and browsing news media websites, we have identified 11 different types of storytelling with AR (Table 13.2). The list is not a comprehensive account of AR cases around the world, but it gives an idea of what has been done in recent years.

Overall, the volume of AR productions has remained low, and smaller or medium-sized newsrooms have mostly stayed out of the whole business. Breaking and hard news may not be the optimal areas for producing AR journalism, whereas sports and travel might be more easily suited for it (Pavlik & Bridges 2013).

We can argue that weather predictions and live sports events have led the way in the adaptation of AR in journalism globally. For example, sports programs in Finland focusing on the Winter Olympics and national ice hockey series have been at the forefront in adapting AR technologies. Both public broadcasters, such as the Finnish Broadcasting Company in 2018, and commercial broadcasting/telecom companies, such as Telia TV in 2019, have utilized AR with live athlete holograms, bringing them to the TV studio from the sports event hundreds of kilometers away.

Producing AR usually requires careful planning, more time, and a bigger team than regular reporting. Use of the technology in TV began with colored lines augmented to sports broadcasts. Media organizations and newsrooms experimented with mobile AR at the beginning of the 2010s. Around the year 2018, applications using 3D models and studio augmentations became more frequent, many of these as collaborations with brands (see e.g. Moses 2017).

Conclusion: still waiting for the AR breakthrough

Nic Newman's study (2018) for the Reuters Institute for the Study of Journalism predicted a breakthrough year for mobile AR in 2018, but "killer apps" in AR journalism are still to be seen.

TABLE 13.2 Types of AR storytelling for journalism.

Type of AR storytelling	*Platforms/devices used*	*Physical environment*	*Examples*
Situated documentary	Backpack, a head-mounted display, and a tablet as part of a user interface (early examples) Smartphone Head-mounted display	In a specific location	Columbia University campus Touring Machine (Höllerer, Feiner & Pavlik 1999) 110stories (110stories 2019)
Localized guides	Smartphone app	In a specific location	*Stella Artois: Le Bar Guide* (Hannaford 2009)
Localized news	Smartphone app	In a specific location	*Talk About Local* (Witkin 2013)
Augmented elements in a TV studio or broadcast	TV/web	Studio	The Weather Channel (LaForme 2018) CNN: Super Bowl (Egripment 2018) ABC News: Royal Wedding (ABC News 2018)
Augmented live event	Smartphone app	In a specific event	Black Eyed Peas concert (CNN 2018)
Printed paper QR code link	Smartphone app	Anywhere	*New York Times Magazine* QR code cover (Pavlik & Bridges 2013)
Printed paper AR extension providing images, video and links	Printed newspaper/magazine and a smartphone app	Anywhere	*Esquire* magazine AR issue (Esquire magazine 2009) *Time* magazine *Optimism* issue (Bosworth & Sarah 2018)
Virtual objects superimposed on the user's environment	Smartphone app	Anywhere	*New York Times*: Statue of Liberty (Stapinski 2018) *New York Times*: Four of the Best Olympians (Branch 2018) ABC: Space Discovery (Bazley 2018)
A story with virtual objects superimposed on the user's environment	Smartphone app	Anywhere	*Washington Post*: Freddie Gray's case (WashPostPR 2016)

TABLE 13.2 (Cont.)

Type of AR storytelling	*Platforms/devices used*	*Physical environment*	*Examples*
News video inside augmented reality	AR glasses	Anywhere	CNN app in Magic Leap (Roettgers 2019) Cheddar app in Magic Leap (Strange 2018)
AR as a reporting tool			*Hindustan Times*: Using Snapchat filters for anonymizing interviewees (Scott 2016)

According to our findings, the main implications of AR for journalism can be seen in smartphone apps and TV broadcasts. As smartphones have become ubiquitous and mobile AR technology is developing, content providers can easily reach a vast number of users all over the world: there were about 990 million ARKit- and ARCore-compatible smartphones at the end of 2018, with 129 million monthly active users (Boland 2018). The same report predicts that these numbers will double in 2019. When compared to the problem of the low penetration percentage of VR gadgets like HMDs in the mass market, AR will soon be available for all smartphone users.

At the turn of the 2020s, we argue that the most powerful AR experiences so far have been focused on weather predictions, especially by The Weather Channel, and live sports events. As climate change has become one of the most urgent news topics of our times, it is easy to predict that other news producers, especially those with a decent budget for testing new technologies and innovations, will probably follow suit. The big sports broadcasters have also always been at the forefront of journalistic innovations globally due to their enormous budgets and intensive competition.

Over the last ten years, the potential of AR for storytelling and journalism has grown. However, as our interviewee mentioned at the start of this chapter, it remains to be seen when the use of AR will be as ubiquitous as smartphones are nowadays.

References

110stories. 2019. "110stories: Harnessing the storytelling power of immersive mobile media." 110stories, April. www.110stories.com/ [Accessed 15 March 2020].

ABC News. 2018. "The royal wedding augmented reality experience." ABC News, 12 December. https://abcnews.go.com/US/royal-wedding-augmented-reality-experience/story?id=59750374 [Accessed 15 March 2020].

Allum, Cynthia, Elyssa Goldberg, Matthew Weinberg, Rashmi Bhagwat, & Siddharth Shanbhag. 2018. "The state of augmented reality." *NYC Media Lab/RYOT Studio white paper*. www.ryotstudio.com/whitepaper/RYOTStudio-CBS-AR-WhitePaper.pdf [Accessed 15 March 2020].

Augment.com. 2016. "Did sports pave the way for augmented reality?" 7 July. www.augment.com/blog/sports-pave-way-augmented-reality/ [Accessed 15 March 2020].

Azuma, Ronald. 1997. "A survey of augmented reality." *Presence: Teleoperators and Virtual Environments 6*(4), August: 355–385.

Azuma, Ronald. 2015. "Location-based mixed and augmented reality storytelling" In: Woodrow Barfield (ed.), *Fundamentals of Wearable Computers and Augmented Reality*. Boca Raton, FL: CRC Press, pp. 259–276.

Baluja, Tamara. 2013. "Augmented reality: The latest fad for newspapers or a real innovation?" *J-Source.ca*. https://j-source.ca/article/augmented-reality-the-latest-fad-for-newspapers-or-a-real-innovation/ [Accessed 15 March 2020].

Bazley, Nathan. 2018. "Backstory: Exploring the potential of augmented reality with the launch of Space Discovery app." ABC Backstory, 22 May. www.abc.net.au/news/about/backstory/digital/2018-05-22/making-ar-space-discovery/9786402 [Accessed 15 March 2020].

Beech, Hannah. 2018. "Step Inside the Thai Cave in Augmented Reality." *The New York Times*, 21 July. www.nytimes.com/interactive/2018/07/21/world/asia/thai-cave-rescue-ar-ul.html [Accessed 15 March 2020].

Berryman, Donna R. 2012. "Augmented reality: A review." *Medical Reference Services Quarterly 31*(2), May: 212–218.

Billinghurst, Mark, Hirokazu Kato, & Ivan Poupyrev. 2001. "The MagicBook: a transitional AR interface." *Computers & Graphics 25*(5), October: 745–753.

Bohn, Dieter. 2019. "Microsoft's HoloLens 2: A $3,500 mixed reality headset for the factory, not the living room." *The Verge*, 24 February. www.theverge.com/2019/2/24/18235460/microsoft-hololens-2-price-specs-mixed-reality-ar-vr-business-work-features-mwc-2019 [Accessed 15 March 2020].

Boland, Mike. 2018. "990 Million ARKit & ARCore Smartphones in the Wild." *AR Insider*. 27 December. https://arinsider.co/2018/12/27/990-million-arkit-arcore-smartphones-in-the-wild/ [Accessed 15 March 2020].

Bosworth, Melissa & Lakshmi Sarah. 2018. *Crafting Stories for Virtual Reality*. Abingdon-on-Thames, UK: Routledge.

Branch, John. 2018. "Four of the best Olympians, as you've never seen them." *The New York Times*. 5 February. www.nytimes.com/interactive/2018/02/05/sports/olympics/ar-augmented-reality-olympic-athletes-ul.html [Accessed 15 March 2020].

Cappucci, Matthew. 2018. "Watch a virtual tornado demolish the Weather Channel studio." *The Washington Post*, 20 June. www.washingtonpost.com/news/capital-weather-gang/wp/2018/06/20/watch-a-virtual-tornado-demolish-the-weather-channel-studio/?noredirect=on&utm_term=.374dca3ef796 [Accessed 15 March 2020].

Caudell, Thomas P. & David W. Mizell. 1992. "Augmented reality: An application of heads-up display technology to manual manufacturing processes." *1992 Hawaii International Conference on System Sciences (HICSS'92)*. 7–10 January, Hawaii. https://doi.org/10.1109/HICSS.1992.183317

Cave, Andrew. 2015. "Why Google Glass flopped." *Forbes.com*, 20 January 2015. www.forbes.com/sites/andrewcave/2015/01/20/a-failure-of-leadership-or-design-why-google-glass-flopped/#6182120057ff [Accessed 15 March 2020].

Chaudhary, Apurva. 2012. "Times of India launches another augmented reality app: Times alive." *Medianama*, 18 December. www.medianama.com/2012/12/223-times-of-india-launches-another-augmented-reality-app-times-alive/ [Accessed 15 March 2020].

CNN. 2018. "Enter a new dimension: Will.i.am's augmented reality revolution." *CNN Style*, 8 November. https://edition.cnn.com/style/article/will-i-am-black-eyed-peas-masters-of-the-sun-smart-creativity/index.html [Accessed 15 March 2020].

Dirin, Amir & Teemu H. Laine. 2018. "User experience in mobile augmented reality: Emotions, challenges, opportunities and best practices." *Computers* 7(2), May.

Egripment. 2018. "CNN's Super Bowl Special uses Egripment's augmented reality system." *Egripment,* February. https://egripment.com/news/cnn%E2%80%99s-super-bowl-special-uses-egripment%E2%80%99s-augmented-reality-system/ [Accessed 15 March 2020].

eMacula. 2019. "The world's first human friendly full field of view AR/VR system." *eMacula,* 16 April. www.emacula.io/ [Accessed 15 March 2020].

Emrich, Tom. 2013. "The Toronto Star uses augmented reality to try to go beyond the ink." *Betakit,* 19 September. https://betakit.com/the-toronto-star-uses-augmented-reality-to-try-to-go-beyond-the-ink/ [Accessed 15 March 2020].

Esquire. 2009. "Behind the scenes of augmented Esquire." *Esquire magazine,* 9 November. www.esquire.com/news-politics/news/g371/augmented-reality-technology-110909/?slide=10 [Accessed 15 March 2020].

Fedorovskaya, Elena & Lufei Yu. 2015. "Investigating the effects of publishing approaches using print, electronic and augmented reality media on user experience." *Journal of Print and Media Technology Research 4*(3), September: 217–226.

Feiner, Steven K. 2002. "Augmented reality: A new way of seeing." *Scientific American 286*(4), April: 48–55.

Goyal, Gaurav. 2016. "This 15th August, introducing augmented reality in Jaipur's Dainik Bhaskar with Yeppar." *Medium.com,* 10 August. https://medium.com/@yeppar/this-15th-august-introducing-augmented-reality-in-jaipurs-dainik-bhaskar-with-yeppar-254264a25a1 [Accessed 15 March 2020].

The Guardian. 2012. "Guardian partners with Blippar for augmented reality ad and editorial." *The Guardian,* 20 April. www.theguardian.com/gnm-press-office/guardian-partners-with-blippar [Accessed 15 March 2020].

Hamilton Spectator. 2016. "The Dolphin Way." *Hamilton Spectator,* 11 July. www.thespec.com/community-story/6761980-the-dolphin-way/ [Accessed 15 March 2020].

Hannaford, Kat. 2009. "Stella Artois uses augmented reality in cool iPhone app." *Gizmodo,* 21 December. https://gizmodo.com/stella-artois-uses-augmented-reality-in-cool-iphone-app-5431120 [Accessed 15 March 2020].

Hauser, Andreas. 2010. "Wikitude world browser." *Wikitude.com,* 9 August 2010. www.wikitude.com/wikitude-world-browser-augmented-reality/ [Accessed 15 March 2020].

Heaney, David. 2019. "Report: Facebook's upcoming AR glasses much less bulky than hololens or magic leap." *Upload VR,* 18 January. https://uploadvr.com/facebook-ar-glasses-abrash-report/ [Accessed 15 March 2020].

Hill, Michael P. 2018a. "Al Jazeera English uses AR to map out Holy Land." *Newscast Studio,* 26 January. www.newscaststudio.com/2018/01/26/holy-land-augmented-reality/ [Accessed 15 March 2020].

Hill, Michael P. 2018b. "Augmented reality helps Al Jazeera explain Winter Olympics sports." *NewscastStudio,* 21 February. www.newscaststudio.com/2018/02/21/al-jazeera-augmented-reality-olympics-2018/ [Accessed 15 March 2020].

Höllerer, Tobias, Steven Feiner, & John Pavlik. 1999. "Situated documentaries: Embedding multimedia presentations in the real world." Paper presented at the Third International Symposium on Wearable Computers, San Francisco, CA, USA, 18–19 October. https://ieeexplore.ieee.org/abstract/document/806664 [Accessed 15 March 2020].

Jacobson, Lindsey. 2018. "Behind the scenes on Election Day: 360-degree video of the ABC News election set and AR experience." *ABC News,* 5 November. https://abcnews.go.com/Politics/scenes-election-day-360-degree-video-abc-news/story?id=58942385 [Accessed 15 March 2020].

Kieslow, Damon. 2011. "Boston Globe's augmented reality project an example of quick, cheap innovation." Poynter newsletter. 9 February. www.poynter.org/newsletters/2011/boston-globes-augmented-reality-project-an-example-of-quick-cheap-innovation/ [Accessed 15 March 2020].

Kipper, Greg & Joseph Rampolla. 2013. *Augmented reality: An emerging technologies guide to AR*. Amsterdam; Boston, MA: Syngress/Elsevier.

Knight Foundation. 2018. "Journalism 360 awards $195,000 to 11 winning projects that use immersive storytelling to advance journalism." Knight Foundation press release, 12 September. www.knightfoundation.org/press/releases/journalism-360-awards-195-000-to-11-winning-projects-that-use-immersive-storytelling-to-advance-journalism [Accessed 15 March 2020].

Ko, Sang M., Won S. Chang, & Ji Yong G. 2013. "Usability principles for augmented reality applications in a smartphone environment." *International Journal of Human-Computer Interaction 29*(8), August: 501–515.

Kothari, Jay. 2017. "A new chapter for Glass." *Medium.com,* 18 July. https://blog.x.company/a-new-chapter-for-glass-c7875d40bf24 [Accessed 15 March 2020].

Kunova, Marcela. 2019. "Pros and cons of using augmented reality in the newsroom." *Journalism.co.uk*, 8 May. www.journalism.co.uk/news/pros-and-cons-of-using-augmented-reality-in-the-newsroom/s2/a738521/ [Accessed 15 March 2020].

LaForme, Ren. 2018. "The Weather Channel created a tornado that tore down their walls." *Poynter Tech & Tools,* 26 June. www.poynter.org/tech-tools/2018/the-weather-channel-created-a-tornado-that-tore-down-their-walls/ [Accessed 15 March 2020].

Langley, Hugh. 2018. "The patented history and future of… Google Glass: Quite the spectacle." *Wareable,* 7 April. www.wareable.com/features/the-patented-history-and-future-of-google-glass-656 [Accessed 15 March 2020].

Layar. 2013. "Glacier Media launches massive interactive print rollout with Layar." *layar.com,* 7 February. www.layar.com/news/press-releases/glacier-media/ [Accessed 15 March 2020].

Lemley, Mark A. & Eugene Volokh. 2017. "Law, virtual reality, and augmented reality." *University of Pennsylvania Law Review 166*: 1051–1138.

Levy, Stephen. 2017. "Google Glass 2.0 Is a startling second act." *Wired.com,* 18 July. www.wired.com/story/google-glass-2-is-here/ [Accessed 15 March 2020].

Mahpar, M. Hafidz & Eugene Mahalingam. 2012. "iSnap feature excites media specialist companies." *The Star Online,* 28 April. www.thestar.com.my/business/business-news/2012/04/28/isnap-feature-excites-media-specialist-companies/ [Accessed 15 March 2020].

Mann, Steve, John C. Havens, Jay Iorio, Yu Yuan, & Tom Furness. 2018. "All reality: Values, taxonomy, and continuum, for Virtual, Augmented, eXtended/MiXed (X), Mediated (X, Y), and Multimediated Reality/Intelligence." Paper Presented at AWE 2018, Santa Clara, California, USA, 31 May.

Milgram, Paul & Fumio Kishino. 1994. "A taxonomy of mixed reality visual displays." *IEICE TRANSACTIONS on Information and Systems* 77(12), December: 1321–1329.

Moses, Lucia. 2017. "The Washington Post is diving into augmented reality." *Digiday UK,* 15 May. https://digiday.com/media/washington-post-diving-augmented-reality/ [Accessed 15 March 2020].

The New York Times. 2019. "Your guide to augmented reality in The Times." *The New York Times,* 17 April. www.nytimes.com/interactive/2018/02/01/sports/olympics/nyt-ar-augmented-reality-guide.html [Accessed 15 March 2020].

Newman, Nic. 2018. *Journalism, Media and Technology Trends and Predictions 2018.* Oxford, UK: Reuters Institute for the Study of Journalism, Oxford University. https://reutersinstitute.politics.ox.ac.uk/our-research/journalism-media-and-technology-trends-and-predictions-2018 [Accessed 15 March 2020].

O'Hear, Steve. 2010. "Video: The 'first' dead tree magazine with Augmented Reality support." *TechCrunch,* 19 August. https://techcrunch.com/2010/08/19/video-the-first-dead-tree-magazine-with-augmented-reality-support/?guccounter=1 [Accessed 15 March 2020].

Pahwa, Nikhil. 2010. "Mid Day introduces QR codes for rich content via mobile." *Medianama,* 18 February. www.medianama.com/2010/02/223-mid-day-introduces-qr-codes-for-rich-content-via-mobile/ [Accessed 15 March 2020].

Pavlik, John V. & Frank Bridges. 2013. "The emergence of augmented reality (AR) as a storytelling medium in journalism." *Journalism and Communication Monographs 15*(1), January: 4–59.

Press Gazette. 2013. "Independent claims world first as it uses 'augmented reality' app to enhance daily print content." *Press Gazette,* 23 April. www.pressgazette.co.uk/independent-claims-world-first-as-it-uses-augmented-reality-app-to-enhance-daily-print-content [Accessed 15 March 2020].

Radcliffe, Damian, Christopher Ali, & Rosalind Donald. 2017. "Life at small-market newspapers: Results from a survey of small market newsrooms." *Columbia University Academic Commons,* 16 May. https://academiccommons.columbia.edu/doi/10.7916/D8XP7BGC [Accessed 15 March 2020].

Raso, Rocco, Sebastian Cucerca, Dirk Werth, & Peter Loos. 2016. "Automated augmented reality content creation for print media." In: A. Lugmayr, E. Stojmenova, K. Stanoevska, & R. Wellington (eds), *Information Systems and Management in Media and Entertainment Industries.* International Series on Computer Entertainment and Media Technology. Cham, Switzerland: Springer.

Roettgers, Janko. 2019. "CNN launches app on Magic Leap One headset." *Variety,* 28 February. https://variety.com/2019/digital/news/cnn-magic-leap-one-app-1203151975/ [Accessed 15 March 2020].

Royakkers, Lamber, Jelte Timmer, Linda Kool, & Rinie van Est. 2018. "Societal and ethical issues of digitization." *Ethics and Information Technology 20*(2), March: 127–142.

Schmalstieg, Dieter, Tobias Langlotz, & Mark Billinghurst. 2011. "Augmented Reality 2.0." In: G. Brunnett, S. Coquillart, & G. Welch (eds), *Virtual Realities.* Vienna: Springer.

Scott, Caroline. 2016. "Hindustan Times uses Snapchat filters to enable sexual assault survivors to speak freely on camera." *Journalism.co.uk,* 11 July. www.journalism.co.uk/news/using-snapchat-s-filters-to-conceal-interviewee-identities/s2/a654554/ [Accessed 15 March 2020].

Siriborvornratanakul, Thitirat. 2018. "Enhancing user experiences of mobile-based augmented reality via spatial augmented reality: Designs and architectures of projector-camera devices." *Advances in Multimedia,* April: 1–17.

Southern, Lucinda. 2017. "Quartz adds augmented reality to its app, now with 780k downloads." *Digiday UK,* 9 October. https://digiday.com/media/quartz-finds-augmented-reality-drives-app-downloads/ [Accessed 15 March 2020].

Spark AR. 2018. Spark AR website. https://sparkar.facebook.com/ [Accessed 15 March 2020].

Stapinski, Helene. 2018. "Take a tour of Lady Liberty's torch (right this second)." *The New York Times,* 13 November. www.nytimes.com/interactive/2018/11/13/nyregion/statue-of-liberty-torch-ar-ul.html?action=click&module=RelatedLinks&pgtype= Article [Accessed 15 March 2020].

Statt, Nick. 2019. "These slick new AR glasses project shockingly high-quality visuals." *The Verge,* 9 January. www.theverge.com/circuitbreaker/2019/1/9/18176083/nreal-augmented-reality-ar-smart-glasses-features-pricing-release-date-ces-2019 [Accessed 15 March 2020].

Strange, Adario. 2018. "Magic Leap launches Cheddar Video news channel on Magic Leap One." *Magic Leap News,* 12 December. https://magic-leap.reality.news/news/magic-leap-launches-cheddar-video-news-channel-magic-leap-one-0191260/ [Accessed 15 March 2020].

Sutherland, Ivan. 1965. "The ultimate display." In: *Proceedings of the IFIP Congress*, pp. 506–508.

Swider, Matt & Michelle Fitzsimmons. 2019. "Magic Leap One release date, price and features." *Techradar,* 4 January. www.techradar.com/news/magic-leap-one [Accessed 15 March 2020].

Väätäjä, Heli K., Mari J. Ahvenainen, Markus S. Jaakola, & Thomas D. Olsson. 2013. "Exploring augmented reality for user-generated hyperlocal news content." Paper presented at CHI'13 Extended Abstracts on Human Factors in Computing Systems, Paris, 27 April. https://doi.org/10.1145/2468356.2468529 [Accessed 15 March 2020].

Valcarce, David. P., Concha E. Bolós, & Juan C.M. Recio. 2017. "Analysis of the application of augmented reality technologies in Spanish mass media productive processes." *Revista Latina De Comunicación Social 72*: 1670–1688.

WashPostPR. 2016. "The Washington Post releases augmented reality view of Freddie Gray's case." *The Washington Post PR* blog, 10 May. www.washingtonpost.com/pr/wp/2016/05/10/the-washington-post-releases-augmented-reality-view-of-freddie-grays-case/ [Accessed 15 March 2020].

Wassom, Brian. 2014. *Augmented reality law, privacy, and ethics: Law, society, and emerging AR technologies*. Waltham, MA: Syngress.

Witkin, Kira. 2013. "Independent integrates augmented reality into editorial workflow." *WAN-IFRA* blog, 26 April. https://blog.wan-ifra.org/2013/04/26/independent-integrates-augmented-reality-into-editorial-workflow [Accessed 15 March 2020].

Wolf, Marty J., Frances Grodzinsky, & Keith Miller. 2016. "Augmented reality all around us: Power and perception at a crossroads." ACM SIGCAS *Computers and Society 45*(3): 126–131.

Zhou, Tao. 2018. "Examining user adoption of mobile augmented reality applications." *International Journal of E-Adoption (IJEA) 10*(2), July: 37–49.

PART IV
Education

14

TEACHING IMMERSIVE JOURNALISM

Turo Uskali and Pasi Ikonen

This chapter draws from a study designed for this volume. Its main purpose was to answer two questions: 1) where has immersive journalism been taught? and 2) how to best teach immersive journalism?

This chapter adds value by offering an overview and fresh insights from some of the leading journalism educators in the world, focusing on the interplay of emergent technologies and journalism, especially in relation to immersive journalism. So far, journalism educators have not been at the forefront of immersive journalism studies, although journalists (Watson 2017; Aitamurto 2019), content (Jones 2017; Bosworth & Sarah 2019), and audiences, especially students (Sundar et al. 2017; Shin & Biocca 2018), have received attention.

Traditionally, journalism education has been rather slow in reacting to many technological changes (Deuze 2006). The change needed for journalism education has been emphasized from varying perspectives. Angus and Doherty (2015) have argued for design skills for students to be able to better understand digital platforms. Robinson (2013) has demanded radical changes in core curricula and reporting classes, arguing for teaching "journalism as process". Although technology adoption into journalism curricula has been slow, fresh entrants to the news industry have also been criticized by working veterans for lacking traditional skills, which have been superseded by technological emphasis in the curricula (Ferrucci 2018).

We first map the journalism educators that have been teaching Immersive Journalism courses. We proceed by giving some background information about the five journalism teachers chosen as interviewees. Next we present our results, and finally we summarize and discuss our results in the Conclusions section.

Mapping immersive journalism educators

To begin seeking out those journalism educators who have used immersive technologies in their classes, a desk study was implemented. We searched for global course listings and public announcements in English as well as online news articles on the topic using internet search engines. In addition, we also used the snowball sampling method (King et al. 2019, 62) during the interviews, and asked each interviewee to recommend another knowledgeable interviewee in terms of immersive journalism education.

We could find only a few teachers and courses. In reality, there are most probably many more, but nevertheless this initial listing (see Table 14.1) sketches the current status of the field, at least in the English-speaking parts of the world. Many of the courses have been one-time tryouts or experiments.

To understand how immersive journalism is being taught, a closer look at practice is needed. For this chapter, we conducted a set of interviews with five immersive journalism teachers from five different countries. The interviews were semi-structured (Ayress 2008, 810) and lasted from 25 minutes to one hour. They were conducted face-to-face (one interview) and via phone and video calls (four interviews). Table 14.2 presents the interviewees and their courses in their respective higher education institutions. The interview transcripts were analyzed in a qualitative manner using content analysis, and paraphrases related to teaching virtual reality (VR) were searched for.

In this next section we introduce the five courses in question and their instructors.

Associate Professor of Practice Robert Hernandez from the University of Southern California, Los Angeles (USC) has been teaching immersive technologies for journalism since 2012. He began with augmented reality (AR) before starting the ongoing VR course in 2015. At the same time, TV documentarist Nonny de la Peña, the "godmother" of immersive journalism, and Palmer Luckey, who later founded the head-mounted display company Oculus, were working at the USC's Mixed Reality Lab. During recent years, Hernandez and his students have won several awards, especially thanks to their Jovrnalism app that includes several immersive journalism stories. Jovrnalism has received awards from the Online News Association, the Association for Education in Journalism and Mass Communication, the Los Angeles Press Club, The Webby Awards, and the World Journalism Education Congress. In addition, from March to April 2017, Hernandez ran the very first MOOC (massive open online course) on immersive journalism, "Intro to Immersive Journalism: Virtual Reality & 360 video". It was offered by the Knight Center for Journalism in the Americas at the University of Texas at Austin. During the course, students produced VR, AR, and mixed reality productions, some of which ended up on the project's website and were distributed further.

Senior Lecturer Ben Stubbs of the University of South Australia (UniSA) at Adelaide in Australia created the course "VR Storytelling" in 2017. It is being taught for the third time in autumn 2019. In the course, students learn about VR in general, the use of 360-degree cameras, editing, creating their own stories, and

TABLE 14.1 A selection of journalism schools teaching immersive journalism

Country	*University*	*Teacher(s)*	*Course/class (or part of a course)*	*Active?*
Australia	University of South Australia	Ben Stubbs	Virtual Reality Storytelling	2017 -
Belgium	University of Antwerp	Kristof Timmerman and others	Summer course "Storytelling in Virtual Reality"	2019
Denmark	Danish School of Media and Journalism	Mette Sejsbo	Virtual Reality Storytelling	2018 -
Finland	University of Jyväskylä	Panu Uotila	Part of a Multimedia Journalism course	2018
Norway	University of Bergen	Lars Nyre	Journalistic Prototyping (VR journalism using Samsung Gear)	2018
			Design for Media Use (focus on VR narratives for HTC Vive)	2019
	University of Stavanger	Sigmund Trageton and others	Part of a Multimedia Storytelling course	2018
			Part of an Audiovisual Storytelling course	2019
Sweden	Södertorn University	Malin Picha Edwardsson and others	Part of the Storylab project	2015
			Part of a course at the Media Technology department	2019
United States	University of Southern California, Annenberg School of Communication	Robert Hernandez	Emergent Technologies in Journalism	2012 -
	Stanford University	Geri Migielicz, Janine Zacharia	Immersive Journalism class	2016
	Syracuse University	Dan Pacheco	Virtual Reality Storytelling	2015 -
	Hofstra University School of Communication	Aashish Kumar	Virtual Reality Storytelling	2017 -
	University of California, Berkeley	Melissa Bosworth, Lakshmi Sarah	Workshop: VR: Immersive 360-Degree Video Storytelling	2018 -
United Kingdom	Coventry University & Birmingham City University	Sarah Jones	Part of Innovation Journalism courses	2015 -

ethical questions related to this form of storytelling. Stubbs has acquired AUD 50,000 in grants to explore VR in journalism education. The course won the 2018 Innovation in Journalism award from the Journalism Education and Research Association Australia, awarded by *The Guardian*. The university is currently the only one in Australia with a Practical VR Journalism course. The course is 12 weeks long (with a two-hour seminar every week) and has 15 students from Journalism and Media Arts. They use seven Insta 360 One cameras and have created their own editing software Immerse, which enables the use of interactive storytelling for 360-degree videos. As coursework, students produce six-minute videos with interactivity included.

Lecturer Mette Sejsbo of the Danish School of Media and Journalism (DJMX) at Copenhagen in Denmark teaches in the Department of TV and Media Direction. They provide basic training in producing and directing journalistic and documentary productions in VR, more specifically 360-degree videos. The course was run for the first time in 2017 with 40 students. The intensive course lasted for three weeks, focusing on creativity. In 2018, the VR workshop was held as part of a six-week Documentary course. During the course, the students used ten sets of Samsung equipment, including a phone, a pair of VR glasses, and a camera. The students produced documentaries and made one scene from the film also for VR. Sejsbo teaches the course with other lecturers as well as some outside visitors, for example former students and Danish Broadcasting Company journalists.

Senior Lecturer Malin Picha Edwardsson of Södertörn University at Stockholm, Sweden has taught courses that incorporate new technology, including VR, into journalism classes. While working at KTH Royal Institute of Technology in Stockholm, she taught in a Storylab class (Hultén & Picha Edwardsson 2017) in cooperation with Stockholm University. In this class, Media Technology Engineering students worked together with Journalism students, creating stories using different technologies. One group used VR to tell a story about parental leave. The course started with five weeks of lectures, followed by a workshop. They then worked eight weeks on the group projects.

Assistant Professor Sigmund Trageton of the University of Stavanger in Norway teaches VR and 360-degree filming as part of an Audiovisual Storytelling course. The course is for third-year bachelor students of Television and Multimedia Production. The course lasts the whole autumn term, and students acquire ten points in the European Credit Transfer and Accumulation System (ECTS) from it. The section on multimedia, in which VR is introduced, takes about 40 percent of the time of the full course. There are 16 students in the class this year, and Trageton is leading the course with two colleagues. The course combines lectures, seminars, and workshops. They are equipped with one GoPro Omni camera, Kolor stitching software, and they use Premiere Pro and Pro Tools for editing. In 2018, Trageton and Espen Reiss Mathiesen taught a similar but smaller-scale VR class for Journalism and Television Production students, as part of a Multimedia Storytelling course.

Having introduced our interviewees, we present the results from the qualitative interviews. We identify some recurring themes, including practical skills,

TABLE 14.2 Immersive journalism educators interviewed

Interviewee and institution	*Course description*
Robert Hernandez Associate Professor of Practice University of Southern California (USC)	Journalism course. Using VR, AR, and mixed reality technologies.
Ben Stubbs Senior Lecturer University of South Australia (UniSA)	VR Storytelling course since 2017. 12-week course with 15 students producing 360-degree videos with interactivity.
Mette Sejsbo Lecturer Danish School of Media and Journalism (DJMX)	Virtual Reality Storytelling with varying forms. Currently as a one-week part of a larger Documentary course.
Malin Picha Edwardsson Senior Lecturer Södertörn University	Introducing VR as a part of a more general Journalism and Media Technology course.
Sigmund Trageton Assistant Professor University of Stavanger	Introducing 360 filming and VR as a part of a course on Audiovisual Storytelling. One student group doing their coursework as a 360-degree video.

multidisciplinary cooperation, challenges with technology and time, course updating, larger questions to be addressed, and selecting the right technologies for classes. A few main challenges concerning teaching were also highlighted: learning the technology, motivating students to invest in the medium, time constraints, and the lack of examples from other universities.

The challenge of emergent technologies in teaching

How immersive storytelling is taught varies in scale and style. Reading the interviews reveals how teachers emphasize the importance of a hands-on approach and the role of students in learning. While immersive technologies are new to most students, enough time is required for them to be able to try out the equipment, experiment with filming in 360-degrees and work through the difficulties posed by new hardware and software. At the same time as students are learning the equipment, it is aging quickly. Most mid-range cameras used five years ago do not offer sufficient quality anymore.

Thus, one challenge is how to enable students to learn valuable skills and competences that are not tied to specific equipment. Many interviewees noted the variability of the hype around VR and changing forecasts on whether the technology will remain relevant in journalism or be forgotten. Nevertheless, students can learn valuable things from these courses, as was noted by Ben Stubbs and Sigmund Trageton.

During two years of teaching VR at UniSA, Ben Stubbs has noted the value of practical skills for students. They start with an introduction, talking about VR's history and its connection to journalism. The next two weeks are spent learning the cameras, followed by a week of learning how to edit in Premiere Pro. The following weeks are dedicated to using their own editing software Immerse, interactivity, ethics, troubleshooting, and visiting an industry partner. The rest of the time is left open for students to work on their projects.

The UniSA course is taught with two teachers equally sharing the teaching load. The teachers have found that it is also beneficial to join each other's seminars for learning. Ben Stubbs notes the benefit of the small class size. Giving a strong foundation for the basic elements of 360-degree storytelling is crucial, so that the students are able to produce high-quality works. Before they start working on actual footage, the students do a written assignment, where they go through a set of questions, including why the story suits VR, what the role of the viewer is going to be, how the shots are planned, how interactivity will be used, and whether the topic could be filmed in another way.

Similarly, at the University of Stavanger, the VR part of the course, led by Sigmund Trageton, begins with a historical perspective, examining the differences in the VR medium compared to other formats. Then it proceeds to workshops about the equipment and software, and finally a course assignment for a real-life client. Although the end product of the assignment is fact-based immersive storytelling, it is not strictly a journalistic product, as it is aimed as educational material for eighth-grade primary school students.

Multiple teacher roles

Immersive journalism teachers may have multiple roles. During the time Robert Hernandez has been teaching his course since 2012, he has developed special methods and pedagogical insights for higher education that deserve to be explained in detail and at length. His teaching strategy mixes journalistic, managerial, diplomatic, and entrepreneurial skills in a way that could be seen as a rarity or even unique in journalism education.

First, as an educator he works like a journalist.

> I'm still a journalist. I'm still looking at when the story or a trend is happening. And I find a way [...] As a reporter, I get informed. It is an informed, educated hunch. Right, so I have learned enough. If I start to think that I know all the answers without interviewing and learning [from] the community, that's the problem.

Second, Hernandez says that he has applied previous managerial knowledge to his Journalism courses. This could also be interpreted as part of an entrepreneurial mindset. Giving the course participants autonomy in their work is one important aspect.

Third, he gives a lot of power and trust to his students. He has tried to work with his colleagues, inside industry and inside the university, but it did not work out.

> They [students] bring us the skills and passions and they produce things. Even if I have a really creative imagination [and a] thinking, innovative mind, they bring it forward. We bring each other forward.

Hernandez acknowledges that if one gives too much freedom to the students it could paralyze them, so it is important to find the right balance.

> So, I found ways to put a framework around it. Okay, you have a canvas about homelessness. You have a canvas [about] making it work with this media company. These are the limitations, but there is still this freedom and those limitations to create, but it is not paralyzing.

In addition, he says that the students are also the key to changing the industry in the near future.

> My students that may have graduated, let's say, five years ago, are eventually going to be the boss. And they're going to apply the mindset there. So playing the long game and hopefully inspiring and innovating the media companies that are slow to do that.

As good examples of news media organizations that are constantly innovating, Hernandez mentions *The New York Times*, *USA Today*, and Al Jazeera.

Fourth, Hernandez clearly works like a producer and a hub-builder. Even if his employer is one of the best-funded universities in the world, his courses have not enjoyed vast resources. They have needed to create their own innovator hub strategy, bringing together an academic institution, industry, and media partners. He constantly connects media organizations and technology companies together in order to test new emergent technologies via journalism education.

> So, the traditional professor-academic industry relationship was to ask industry, "What do you need?" I would train people to give them. Industry now, [it] does not know what it needs. It is not funded enough to think ahead. So, I'm taking advantage of that and saying, "I know what the industry needs". I'm going to create. I wanna be the R&D for the industry.

Hernandez and his students have freedom to experiment with new formats. They can also work simultaneously with industry partners that usually do not cooperate. For example, in the case of President Donald Trump's inauguration and the women's march in January 2017, Hernandez and his students produced content both for *The New York Times* and National Public Radio (NPR). In addition, Samsung funded the 360-degree cameras for the students.

To sum up, Hernandez's teaching strategies could be defined as long-term innovation pedagogy. Even if emergent technologies come and go and cycle through different maturation phases, journalism schools could be innovative test labs for the future of journalism. This could be done with the help of the students' creativity and risk-taking, supporting media-tech industry hubs, and the journalist/manager leading the project.

Multidisciplinary approach

Australian Ben Stubbs argues that bringing in students from different disciplines has been beneficial. Students with Communication and Media degrees are joining the course alongside Journalism majors. Stubbs finds the whole nature of immersive journalism so different from conventional journalistic storytelling, and that the different skillsets brought by students benefit the group work.

For Senior Lecturer Malin Picha Edwardsson, group work combining four Engineering students with one Journalism student proved to be challenging. She attributes this to the students from different backgrounds "speaking in different languages", and having trouble with group collaboration: "By the time we got them [the groups] to actually function, then time had run out for making the final result". Obviously, this was a valuable learning experience for the students.

In their Storylab class project, Edwardsson and her colleagues gained insights into various challenges that new technology can introduce. As immersive technologies were introduced on a small scale as part of a larger class, technical issues often came up. Lack of time to test the equipment as well as teach how to use it can frustrate students, and the full potential for learning storytelling is missed. Moreover, VR was only part of the course, and learning the technology became a major challenge for successful work. The students did not have the right equipment nor anyone to teach them how to work with that technology properly, so they were facing a tough test.

Getting new software to work also caused problems during the first year of Sejsbo's course at DJMX. The programs worked slowly, causing students to spend hours of time just waiting. Taking the VR class for the first time, Sejsbo's students were not very excited. The equipment was not working properly, and for some groups not at all: "So their experience of, 'Can this do something?' was very limited – it was an eye-opener to all the difficulties".

In the following year, VR storytelling was incorporated into a longer six-week course in which the students produced flatscreen documentaries. They were instructed to make an extra VR production of one scene from the documentary. This time, as students were occupied in working with the flatscreen documentaries, they did not put energy into the VR production, and felt that it was an "irritating appendix". In autumn 2019 the course has been adjusted again so that the last week of the Documentary course will be reserved for VR storytelling. Based on the previous experiences, the teachers are now very aware of the limitations with the equipment, and are aiming to avoid frustrating the students.

Sigmund Trageton has found that the students need more time for the planning phase of the filming. Another point he notes is understanding how to structure stories with this technology.

> I don't think the students knew how much work it would take, from a technical point of view. And maybe they also thought that it would be easier in a way, to tell compelling stories, because of the medium itself [...] If we want to have a better quality of the end product, we also need to give them more time and more teaching about this medium. But like the plan is now for this semester, it's [that] we have so much other things to teach them.

Ben Stubbs has recognized that there is much to be taught in a short time. Overburdening the students with too much information is a risk, he states. It is challenging to get students to handle all the storytelling aspects, including the use of interactivity.

> Because a lot of what they are going to learn comes from experimenting, during that month during the teaching break, where they are going to take the camera and go out and make some mistakes. And they come back to the edit suite, and they realize, "Hey, we should've done this." So, it's kind of balancing.

Bigger questions at play, such as ethics

Stubbs noted that setting proper requirements for the students' coursework is important. Previously, students were producing only linear stories. From 2019, the UniSA course requires use of interactivity. Students can add branching storylines in the Immerse editing application using hot spots that can be accessed via focusing the user's gaze on them.

> Just playing with that idea, that what a story in VR can be. That journalism normally is that beginning, middle, and end, but this allows [them] to do something different.

Even though the course held by Mette Sejsbo at DJMX is an introduction to the technology, bigger questions are immediately also at play. These include topics such as the role of VR in journalism and what it should be used for. Students are eager to discuss these dilemmas.

Final coursework from students of Sejsbo's documentary class in 2018 was very varied in quality and style. Some of the best works included small stories where the viewer was taken into a place not very well-known to many, for example showing a wheelchair-user's view of the world. For Sejsbo, an intriguing aspect in teaching VR storytelling is the question of what it means for our way of telling stories. She asks what the effects of this are on learning and engaging people:

> If we want to speak so much as VR supposedly does, or that's what the producers hope it does, engage people more, what is the cost on the information level? [...] And also, to say, if we use VR, if we go for it, what kind of things should it be for?

Therefore, when teaching VR journalism or documentary-making, it is important also to consider why the format is being used. Sejsbo wants to teach the students to tell stories in a new way and understand 360-degree stories and their consequences in portraying our world. Finding the proper narrative tools for VR journalism is important.

Sigmund Trageton feels that the students need to experience the medium in order to understand it properly.

> I think if you're gonna use VR or 360, you have to experience it in a head-mounted display. If not, it's a little bit, you know, in between.

Ethical questions are part of the UniSA coursework. Stubbs wants the students to be aware of what the so-called gray areas in VR ethics are. Stubbs hopes that students make deliberate choices concerning ethics while they produce their own course assignments.

Stubbs states that the notion of what a journalist is can and should be questioned to some extent. As future roles of journalists are still debatable, journalism educators should remain alert to how the field is changing.

Selecting the right technologies to work with

There are emergent technologies coming up all the time. For these technologies to be picked up by Hernandez's class at USC, they need to be interesting, currently available, affordable, modifiable, and not locked to a specific environment. The class should be able to make their own product and brand it as such. In essence, Hernandez's class is not trying to come up with new technologies but adapting affordable emergent technologies and innovating new forms for journalism.

> I focus on all the emergent technologies, [with] immersive as a focus [...] 360-degree video is still a valid platform, [an] incredible medium that can tell stories no other medium can tell. It is also a fantastic way to onboard people to the immersive platform.

UniSA students appreciate the future-oriented nature of the VR course, Stubbs notes. Even if the hype for VR journalism has cooled down in recent years, Stubbs sees learning 360-degree storytelling as an advantage for students' future careers. These kinds of skills might not be in use in many newsrooms, but having a "bag of tricks" that the newsrooms do not yet possess might come in handy later on.

Trageton emphasizes that teaching about VR also teaches students about other forms of audiovisual communication that they are learning at the same time. Making the students conscious about the differences in each medium takes time.

> So, then my main philosophy is that [...] by learning this new medium, they learn that it's a different medium, and by learning a different medium, they also learn more about the older media, like film and still photography [...] I think it needs quite a long time for the students to understand this.

Future prospects

In 2019, as the VR hype cooled down, Hernandez again focused more on AR in his Emergent Technologies class. Hernandez is convinced that, with fast mobile 5G internet networks, immersive technologies will prevail, even though quality content that excites the average consumer is still needed for a breakthrough.

> AR, for me and all in the industry, is the long game. That will have more mass adoption than VR [...] And when we are living in [a] mobile first world, AR is mobile-friendly. You already have the devices. So, then we talk about what kind of experiences you do wanna create and what kind of assets you need to create.

Hernandez noted that AR technology has matured on a variety of fronts, including mainstream developer platforms available from Apple and Google as well as Unity plugins. Making 3D models is becoming easier and more accessible. To also investigate how immersive journalism is distributed, Hernandez is utilizing different platforms, including Snapchat.

Due to the evolving nature of the technology, Stubbs notes, the UniSA course requires constant updating, both of the equipment and of what to teach.

> It does require more attention than other courses. Just in terms of tweaking and making sure that we are aware of new things in the industry as well. Because, even from the lectures I wrote three years ago, things have changed quite a lot. I think the optimism has dimmed a little.

On another note, according to Stubbs, course expenses have come down. For example, the cameras are much cheaper than three years ago, the editing is easier, and the picture quality is better.

To develop teaching, getting insights from other universities would be beneficial. In Stubbs' view, this would enable him to benchmark courses and also to collaborate. Currently, UniSA is the only Australian university with a Practical VR course.

Trageton remains unsure about continuing the 360-video part of the course during the coming years. They might add more emphasis on the medium, buy some cheaper, handier cameras, or, alternatively, remove it completely to have more time for other parts of the course.

Conclusions

From web-based searches and five experts' semi-structured interviews, we can argue that teaching immersive journalism is still a rarity in the world. Journalism educators have tended to be followers and not proactive innovators in terms of adapting new tools or practices in their education work (Deuze 2006). This is also true in terms of immersive journalism. Technology alone, be it VR or some other, will not save journalism or journalism education (Creech & Mendelson 2015); but still we argue that it would be unwise to ignore any new technologies' potentiality for transforming or at least influencing journalistic storytelling.

Nevertheless, according to our findings, there has been a small number of journalism schools and professors willing to be at the forefront of VR journalism, 360-degree journalism, and even AR journalism. It seems that leading journalism schools, especially in California, have adapted and adopted the idea of Deuze's (2006) innovator model in their journalism education. The Annenberg School of Communication at the University of Southern California in Los Angeles, Stanford University's Virtual Reality Lab's collaboration with Stanford's Journalism Master of Arts (MA) program, and also the School of Journalism at the University of California, Berkeley, have all taught immersive journalism. Not surprisingly, many of the first VR companies were started either in Silicon Valley or near Los Angeles (Lanier 2018; Bailenson 2018).

Moreover, in other parts of the world, from Australia to the United Kingdom and Nordic countries, immersive journalism has been in the curricula. One of the shortcomings of this chapter clearly is that we did not get any information about immersive journalism teaching in Asia, Africa, or South America. Further explorations of global immersive journalism education are needed.

Five immersive journalism teachers from Australia, Denmark, Norway, Sweden, and the United States were interviewed, with the main question being how to best teach immersive journalism. The answer was manifold. In other words, there is a great variety of models of how to teach immersive journalism, but they all relate to innovation pedagogy, which emphasizes exploration and risk-taking. As immersive journalism is still small in its scope, only a few universities have created dedicated courses. There is room for the development of VR journalism around the world; for example, Stubbs (2018) has argued that mastering VR techniques would be a valuable asset for Australian journalism students.

Clearly, we need more research about the importance and role of online communities in terms of adapting new emergent technologies in journalism.

References

Aitamurto, Tanja. 2019. "Normative Paradoxes in 360-degree Journalism: Contested Accuracy and Objectivity." *New Media & Society 21*(1), January: 3–19. doi:10.1177/1461444818785153

Angus, Daniel & Skye Doherty. 2015. "Journalism Meets Interaction Design: An Interdisciplinary Undergraduate Teaching Initiative." *Journalism & Mass Communication Educator 70*(1), March: 44–57.

Ayress, Lioness. 2008. "Semi-Structured Interview." In: L.M. Given (ed.), *The SAGE Encyclopedia of Qualitative Research Methods* Volumes 1–2. Thousand Oaks, CA: SAGE.

Bailenson, Jeremy. 2018. *Experience on Demand: What Virtual Reality Is, How It Works, and What It Can Do*. 1st ed. New York: W.W. Norton & Company.

Bosworth, Melissa & Lakshmi Sarah. 2019. *Crafting Stories for Virtual Reality*. Abingdon-on-Thames, UK: Routledge.

Creech, Brian & Andrew L. Mendelson. 2015. "Imagining the Journalist of the Future: Technological Visions of Journalism Education and Newswork." *The Communication Review 18*(2), May: 142–165.

Deuze, Mark. 2006. "Global Journalism Education: A Conceptual Approach." *Journalism Studies* 7(1), August: 19–34.

Ferrucci, Patrick. 2018. "'We've Lost the Basics': Perceptions of Journalism Education From Veterans in the Field." *Journalism & Mass Communication Educator 73*(4), December: 410–420. doi:10.1177/1077695817731870

Hultén, Gunilla & Malin Picha Edwardsson. 2017. "Storylab Lessons: A Collaborative Project Between Courses in Journalism and Media Technology." *Nordicom Review 39*(1), May: 3–17.

Jones, Sarah. 2017. "Disrupting the Narrative: Immersive Journalism in Virtual Reality." *Journal of Media Practice 18*(2–3), July-November: 171–185.

King, Nigel, Christine Horrocks, & Joanna Brooks. 2019. *Interviews in Qualitative Research*. 2nd ed. London: SAGE.

Lanier, Jaron. 2018. *Dawn of the New Everything: Encounters with Reality and Virtual Reality*. New York: Henry Holt and Co.

Robinson, Sue. 2013. "Teaching 'Journalism as Process': A Proposed Paradigm for J-School Curricula in the Digital Age." *Teaching Journalism & Mass Communication 3*(1), Winter: 1–12.

Shin, Donghee & Frank Biocca. 2018. "Exploring Immersive Experience in Journalism." *New Media & Society 20*(8), August: 2800–2823. doi:10.1177/1461444817733133

Stubbs, Ben. 2018. "Virtual Reality Journalism: Ethics, Grammar and the State of Play." *Australian Journalism Review 40*(1), July: 81–90.

Sundar, S. Shyam, Jin Kang, & Danielle Oprean. 2017. "Being There in the Midst of the Story: How Immersive Journalism Affects Our Perceptions and Cognitions." *Cyberpsychology, Behavior, and Social Networking 20*(11), November: 672–682.

Watson, Zillah. 2017. *VR for News: The New Reality*? Digital News Project. Oxford, UK: Reuters Institute for the Study of Journalism, Oxford University. https://reutersinstitute.politics.ox.ac.uk/our-research/vr-news-new-reality [Accessed 15 March 2020].

15

IMMERSIVE JOURNALISM AS WITNESSING[1]

Lars Nyre and Joakim Vindenes

VR is nothing if not spectacular. It may be difficult to envision that, instead of getting mobile news via written text, photos and videos, and phone-size screens, you would get the news in the perceptual richness of head-mounted displays that allow a 360-degree visual and auditory sphere in which the body of the user is immersed. Technologies are launched in improved versions, and the skillsets and creativity of content producers are also growing.

What's in it for journalism? It is established knowledge that VR narratives are effective for creating first-person perspectives, or what we propose to call "witnessing" (Peters 2001). In the context of immersive journalism, de la Peña et al. (2010, 299) write that "virtual reality systems are uniquely fitted to deliver first-person experiences of stories that appear in the news", and that "immersive journalism offers the opportunity of a uniquely different level of understanding contrasted to reading the printed page or passively watching audiovisual material".

Witnessing seems to be a storytelling technique with potential in a still emerging journalistic practice. In their 2015 report on VR Journalism, the Tow Center writes how VR "represents a new narrative form, one for which technical and stylistic norms are in their infancy" (Owen et al. 2015) and where audience behavior is undecided. For example, traditional visual aesthetics are oriented to the rectangular frame. In 360-degree video it is a striking storytelling dilemma that there is no rectangular frame for the photojournalist in which to place the motif and action. Another example is that 360-degree video makes the journalist/cameraperson visible in the footage unless steps are taken to avoid it by placing the camera on a tripod, or having a cameraperson wear it on their head. There is a need for conceptualization and analysis that would help to clarify things and give audiences a more directed and meaningful experience. Otherwise VR stories may risk feeling empty and shallow, and therefore unable to engage audiences in a proper way. The Knight Foundation's 2016 report on Virtual Reality in Journalism states that the expressive novelties may be a "challenge to journalistic storytellers more familiar with taking the audience along a single narrative ride" (Doyle et al. 2016).

The media industry will no doubt continue to explore storytelling possibilities by trial and error, regulated by their rate of market popularity and technological developments. And in addition to journalistic innovation there is room for more education-driven design experiments. We believe that higher education institutions (HEIs) should explore VR journalism at the bachelor and master level, so that students could contribute with genuinely valuable skillsets and techniques that will have been developed under more open, self-critical, and reflective conditions than what the hectic media industry is able to provide.

In this chapter we report on a design experiment where VR stories were made as mandatory coursework. Four quite different journalistic stories are analyzed in light of two theoretical traditions. Phenomenology explains the experience of being present at the scene and helps to describe what witnessing means in this context. Narrative theory shows the importance of the position that is implied for the user in the narrative. We apply these theoretical perspectives in an analysis of the VR stories scene by scene and show what type of witnessing they should be characterized as being. At the end, there is a discussion of the journalistic value or appropriateness of such types of witnessing.

Method: a pedagogical design experiment

The material we analyze in this article was created in a pedagogical design experiment conducted in 2018. In the learning sciences there is a longstanding tradition of doing design experiments with student groups, trying to teach them new skills and techniques (Brown 1992) and design-based research (Barab & Squire 2004; Collins, Joseph, and Bielaczyc 2004). Such studies involve making interventions in existing educational settings by introducing new technologies, and they are intended to create positive changes in the learning practices and at the same time allow researchers to study the implications of the intervention. Teachers want to make changes to the mediating technologies involved in coursework, such as introducing 360-degree video where the course previously used 16:9 frame video, and to the organizing of learning activities inspired by a given pedagogical goal, like challenging the students to narrate in VR while simultaneously adhering to established journalistic values. In an earlier design experiment, Nyre, Guribye, & Gynnild (2018, 82–83) combined innovation pedagogy with drone-flying and 3D-modelling for journalism. Building on experience from the former study, the method for the present design experiment was as follows:

1) Students were given plenty of time to use the technology and develop new skills. Students needed to acquire the necessary motor skills for dealing with the creative possibilities of using the novel technology. The students had to use the equipment provided by the university. For each group, this comprised a Samsung GEAR VR Head-Mounted Display, a Ricoh Theta V 360 camera,

and a monopod stand. The students were also required to attend mandatory technical training, wherein they were taught VR programming, principles of 360-video production (such as placement of camera, editing, and tips and tricks), and 3D modelling through photogrammetry. The students also attended sessions on storyboarding and visual aesthetics for each separate scene.

2) Teachers made a working definition of journalism. The students were supposed to create genre-consistent journalism with the new tools. A working definition of journalism was formulated in communication with the students: 1) use proper sources for all information presented, 2) no use of hidden microphones or cameras, and 3) be careful not to violate people's right to privacy. 4) Realistic reconstructions are allowed. Notice that the concept of "witnessing" was not central to the design experiment, but emerged analytically after the fact.
3) Students storyboarded, shot, and edited everything themselves. Principles from innovation pedagogy say that students should make as many decisions as possible, while teachers should make as few as possible (Darsø 2011, 15). The presumption is that students will learn more intensely under conditions where they are responsible for exploring the uncertain terrain. We accomplished this by asking the groups to present their productions five times during the semester, with specific requirements and deadlines for each. They received criticism and technical feedback from lecturers, media industry guests, and fellow students. At the end of the course there was a public demo in Media City Bergen attended by around a hundred people who could all trial the VR stories.

The team of researchers and teachers was aware of an ethical dilemma with our approach. The primary author of this text was the main lecturer on the course, and the second author was the main VR instructor. There was a risk of blurring the boundary between teaching and research, so that the students could see us as powerful graders and collegial researchers. We needed to make clear demarcations between our roles. At the beginning of the course we informed the students about the design experiment governing the course, and they attended several research events where VR journalism was discussed. In order not to confuse the student productions with empirical material generated by researchers, we made sure that their VR stories were presented as autonomous productions with due credit given at a public event and on the ViSmedia website. Students and lecturers are all thanked in an afterword to this chapter to further emphasize their contribution. The following analysis was conceived and conducted several months after the course had been completed, and our considerations therefore did not influence the production of the stories.

Four VR journalism stories

Eighteen students were divided into four groups and given the following design challenge: Create a journalistic narrative in the medium of virtual reality, using sound, 360-degree video, and animations. The end product should be a three-minute experience tested by members of a live audience. This design experiment resulted in four original VR stories. Since these stories are integral to our argument in this chapter, they are summarized below:

> "Plastics" is a factual, documentary story told to children around 8–12 years old. The topic is the environmental crisis, with plastic waste in focus. The story is based on journalistic research into pollution, recirculation, and other environmental issues. There is an explicit narrator hovering above the 360 universe, with a calm, friendly, authoritative, adult voice. "Plastics" belongs to the genre of educational program or enlightenment.
>
> "Cryonics" is a factual, documentary story told to young adults. Four different human avatars present their opinions about cryonically freezing your body when you die. The program offers no conclusions. The information is based on research with a priest, ethical philosopher, medical doctor, and cryonics enthusiast. "Cryonics" tentatively belongs to the genre of science journalism or infotainment.
>
> "Drug Addict" is a socially realistic, dogmatic, rough aesthetics documentary. A series of quick scenes pulls us into the dramatic overdose of an average drug addict. The story is based on research and conversations with drug addicts and is filmed on location. The group had to handle ethical issues regarding identification and used actors to recreate the life of a drug addict. "Drug Addict" belongs to the genre of "social documentary" that has existed for decades on television and film.
>
> "Schizophrenia" is an educational first-person simulation of the reality-shattering disorder of schizophrenia, giving the user an experience of visual and auditory hallucinations suffered by patients of this mental disorder. It is based on interviews with doctors and patients, and stages a three-part dramatization of the psychiatric disorder. "Schizophrenia" also belongs to the genre of "social documentary", but the first-person perspective makes it particularly striking.

Theories that explain witnessing

Media phenomenology considers that there is an intimate relation between human perception and media technology. Perceptual phenomenology describes the general features of individual bodily experience, and it argues that perception is an active search for information about the environment. Individuals apply their bodily skills and explorative strategies toward the object in question (Merleau-Ponty 1945). Merleau-Ponty stresses that your body has a temporal horizon – past, present, future – and a spatial horizon – near and far away. While being present you are at all times also in the middle of an experience.

During interactions with media our human perception becomes mediated or augmented by technical means. As Carr (1995) puts it: "taking virtual reality seriously means understanding the process by which technology can fool our perceptions" by "creating a synthetic environment" (3). He argues that virtual reality can be understood as "the stimulation of human perceptual experience to create an impression of something which is not really there" (5). The experience that is stimulated must be a very complex one if it is to fool perception.

Witnessing is an established reporting technique in radio and television. The speaker acquires authority because he is present at the scene of an important event, and the public gets a realistic description of it (Nyre 2008). When someone witnesses an event it is in a sense the event itself that speaks. It demands a realistic description of its properties, and the speaker is in what Erving Goffman (1981, 233) calls a "slave relation" to it. To witness something has two aspects: the passive one of seeing and the active one of saying. Witnessing in the rhetorical sense is therefore "the discursive act of stating one's experience for the benefit of an audience that was not present at the event and yet must make some kind of judgment about it" (Peters 2001, 709). The listener is in no position to challenge the truth claim of the story and is likely to trust it. Peters (2001, 710) says that witnessing presumes a discrepancy between the ignorance of one person and the knowledge of another.

On the basis of this explanation of witnessing, we can conceptualize a first-person witness that experiences the event by being placed in a synthetic, 360-degree audiovisual version of it. Instead of a journalistic reporter recounting what happened, the user experiences it first-hand. Nash (2018, 119) uses the concept of "immersive witness" in a way that fits with Peters' description: "The notion of immersive witness underpins much of the exploration of virtual reality (VR) by journalists and humanitarian organisations. Immersive witness links the experience of VR with a moral attitude of responsibility for distant others". Damiani and Southard (2017) argue that:

> Presence in VR is the sensation of being in the space of a given experience, of sharing that space with characters, of *being there*. [...] Your audience will feel an increased sense of responsibility [...] *Why am I here?* and *What should I do?*
>
> *Damiani & Southard 2017*

To make good witnessing, the producers need to create more than a realistic feeling of presence; there must also be a story with an address and a plotline. Chatman (1978) shows how a story is directed towards the users to persuade them to take up the desired subject position. First, the implied author is "reconstructed by the reader from the narrative" (148). In our case it is the institution of news journalism, and the requirements for trustworthiness, truthfulness, and relevance. Second, the implied reader is written into the narrative as a subject position that the reader can take up to varying degrees. Iser (1978) points out how "The text must therefore *bring about* a standpoint from which the reader will be able to view things that would never have come into focus as long as his own habitual dispositions were determining his orientation" (Iser 1978, 35).

Analysis: witnessing in various shapes and strengths

The first part of our analysis consists of a description of the qualities that create an implied witness in various shapes and strengths in the four journalistic stories made by students. We point to the many different structural and material organizations that allow a VR spectator to accept the idea that she is personally on the scene, even though she sits in a chair wearing a VR headset.

Learning like a child

In "Plastics" the implied reader is a witness in the passive sense. You are positioned as a child at the age of approximately eight to twelve years who is interested in learning about plastics pollution in the Norwegian environment. The child is positioned as listening to a kind of teacher. There is time to explore and orient oneself in the virtual environment as the narrator tells a story. The position is that you are interactively involved in exploring the factual information, which can generate learning. But the learner is not a particular person in the story.

Scene 1: You are at a beach on the Western coast of Norway. The beach is apparently spotless, but as you turn your head around you see pieces of plastic. A voice gives an introduction to the plastic problem and the damage it does to sea and wildlife. The sound is recorded on location, and there are sounds of waves and seagulls. When the voiceover is complete, the user can move on to Scene 2.

Scene 2: You are at a football pitch. Modeled plastic objects slowly but surely fill the football pitch, giving you a feeling of being "locked in" by plastic – such as, presumably, the fish in the sea also feel. There is a locative sound indicating that a new object has popped up, and applause and ballpark shouts that gradually diminish as more plastic piles up on the pitch.

Scene 3: You are at a big recycling station with noisy factory sounds, bright lights, and things moving around on conveyor belts. You can fix your gaze on different objects in the factory space, and click on them with the hand controller to hear and see more. You can click and listen for around a minute before you have tried all the material.

Imagine being dead and cryonically frozen

In "Cryonics" the implied reader is also a witness in a rather passive sense. You are supposed to lie on a reclining chair to have the best starting position. First you are positioned as an adult lying on an operating table dying, and after your death you are addressed by four explicit narrators with strong opinions about cryonics. You are obviously involved, since you are supposedly dead and in the cryonic tube, but nevertheless you only overhear or witness the statements from the speakers.

Nothing happens to you along the way, and you cannot act beyond launching the different speeches.

> Scene 1: You start the experience on an operating table. You see stressed doctors, an X-ray, a heart monitor, and a blood bag. The situation of the patient is critical and he is about to die. The scene ends by one of the doctors "closing your eyes", an indication that you are dying. For a short while you are in a kind of "intermediate stage" floating through space before entering a mysterious tube.
>
> Scene 2: You are in a tank of frozen liquid nitrogen. To create the mood in the tank, there are different sound effects. One is a constant, low-frequency drone sound, another is of dripping water. Sometimes you can also hear hydraulics pushing out air. The tank has a blue tint, and there are chilling smoke effects inside it. First you get an explanatory speech on why you are in the tank. Wherever a symbol appears, when you look at this, the symbol will be turned into a face. The information is presented in an abstract rather than realistic way. The symbols in the three-dimensional environment find their meaning as references to an outside world, comparable to the abstract role of imagery in VR Memory Palaces (Vindenes, de Gortari, & Wasșon 2018). Each person will confront you with their opinion on freezing a human body. In total there are four persons spaced around the sphere: one with a positive view of cryonics, a priest, a philosopher, and a medical doctor.

Overdosing on heroin

In "Drug Addict" the implied reader is a first-person witness. You are moving from place to place in the city, scene by scene. Notice that the user does not have any real freedom to move in 3D space, but "moves" through the events in transitions between the scenes. You are a drug addict who buys heroin and shoots an overdose, probably eventually dying. This is a more active witnessing than in "Plastics" and "Cryonics". The protagonist is also displayed as an explicit narratee in the story due to such features as seeing his arm instead of your own (or no arm). You are positioned as a full-bodied person with a subjective experience of the stress and unpleasantness. This is further accomplished by the use of realistic, cold filters, shabby, rundown locations, and visual disturbances that simulate a sense of losing consciousness. The group chose to make a sequence at the start where an explicit narrator explains what will come. While it heightens the journalistic seriousness of the piece, it also creates an initial distance from the person we are about to become.

> Scene 1: You are sitting in a public square in the heart of the city. Here you are in one of the city's most popular places, but without being able to establish eye contact with anyone.
>
> Scene 2: You are on the Light Rail from the city park to the city bus station. During the tram ride you will notice that a passenger sits down in the seat

next to you, gives you a judgmental look and get up again to stand in the corridor for the rest of the trip. Outcast, subhuman.

Scene 3: You are in a pedestrian subway at the city bus station. Here you are greeted by an approaching person and you receive drugs in the form of heroin.

Scene 4: You are in a public toilet in the subway, where you shoot heroin into your arm. The arm and body are visible in the video. In this scene the colors turn more saturated, and you can hear your increasing heartbeat. Various clips from different parts of the city are presented with a few seconds' delay, each fading to black shortly after introduction. Then there is a dip to a black transition to the next scene.

Scene 5: You are lying in an alleyway. Your overdose may result in death. The video ends with text explaining more about drug addicts in Norway.

Suffering from schizophrenia

In "Schizophrenia" the implied reader is a victim of a mental disease. You are positioned as somebody in a neutrally furnished apartment, and you experience increasingly hallucinatory impressions in both visual and auditive forms. Depending on the degree of immersion, you can either feel like the sufferer does for a short while, and sense its impact on your body and mind, or you witness the condition over the shoulder of the sufferer without identifying as him/her.

Scene 1: You are at the kitchen table in an apartment. The first symptoms of the disorder begin to emerge. There is an auditory hallucination in that the radio host suddenly addresses your situation directly: talking about the bread on your plate. There is a visual hallucination in that, if you look directly at the slice of bread, the cheese will start to mold. You hear a low voice "inside your head" that is somewhat hard to discern.

Scene 2: You are in the laundry room. Now the voices are multiple and louder. An aggressive man shouts: "Did anyone say you're allowed to do this? You know who decides! End it there! Are you listening? I said STOP! Turn off the washing machine! You [...] now you listen to me, I'm the one who decides [...] turn it off!" A panicked woman screams: "Can you hear that sound? They know where you live, they are here now, they are coming to get you!" If you keep your eyes on the floor drain, spiders will start to come up through it. Someone is shouting and cranking the door handle, trying to get in.

Scene 3: You sit on the sofa in the living room. The voices are at their most intense in this scene, at one point urging and guiding the user to kill himself. Paintings on the wall come to life if you look at them. The prince depicted in a painting blinks to the user, and spits out a frog. Another painting shows a number of men, and they suddenly begin to move. Suddenly the phone rings. The scene fades into black and we hear a voicemail that is played on the mobile. The voicemail is from a friend who wanted to check if everything was OK, and wanted to meet up soon. This was intended as a relief from the incessant voices, and to give closure for the user.

Discussion

We started from a question posed by Chatman (1978, 147):

> By what convention does a spectator or reader accept the idea that it is "as if" he were personally on the scene, though he comes to it by sitting in a chair in a theater or by turning pages and reading words?
>
> *Chatman 1978*

In this chapter we propose that for journalism an important part of the answer is the subject position called "witnessing". The design experiment with bachelor students was productive in that it showed us a range of technical and narrative solutions that can be considered witnessing. The experiment helped us to make two important distinctions.

First, it is important to formulate the difference between a subject position, where the user becomes a listener, and the reporter-witness, where she instead experiences the events as one of a protagonist. Jones (2017, 180) has written about this issue. She argues that there are two distinct narratives that have evolved within immersive journalism: "reporter-led narratives and those led by characters or told in the first person". In the reporter-led approach you work with the implied author and an explicit narrator. "You simply take on an 'objective', detached perspective (third-person POV)", say Damiani and Southard (2017). "Plastics" and "Cryonics" belong to the reporter-led narrative with their voiceovers. In contrast, the narrative can be designed so that you "see things through a specific character's eyes (first-person POV)", as Damiani and Southard (2017) put it. This is the direction that two other productions take. "Drug Addict" and "Schizophrenia" both organize a first-person perspective where you are the victim of events happening to you. As a spectator you are placed alongside the victims, or perhaps even inside them.

Second, it is also important to distinguish between different degrees of embodiment of the subject position. Damiani and Southard (2017) make an interesting point relating to embodied position. "Will the viewers' avatar have a body? In other words, if I look down, will I see a body?" "Drug Addict" has a scene where the first-person administers an injection into his arm. The arm is located just where your own arm is, and some spectators might almost feel that the injection goes into their own arm. In this sense we can talk about "embodied witness" in the victim position: feeling like you are inside the person's body. Sánchez Laws (2017) refers to a VR story depicting harsh interrogation of prisoners, suggesting that the production team had been too ambiguous in positioning the user.

> Whose role did participants take in the stress position scenario, did they enter a real other's skin, or were they themselves? One of the participants mentioned that he did not know whether he was the man crouching in the box or not, but he felt like he was meant to be him.
>
> *Sánchez Laws 2017*

"Schizophrenia" also constructs a type of embodied presence in the story, but it feels more mental than physical. Instead of embodiment it is some kind of "enbrainment", in which you are placed into subjective mental phenomena instead of physical bodily experience. The user can have a strong emotional attachment to a sufferer during and after seeing the production. The simulated hallucinations in the apartment give you a glimpse into an everyday life that you hope you will never experience, but you see its potential in your own life.

Conclusion

The material we analyzed in this article was generated in a pedagogical design experiment conducted in 2018. It is a follow-up to the drone journalism experiment conducted in 2016 (Nyre, Guribye, & Gynnild 2018). In both cases it was bachelor students in New Media who created all the narratives and their expressive nuances.

In this chapter we have used the material from the experiment to explore the reporting technique called "witnessing" in VR journalism. Beyond helping us to define this technique for immersive journalism, our analysis and discussion are also intended to show how rich and subtle the creativity among students can be. New skillsets emerge with the students' exploration, and, if researchers are able to describe them constructively in publications afterwards, these novel skillsets are more likely to trickle out into the journalism profession in the long run. Skillsets for journalism may be discovered and formulated in academia, but their true value only emerges as user practices in the public sphere.

Along with these emerging skillsets for witnessing comes great responsibility for their ethical implications. It may not be controversial to create witnessing of current events such as an earthquake or a presidential press conference, but immersive journalism gives us access to so much more subjective experience too. What are the ethical ramifications of allowing anyone to witness the life of a schizophrenic person or someone being tortured in prison or dying in the street? Such powerful subject positions are sensitive, and must be used with care. Furthermore, they can also be used for propaganda and fake news exactly because they can be so emotionally powerful. As John Durham Peters (2001) reminds us, with witnessing comes a moral responsibility because the technique can be used to trick people into believing things based on "seeing it with my own eyes". While he was referring to live news reporting on television and radio, his appeal to responsibility is even more needed in immersive journalism. When teaching students to make new and daring journalism with VR tools, we also have to teach them a cautious attitude towards making stories that position the user as a subject in dramatic life experiences.

Note

1 This chapter is supported by ViSmedia, a research project funded by the Norwegian Research Council. We want to thank the following teachers and students from the INFOMEVI173 course on Journalistic Prototypes, spring 2018, at the University of Bergen: Zulfikar Fahmy, Audun Klyve Gulbrandsen, Erlend Skorpetveit Aga, Trym Røed Arvesen, Michael Fabregas Breien, Vemund Fjeld, Ingvild Vara Hagen, Mathias Dyrkolbotn Haukjem, Sindre Haveland, Stine Olsen Helland, Simen Larsen Johansen, Andrea Iversen Karlsen, Edvard Muli Langen, Jonathan Lindø Meling, Stian Holm Nordahl, Martin Norvoll, Preben Ørpetveit Solberg, Ida Charlotte Solvig, Helene Sofie Borthen Stenstadvold, and Malene Berg Sundsøy.

References

Barab, S. & K. Squire. 2004. "Design-Based Research: Putting a Stake in the Ground." *Journal of the Learning Sciences 13*(1): 1–14. http://doi.org/10.1207/s15327809jls1301_1.

Brown, A.L. 1992. "Design Experiments: Theoretical and Methodological Challenges in Creating Complex Interventions in Classroom Settings." *Journal of the Learning Sciences 2*(2): 141–178. http://doi.org/10.1207/s15327809jls0202_2.

Carr, Karen. 1995. "Introduction." In: K. Carr & R. England (eds), *Simulated and Virtual Realities: Elements of Perception*. London: Taylor and Francis, pp. 1–10.

Chatman, S. 1978. *Story and Discourse: Narrative Structure in Fiction Film*. Ithaca, NY: Cornell University Press.

Collins, A., D. Joseph, & K. Bielaczyc. 2004. "Design Research: Theoretical and Methodological Issues." *Journal of the Learning Sciences 13*(1): 15–42. doi:10.1207/s15327809jls1301_2

Damiani, Jesse & Dylan Southard. 2017. "Writing for VR: The Definitive Guide to VR Storytelling." *VR Scout*, 2 October. https://vrscout.com/news/writing-vr-definitive-guide-vr-storytelling/ [Accessed 15 March 2020].

Darsø, L. 2011. *Innovationspædagagogik:Kunsten at fremelske innovationskompetence*. Copenhagen: Samfundsliteratur.

de la Peña, Nonny, Peggy Weil, Joan Llobera, Elias Giannopoulos, Ausiàs Pomés, Bernhard Spanlang, Doron Friedman, Maria V. Sanchez-Vives, & Mel Slater. 2010. "Immersive Journalism: Immersive Virtual Reality for the First-Person Experience of News." *Presence: Teleoperators and Virtual Environments 19*(4): 291–301.

Doyle, Patrick, Mitch Gelman, & Sam Gill. 2016. *Viewing the Future? Virtual Reality in Journalism*. Knight Foundation. https://knightfoundation.org/reports/vrjournalism/ [Accessed 15 March 2020].

Goffman, Erving. 1981. "Radio Talk." In: *Forms of Talk*. Philadelphia: University of Pennsylvania Press.

Iser, Wolfgang. 1978. *The Act of Reading. A Theory of Aesthetic Response*. Baltimore, MD: Johns Hopkins University Press.

Jones, Sarah. 2017. "Disrupting the Narrative: Immersive Journalism in Virtual Reality." *Journal of Media Practice 18*(2–3): 171–185. doi:10.1080/14682753.2017.1374677

Merleau-Ponty, Maurice. 2001. [1945] *Phenomenology of Perception.* Trans: Colin Smith. London: Routledge Classics.

Nash, Kate. 2018. "Virtual Reality Witness: Exploring the Ethics of Mediated Presence." *Studies in Documentary Film 12*(2): 119–131. doi:10.1080/17503280.2017.1340796.

Nyre, Lars. 2008. *Sound Media: From Live Journalism to Recorded Music.* London: Routledge.

Nyre, Lars, Frode Guribye, & Astrid Gynnild. 2018. "Taking Risks with Drones: Responsible Innovation Pedagogy for Media Education." In: A. Gynnild & T. Uskali (eds), *Responsible Drone Journalism.* Abingdon: Routledge Focus, pp. 71–85.

Owen, T., F. Pitt, R. Aronson-Rath, & J. Milward. 2015. "Virtual Reality Journalism." Columbia Journalism School, Tow Center. http://towcenter.org/ research/virtual-reality-journalism/ [Accessed 15 March 2020].

Peters, John Durham. 2001. "Witnessing." *Media, Culture & Society 23*(6): 707–723.

Sánchez Laws, Ana Luisa. 2017. "Can Immersive Journalism Enhance Empathy?" *Digital Journalism 5.* doi:10.1080/21670811.2017.1389286

Vindenes, J., A.O. de Gortari, & B. Wasson. 2018. "Mnemosyne: Adapting the Method of Loci to Immersive Virtual Reality." In: L. De Paolis & P. Bourdot (eds), *Augmented Reality, Virtual Reality, and Computer Graphics.* AVR. Lecture Notes in Computer Science *10850.* Cham, Switzerland: Springer.

16

FORECASTING FUTURE TRAJECTORIES FOR IMMERSIVE JOURNALISM

Turo Uskali, Astrid Gynnild, Esa Sirkkunen, and Sarah Jones

In this book we have critically explored the emerging practices of immersive journalism. In the news business, experimenting with new forms of storytelling has become the new normal. After spending a decade to get familiar with simple virtual reality tools, however, the future of immersive journalism is still considered uncertain. Immersive storytelling appears to become more concentrated on special events and locations. Journalistic virtual reality skills are increasingly crafted away from the newsrooms by small and specialized subcontractors. Sponsoring VR by the big tech companies tends to diminish in parallel with a growing move towards augmented reality investments.

An early VR experiment by the Finnish Broadcasting Company (YLE) highlights some crucial challenges with implementing VR within news. In 2019, the public broadcaster funded a VR experience that imitated the first explosion of the hydrogen bomb Ivy Mike in 1952 in the Pacific Ocean. The video was produced by Tea Time Productions and promoted in YLE´s main news program. The piece experiment was heavily criticized and considered a waste of time. It was too difficult for the viewers to grasp what was going on. In the broadcast the journalist wore the head-mounted display and moved around the studio, whilst the background showed the atoll and the explosion. Users could also download the video from the broadcaster's website. The only dilemma was that most people in the audience did not own high-end VR devices, so later on YLE decided to offer the video experience at various events such as city fairs. The strategy was clear: to create the experience, demonstrate it in a traditional news format, then offer as a download and allow more people to experience the video in exhibition formats. The strategy uncovered the difficulties of promoting new visual technologies on established platforms. Television obviously cannot really support VR affordances such as presence and immersion. Additionally, the TV audience got the feeling of being ignored for a few valuable minutes by the public broadcaster.

In science and technology studies there is a growing interest in understanding the social consequences of technologies more reflectively. Lievrouw (2014, 46–47) sketches a triad of *artifacts, practices, and arrangements* with which we can start to seek answers to the slow development of VR technology in a broader societal context.

As a thought experiment, we apply this model to the existing research findings of this book. An important aspect of VR as material artifacts is the poor usability of the low-end VR devices. The HMDs have been rather clunky to use, the visual footage has been blurry, audio monaural, etc. The offering of free cardboard HMDs was a sympathetic, shoelace-budget idea to introduce users to this new medium, but it came at a price. The smartphone can slide away easily from the cardboard, the footage is rather fuzzy, and the feeling of immersion limited. These experiences may partly explain the low interest in VR content or devices. In addition, fears of simulation sickness, especially when using low-end devices, has made users suspicious and less eager to try new gadgets. Chapter 11 on the hierarchy of user experience articulated clearly the importance of understanding the material usability of VR artifacts.

The usability of VR devices has been previously up for discussion as well. The technological lag between expectations and reality created much disappointment during the second appearance of VR in the 1990s (Evans 2019). The costs of high-end devices with better usability have remained high. Thus, VR is still far from being the democratic medium as was previously predicted.

Following Marshall McLuhan's famous tetrad of media effects (McLuhan & McLuhan 1988), we can ponder what kind of media practices the use of VR would render obsolete? Television still has important cohesive meaning in modern societies, although cloud-based services like Netflix have been challenging the ritualistic television usage. The good side of conventional TV is that it allows multitasking, which is, at the moment, impossible with VR. The social applications of VR are limited compared to social media apps. Users are left mostly alone in the VR environment, although AltSpaceVR and Facebook Spaces exemplify attempts to make VR more social. Therefore, we predict that VR as a practice starts as a complementary, rather than an eliminatory, media practice.

Journalism follows its own production logics and ethics. The ethical premises of accuracy and transparency create tensions among journalists about how to be ethical storytellers in the virtual reality universe. Being transparent means making the users understand how immersive technologies work and how the users are affected by them. The underlying idea is that when users become more VR-literate they will become aware of the epistemic differences between genres such as immersive news and more interpretative immersive documentaries.

When thinking about *arrangements* and institutions, we enter into the world of digital economy. The global techno-giants' Google, Facebook, Microsoft, and Samsung drive towards VR is a continuation of their general battle for market dominance of the emerging consumer VR market and the future of the digital economy, as Evans (2019, 46) states. The already functioning VR platforms demonstrate how the relations between users and companies are being arranged. When building is closed, proprietary platforms are able to control the contents and collect data from the reactions of users – as they have been doing with various other services. If the business model of data collection is transferred into VR usage, the concerns around privacy and user-profiling become paramount also in this field. The situation resembles the process around 2006–2008 when the social media platforms were established without public knowledge about their business model and its consequences. In the same way the platforms are setting the field and controlling the emerging practices of VR. However, structures and norms on how to regulate this new medium are still far into the future.

Our experiment with Lievrow's model shows that in VR there is much improvement to be made. The material artifacts must be easier to use to become part of our daily practices. Immersive journalism needs to further develop storytelling approaches that are in alignment with journalism principles of accuracy and transparency. The affordances of technology and journalism are challenged to merge in new ways. At the same time, some kind of regulation is needed to protect the users from emotional manipulation and exploitation. To a large extent the giant tech companies rule out the emerging practice for immersive technologies in journalism as well as in other business, without too much interference from the content producers themselves.

From the time that podcast was first developed as an immersive medium, it took ten years before it was adopted by journalism. The main factors that contributed to the breakthrough were: interesting content, enthusiastic producers, usable and widespread technology, users who knew how to use the devices, cloud services, fast connections, and channels of distribution that are independent of the producers of technology (Hammersley 2004; Berry 2015; Berry 2016; Bottomley 2015).

Future trajectories

In the years to come immersive journalism might gravitate in different directions depending on the variables above and more. We conclude this book by suggesting six potential trajectories for the adoption and adaption of immersive technologies in journalism in the near future.

1. Researching audiences will open new avenues for development

The question at the heart of any journalism scenario lies in the audience. There has been plenty of "buzz" in the aftermath of Milk's TED talk in 2015, and also in the impact of the *New York Times*' NYTVR app, which was the most downloaded on its first weekend in the same year (Jaekel 2015). But what happened to longevity? Has immersive journalism found a growing audience or are the enthusiasts still searching for more users?

An ImmerseUK survey in 2018 found that "audiences loved that they had their own story to take away with them – something they did rather than something they saw" (ImmerseUK 2018, 10). The challenge is getting them into the spaces to view stories in the first place. The survey also found that of all of the immersive pieces studied, from education to gaming to social, the most popular in the audience were the perspective-shifting pieces. These videos were mostly found in immersive journalism or documentary formats. These were the Iexperiences, exemplified through videos such as *Clouds Over Sidra* (Milk 2015) and *In My Shoes: Intimacy* (Gauntlett 2016), that created physiological feelings in the audience, for instance heart rates increasing. The impact that immersive experiences have on an audience is clear: "Participants explained in discussion that they were 'in' rather than simply watching a story".

Another study found that immersive journalism in which there was an element of perceived interactivity, with a character making direct eye contact with the viewer, engaged users more often and for longer periods of time. The study (Steed et al. 2018) used an immersive journalism experience by the BBC called "We Wait". Nick North, Director of Audiences at the BBC, said: "whilst this was a small study, a 25 percent conversion rate from the We Wait VR experience is very impressive, and potentially indicative of the significant impact VR could have at scale" (Steed et al. 2018).

A recent study of users' impressions of and reactions to immersive journalism in virtual reality found that users think VR can add considerable value to mainstream journalistic productions, potentially boosting engagement and trust (Nielsen & Sheets 2019). Through a study utilizing a use-and-gratifications framework, focus groups looked at different immersive experiences. Even though they were critical towards the technology itself, they saw a potential within journalism.

One particular concern raised in this study is echoed in other studies and in anecdotal evidence collected at various VR events, namely the social perception of VR. Users feel embarrassed when putting on a headset. It is an isolating experience and one that can make people feel self-conscious. A study by the BBC found a similar audience concern, which suggested that the limitations were the "clunky user experiences of the headsets" (Watson 2017, 37). To sum up, just because a story is told on the platform, it may not be told in the way most users want to receive it. The various media technologies are to a large extent complementary platforms and not actually competitors; users have different preferences and there is no longer a "one size fits all".

In a year-long study as an RJI Fellow at the University of Missouri, *Euronews*' Thomas Seymat set out to develop tools that would facilitate audience research for 360-degree or VR content. He wanted to provide evidence-based best practices for immersive storytelling. By interviewing immersive journalists, he found that 41 percent either agreed or strongly agreed that they knew what their audience liked. Only 30 percent knew what their audience wanted. Right here we have a gap in knowledge. To determine where immersive journalism is going, how it is to be experienced, and how narratives are formed, we need more research in order to understand. Seymat is creating tools to help immersive journalists get better audience feedback. If we are to see immersive journalism thrive, we think that such tools are needed across the industry.

2. Authenticity and transparency remain core values of immersive journalism

Questions of authenticity in immersive journalism stories are essential. Already in the first immersive journalism experience by Nonny de la Peña, *Hunger in LA* (2012), authentic audio recordings and animation were used to reconstruct the human drama at a food bank line. When *The New York Times* produced its first immersive journalism documentary, *The Displaced,* in 2015, the critics, mostly from other news media organizations, commented that VR journalism needed more collaboration between the journalist and the subject than traditional video journalism, even repetition of the action. *The New York Times*' production team emphasized that they went "through the film piece by piece to make sure that it fairly represented reality" (Sullivan 2015; Robitzski 2017). Many experts have emphasized the importance of transparency: that the journalists tell openly about the journalistic processes that preceded the output and what kind of decisions are made, especially relating to authenticity and ethics.

As the resolution of the immersive journalism experience still evolves, the question of reality versus virtual reality is getting even more serious. For example, the Finnish company Varjo developed their first headset with a display that delivers human-eye resolution: 60 pixels per degree, the equivalent of 20/20 vision (Varjo.com 2019).

What happens when the quality of virtual reality is the same as our own vision? Actually, one of the biggest challenges for the future of immersive journalism will be how to detect forgeries. There is already a special term, "deepfakes", coined for a new kind of digital hoax. Fillion (2018) defines deepfakes as "realistic videos created with artificial intelligence software". So far, the known cases of deepfakes have used a variety of technologies, for example faceswaps, creating a lip-syncing facial expression onto someone else's face (ibid.). *The Wall Street Journal* has been among the first to establish a special section called a Media Forensics Committee in order to tackle the deepfakes already evidenced in 2018. In 2019, it had about 20 members from different parts of the newsroom, including photo, video, editorial, R&D, audience/analytics, and standards/ethics (Lomdatze 2019). Arguably, it is only a matter of time before deepfakes in the form of immersive journalism news or documentaries will be created and circulated.

3. Ethical reviews as tools, increased awareness of emotional data

It has been interesting to note the findings of reviews into immersive technologies and how these may inform future practices. In 2019, a six-month inquiry was held by the UK Government into Immersive and Addictive Technologies. The recommendations included calling for technology companies to look at how they protect the audience from harm, and for a new "Online Harms" regulator that would hold social media platforms accountable for content or activity that harms individual users. Alongside this, there must be clear procedures to take down misleading "deepfake" videos. This may have an impact for developments within immersive journalism as technology evolves and more interactivity and social interactions within the news stories emerge.

Furthermore, as the platform companies are already seriously investing in the future of immersive technologies such as virtual reality, it is important also to start ethical discussions about their practices, especially in terms of emotional data collection. For example, by signing Facebook's data use policy the users potentially expose themselves to various experiments that could target, for instance, the users' emotions without informed consents (Jouhki et al. 2016, 79–81). As the tech companies have their own ethical rules and practices, and business secrets, critical academic research should continuously emphasize the importance of ethical questions in terms of the use of new technologies.

4. Global co-learning on immersive journalism is growing

It is important to add that global online networks and communities like special Facebook groups or ad-hoc Twitter accounts continuously foster and curate our knowledge about the new implications of virtual, augmented, and mixed reality in journalism. These virtual social media communities are increasingly identified as important global education hubs and information networks for immersive journalism.

One of the largest online communities focusing on VR is a Facebook group called Virtual Reality with more than 50,000 members in September 2019, seven years after it was started. There are also plenty of niche groups in social media platforms, like a Facebook group named as Film 360VR/MR – Los Angeles, which spreads across wider California. The group was founded in August 2017 and it had almost 400 members in September 2019. The main aims of this group are to 1) explore immersive media through interactive and robust events, 2) inform members about new tools and workflows at the intersection of media, entertainment, and technology, and 3) curate resources and solutions for immersive storytellers and innovators.

5. Ways of storytelling are changing, eventually with the 5G

Many experts have argued that especially the fifth generation of cellular networks (5G) is needed before the immersive technologies will take off on a large scale. *The New York Times* launched among the very first newsrooms its 5G Journalism Lab in 2019. The company predicts that "Over the next few years, the transition to 5G will provide Internet speeds at least 20 times faster than 4G networks, enabling smartphones to download entire movies in seconds or stream massive multiplayer games without latency" (NYTimes.com 2019).

When preparing this book we asked those working within immersive journalism for their thoughts on where the industry will be heading. What are their own ideas about how it may develop as the technological infrastructures and gadgets evolve?

> Because of 5G and wearables, we're going to see an increasing intersection between biometric information and media. Users will be controlling media environments with their brainwaves and heart rate. In addition, media will be recommended to the user based on the data that's coming from their wearables.
>
> *Sarah Hill, Story-Up*

> I think the onset of 5G and the possibilities of immersive "glasses" that achieve what Google Glass couldn't may prove to be sparks that finally set this brand of journalism on fire. The one thing "traditional news" still can't do is put the viewer in the middle of the story. Well shot and produced 360 video can do that. Throw in all the other potential bells and whistles that VR and AR can offer, and I'm still convinced storytelling will be changed forever by this technology. Great work is being done, we just need a broad audience with the ability to watch it in its best form.
>
> *George Sells, MetroSTL.com*

> We took VR on a tour this summer to 160 local libraries – slightly against my expectations the Congo films were the most appreciated by audiences – so that's a great endorsement of the power of VR journalism.
>
> *Zillah Watson, BBC*

> Predictions are particularly hard in the immersive field, even for 5 years in the future, because, if you glimpse back 5 years ago, you will be baffled at how fast hardware, software and content have evolved. One thing is clear for the next five years though, if they hope to reach the Promised Land of a mainstreamed technology, hardware manufacturers, software companies and content producers must put the audience at the centre of every decision they make from now on.
>
> *Thomas Seymat, VR editor at* Euronews, *RJI Fellow 2018–2019*

6. *The promises of immersive journalism are still pertinent*

Immersive journalism is an evolving field. This book draws together research from scholars around the world highlighting the opportunities that the field presents, while acknowledging the challenges and concerns it brings as well. With greater adoption and the potential of 5G, the field may find many new users but most likely only as an addition to a growing portfolio of journalistic platforms.

Clearly, there is a need for more research about the importance and role of online communities in terms of adapting to new emergent technologies in journalism, as well as the ethical challenges that this medium presents. Immersive journalism has the potential to reach new audiences, change the way stories are told, and provide more interactivity within the news industry.

References

Berry, Richard. 2015. "A Golden Age of Podcasting? Evaluating *Serial* in the Context of Podcast Histories." *Journal of Radio & Audio Media 22*(2): 170–178.

Berry, Richard. 2016. "Podcasting: Considering the Evolution of the Medium and its Association with the Word 'Radio'." *The Radio Journal: International Studies in Broadcast & Audio Media 14*(1): 7–22. doi:10.1386/rajo.14.1.7_1

Bottomley, Andrew J. 2015. "Podcasting: A Decade in the Life of a 'New' Audio Medium: Introduction." *Journal of Radio & Audio Media 22*(2): 164–169.

Evans, Leighton. 2019. *The Re-Emergence of Virtual Reality*. 1st ed. London: Routledge.

Fillion, Rubina M. 2018. "Fighting the Reality of Deepfakes. Predictions for Journalism 2019." *Niemanlab.org* [Accessed 19 December 2019].

Gauntlett, Jane. 2016. "In My Shoes: Intimacy. A Virtual Reality Experience for Two." https://jane-gauntlett.squarespace.com/ [Accessed 5 January 2020].

Hammersley, Ben. 2004. "Audible revolution." *The Guardian*. www.theguardian.com/media/2004/feb/12/broadcasting.digitalmedia [Accessed 14 October 2019].

ImmerseUK. 2018. "Immersive Economy Report." www.immerseuk.org/resources/immersive_economy_report/ [Accessed 15 March 2020].

Jaekel, Brielle. 2015. "NY Times' VR Play is Publisher's Most Successful App Launch." *Mobile Marketer*, 12 November. www.mobilemarketer.com/cms/news/video/21676.html [Accessed 14 October 2019].

Jouhki, Jukka, Epp Lauk, Maija Penttinen, Niina Sormanen, & Turo Uskali. 2016. "Facebook's Emotional Contagion Experiment as a Challenge to Research Ethics." *Media and Communication 4*(4), October: 75–85.

Lievrouw, Leah, A. 2014. "Materiality and Media in Communication and Technology Studies: An Unfinished Project." In: Tarleton Gillespie, Pablo J. Boczkowski, & Kirsten A. Foot. *Media Technologies: Essays on Communication, Materiality and Society*. Cambridge; London: The MIT Press.

Lomdatze, Ana. 2019. "The WSJ on DeepFakes. 'It's a Cat and Mouse Game'." *Medium.com*/Global Editors Network. https://medium.com/global-editors-network/wsj-on-deepfakes-its-a-cat-mouse-game-212c3c7c6a4 [Accessed 14 October 2019].

McLuhan, Marshall & Eric McLuhan. 1988. *Laws of Media*. University of Toronto Press.

Milk, C. 2015. "How Virtual Reality Can Create the Ultimate Empathy Machine." *TED Talk*, March. www.ted.com/talks/chris_milk_how_virtual_reality_can_create_the_ultimate_empathy_machine?utm_campaign1/4linkplug&utm_source1/4linkplug&utm_medium1/4linkplug&utm_content1/4linkplug&utm_term1/4linkplug#t-5120 [Accessed 15 March 2020].

Nielsen, S.L. & P. Sheets. 2019. "Virtual Hype Meets Reality: Users' Perception of Immersive Journalism." *Journalism*. https://doi.org/10.1177/1464884919869399.

NYTimes.com. 2019. "Exploring the Future of 5G and Journalism." https://open.nytimes.com/exploring-the-future-of-5g-and-journalism-a53f4c4b8644 [Accessed 14 October 2019].

Robitzski, Dan. 2017. "Virtual Reality and Journalistic Ethics: Where Are the Lines?" *Undark.org*, 27 September. https://undark.org/article/virtual-reality-and-journalistic-ethics-where-are-the-lines/ [Accessed 15 March 2020].

Steed, Anthony, Ye Pan, Zillah Watson, & Mel Slater. 2018. "'We Wait': The Impact of Character Responsiveness and Self Embodiment on Presence and Interest in an Immersive News Experience." *Frontiers in Robotics and AI 5*.

Sullivan, M. 2015. "The Tricky Terrain of Virtual Reality." *The New York Times*. www.nytimes.com/2015/11/15/public-editor/new-york-times-virtual-reality-margaret-sullivan-public-editor.html [Accessed 9 March 2019].

Varjo.com. 2019. https://varjo.com/ [Accessed 14 October 2019].

Watson, Z. 2017. *VR for News: The New Reality?* Digital News Project. Oxford, UK: Reuters Institute for the Study of Journalism, University of Oxford, p. 37. https://reutersinstitute.politics.ox.ac.uk/our-research/vr-news-new-reality [Accessed 15 March 2020].

INDEX

Note: Page numbers in *italic* denote figures and in **bold** denote tables.

Made in the USA
Monee, IL
12 November 2026

c057e9fb-b94c-4f8b-89d4-042bdf03d941R01